616.89143 K38b

Kepner, James I.

Body process

DATE DUE

JUL 28 1997		
JAN 2 4 1998		
DEC 0 2 2003		
JUN 0 1 2006		
GAYLORD		PRINTED IN U.S.A.

A GESTALT INSTITUTE
OF CLEVELAND PUBLICATION

*BODY
PROCESS*

JAMES I. KEPNER

with a new prologue
by the author

FOREWORD
by JOSEPH C. ZINKER

BODY
PROCESS

WORKING WITH THE
BODY IN PSYCHOTHERAPY

Jossey-Bass Publishers
San Francisco

Originally published as *Body Process: A Gestalt Approach to Working with the Body in Psychotherapy.* © 1987 by James I. Kepner.

Copyright © 1993 by Jossey-Bass Inc., Publishers, 350 Sansome Street, San Francisco, California 94104. Copyright under International, Pan American, and Universal Copyright Conventions. All rights reserved. No part of this book may be reproduced in any form—except for brief quotation (not to exceed 1,000 words) in a review or professional work—without permission in writing from the publishers.

A Gestalt Institute of Cleveland publication

Substantial discounts on bulk quantities of Jossey-Bass books are available to corporations, professional associations, and other organizations. For details and discount information, contact the special sales department at Jossey-Bass Inc., Publishers. (415) 433-1740; Fax (415) 433-0499.

For sales outside the United States, contact Maxwell Macmillan International Publishing Group, 866 Third Avenue, New York, New York 10022.

Manufactured in the United States of America

10% POST CONSUMER WASTE

The paper used in this book is acid-free and meets the State of California requirements for recycled paper (50 percent recycled waste, including 10 percent postconsumer waste), which are the strictest guidelines for recycled paper currently in use in the United States.

Library of Congress Cataloging-in-Publication Data

Kepner, James I.
  Body process : working with the body in psychotherapy / James I. Kepner.
     p. cm. — (The Jossey-Bass social and behavioral science series)
   Originally published: New York : Gardner Press, c1987.
   Includes bibliographical references and index.
   ISBN 1-55542-586-0
   1. Gestalt therapy. 2. Body image. 3. Mind and body. I. Title. II. Series.
RC489.G4K47 1993
616.89′143—dc20   93-17664
                                                                       CIP

FIRST EDITION
HB Printing   10 9 8 7 6 5 4 3 2 1   *Code 9384*

The Jossey-Bass
Social and Behavioral Science Series

Contents

Part II: Body Phenomena and the Cycle of Experience

Prologue

Since the publication of this book in 1987 as part of a special interest list of a small psychology publishing house, I have had the pleasure of seeing this volume come to be considered a standard in the field. Certainly, the field has lamentably few book-length discussions for the serious practitioner. So it pleases me that others, both professionals and laypersons, have seen the relevance and power of a body-oriented approach to psychotherapy with the particular orientation described in *Body Process: Working with the Body in Psychotherapy.*

I am certainly delighted to have had such a positive response. But I think the book's reception is due only in part to whatever contribution it makes. I believe that there is something more going on here – something to do with the power of this often unacknowledged side of our existence: our experience as embodied beings. The same undercurrent originally called me to learn more about the life and nature of the physical self.

Body Process has joined a tradition that attempts to point into the darkness of denial and unconsciousness at something fundamental to our nature, of such importance to our functioning that it is a wonder we could have left it out of so many of our attempts to understand ourselves. It is our life as embodied beings. Our bodily nature has remained so much "in darkness" because we come from a culture that has split apart human experience, so any study or explanation of human experience is similarly split. This split of human experience and functioning into "mind" and "body," joining similar artificial divisions endemic to our cultural heritage, such as "human" and "nature," leaves us without access to a whole sphere of our being which has now been transformed into mere mechanism.

Yet we know well from Freud's legacy that when something so fundamental to us is ignored or repressed, it by no means disappears. Rather, it calls even more strongly to us from the darkness, but often in ways that are perhaps felt only intuitively, or can be seen only indirectly, or at times expressed in ways that become perverse and twisted by our inner desperation. What is intrinsic to our nature can be ignored, subdued, or hidden under cover of darkness, but it cannot be destroyed. For that would destroy our very self.

The need for us to recognize the holistic nature of "mental" and "emotional" problems has more urgency now than ever before. We are finally, as a culture, able to recognize and support Freud's original insight, which as Judith Herman points out, he was unable to maintain against the pressures of his cultural context, that psychic illness has to do with *real injury* whose source cannot be recognized (Herman, 1992). This injury is often sexual or physical, but by extension is also often emotional. As real injury, it is responded to by a real person, a child shaping his or her body, as well as mind and emotions, around the injury. As healers we must be able not only to face the real nature of such injuries, but also to see the persons in front of us as having brought the full range of their childhood resources to bear as they faced their injuries: their bodies, their minds, and their souls.

A second urgent call for us to continue to explore, understand, and integrate our vision of the person as an embodied being comes from the increasing recognition that health and disease are subtly and fundamentally affected by our attitudes, our tension, our breathing, and our feelings. It is becoming increasingly untenable for us to see people as other than integral beings. Thoughts and attitudes are bodily and muscular, affecting the juices of our organs and rhythms of our cells as well as our moods.

Contrast these trends with others in psychotherapy. Currently, mainstream psychotherapy tends to emphasize mentally and verbally oriented approaches such as cognitive therapy, object relations psychoanalysis, strategic and problem-oriented brief therapies, and systems therapy. The medicalization of psychotherapy, coupled with increasing economic pressures on health services to technologize and standardize treatments, is also influencing the field to become more conventional, and thus more cognitive, in orientation. Yet perhaps this trend is just part of a natural pendulum swing. Our tendency to dichotomize and split up persons is embedded in our culture, as well as in our psychic and physical organization.

In the field of psychotherapy, we can see a historical recognition of the importance of our bodily life in connection with "mental" problems. As an early student of Freudian theory, Wilhelm Reich studied character defenses as manifest in posture and muscular tension. His work is considered classic in psychoanalysis, despite his later break with his mentor's approach and his sad, mad demise. Reich's insistence on the importance of breathing, posture, body armor, and physical vitality (energy) in the process of emotional adaptation helped keep alive the awareness that emotion, movement, and physical expression influence mental health, even as psychoanalysis became more and more detached, intellectual, and mentalistic in character.

One could say that it was precisely this detached, intellectual, and mentalistic trend in psychotherapy that created the conditions for the emergence in the 1960s of approaches with an emphasis on movement, emotional expressiveness, and body awareness such as those in the humanistic psychology movement. Alexander Lowen and Frederick Perls, for example, both students of Reich, incorporated a distinct body emphasis into their own unique approaches to bioenergetic therapy and Gestalt therapy, respectively.

There was also, at this time, a strong interest in dance therapy, Rolfing and massage, nonverbal communication, sensory awareness, T'ai Chi Ch'uan, and other body arts as adjuncts to the growth and healing process. Although many of the trappings of this movement were a rebellious reaction to the button-down conformity of the 1950s, my belief is that this movement reflected a deeper need as well: the need to reach toward a holism of body, mind, and self that was elusive, a holism known intuitively but not always apprehensible because of cultural constraints.

As with any dichotomy, when aspects of a whole cannot be integrated and seen as such, they become polarized. Body-oriented therapy has often seemed to be some sort of faddish swing of the pendulum or has been relegated by the dominant mainstream approaches into the shadows of "fringe" therapies. While it is clear to me that our bodily existence will continue to claim a place in our attempts to understand human process and experience, it is also clear that body and mind are still quite dichotomized within our culture at large, and of course within the field of psychotherapy. Our field, after all, is a reflection of our culture.

But there is no such thing as a one-sided coin. Today, despite prevailing mentalistic trends, the "calling" to us of our physical nature continues to find avenues of expression in the field of psychotherapy. The recognition of the reality of trauma and injury mentioned earlier and the increasingly holistic view of health and disease are indications that the pendulum does not merely swing back and forth, but that there is increasing growth and integration of our viewpoint with each swing.

It is time for more serious work on this integration. The present volume is certainly one such serious discussion of these issues. Interestingly, the Jungian (Mindell, 1982) and psychoanalytic (McDougall, 1989) schools, traditionally leaning toward the symbolic and intellectual modes, are also increasingly recognizing the intrinsic involvement of bodily being in human process. We can add to this the popular interest in holistic health, with the emergence of many hands-on healing approaches, related work in imagery and healing, and other developments, and we can see that there is something here that continues to glimmer with vitality and importance.

The approach described in this book, over the years of its application, has been received well because of the strengths of the Gestalt approach it is based on in the experiential and process realms. Using an experiential and thus noninterpretive methodology, the therapist does not box the client into a body typology system that may be irrelevant to the client's actual body experience. This process approach keeps the therapist open: open to the client's way of being, open to new possibilities, open to the unique solutions creativity and spontaneity can provide. The therapist needs to know *how* to work and *how* to help illuminate the client's body experience, but does not have to analyze character and predict the client's behavior, as in interpretive approaches. This also means that the therapist is not bound into yesterday's interpretive system, which may no longer have relevance to today's experience.*

Additionally, because it is a process methodology, this way of working with body experience can be used to complement more specific techniques of intervention that do not normally focus on the client's body process and experience. Physical therapists, for example, have found this method helpful in understanding how their interventions can create unnecessary resistance in the patient or how patterns of tension are part of the patient's emotional adaptation to disability and disease. They have also found this method helps patients own and take control over their bodily states.

*We have seen this with classical psychoanalytic theory, which became mired in the Oedipal interpretive framework and blinded many analysts to the reality of patients' *experience* of actual incest and sexual abuse.

NEW DIRECTIONS AND DEVELOPMENTS

One of the biggest areas of application for body-oriented psychotherapy that has developed over the last five years, as may be obvious from my earlier comments, has been with adult survivors of childhood abuse.* Despite the emphasis in the field on the psychological aspects of trauma, much of the trauma in such abuse is physical in nature: beatings, sexual intrusion, fondling, witnessing assaults on others' bodies, and so on. Additionally, much of what is "remembered" of such abuse, particularly of what occurred at a preverbal stage, is found through "body memory," often in the form of somatic symptoms, body sensations and feelings, muscular tensions, and habits of movement. Psychotherapists, medical consultants, and others who work with this population have been applying body process work to illuminate such issues and assist survivors in the healing of their bodily trauma.

The approach described in this volume is particularly suited to work with survivors because it posits resistance as a creative part of the person rather than armor to break down, and emphasizes the gradual development of awareness and ownership of one's bodily existence. These principles help insure that work with the body is less likely to be intrusive, the therapist is less likely to pathologize the client's physical symptoms and character structure, and the work can proceed in a manner suited to the client's pace of assimilation. These are crucial factors in the work of healing from abuse, since physical intrusion, being blamed for their victimization, and being subject to overwhelming and unassimilable experience are characteristic of abused children's experience. Therapy should avoid replicating such abuse in its methodology of healing.

Another area of useful application for body process work is with persons in recovery from chemical and other addictions. In addition to the high occurrence of addictions in people with histories of childhood abuse, addiction itself is a form of self-abuse, particularly of one's bodily self. Much of what is being managed through addiction is bodily sensations and feelings that the addicted person strives to deny or control with the use of a chemical. As addicted persons get beyond the initial need to establish sobriety and acquire some basic organization to their lives, they

---

*A future volume will detail this work in an integrated model. See Kepner, J., forthcoming. *Healing tasks in the psychotherapy of adult survivors of childhood abuse.* Cleveland: Gestalt Institute of Cleveland Press.

cannot move on to higher levels of integration and functioning without facing and reowning the body-selves they have denied and, through their addiction, assaulted. Feelings, sensations, hurts and pains, joys and sadnesses—all are part of the life the addicted person must reclaim. The bodily self is the locus of this life.

A newer area of exploration is the application of body process work to illness—chronic diseases. The door is just cracking open to the realm of "psychoneuroimmunology." Along with intervention methods such as imagery work, relaxation therapy, group therapy for chronically ill patients, and biofeedback, the experiential methods of body process work offer alternative ways for people to grapple with their illness.

Many people are struggling with illnesses that medicine has limited capacity to cure, such as rheumatoid arthritis, scleraderma, chronic fatigue syndrome, myofascitus, HIV, and more. Other diseases are coming to be understood as having some emotional component at least influencing their course, such as certain cancers and heart disease. We are just beginning to explore ways of using body experience and process to develop interventions that might influence the course of such diseases. This is an area of exciting potential for people working with these problems. At this early date we can only speculate how meaningful this approach will be and experiment with extending our techniques into new areas.

So, I welcome new readers and old to this new release of *Body Process.* I welcome you to the adventure of integration, to a more inclusive vision of human functioning, and to an abiding tradition that has insisted that our bodily existence not be forgotten. I hope you will find new insights here and find an affirmation of that which you have intuitively felt and understood, even if not before articulated.

Cleveland, Ohio   James I. Kepner
May 1993

SYNTHETIC THINKING

We are living in an age of therapeutic specialization. Emphasis is on individual creativity and innovation, perhaps even improvisation—where a kind of grass-roots eclecticism is born of each practitioner's efforts to accommodate both his/her own need for survival in the consulting room and the desire to respond to the needs of clients.

Thus we have the "thinking" therapies, the "feeling" therapies, the conditioning, the psychoanalytic, the transactional, the systems-oriented couple and family therapies, the group therapies. There are the Reichians, the neo-Reichians, the Rolfers, the Alexander and Feldenkrais people, and the hypnotists. There are the existentialists, Rogerians, transactional analysts, behaviorists, and there are the laser beamers who offer change for the price of a short trip through one's neurolinguistic software; here one can bypass awareness altogether and find, at last, some temporary relief from life's daily stress.

They are all here, thriving and accommodating people's needs for clarity, expression of feeling, muscular relaxation, muscular relearning, movement, and the realignment of adhesively demoralized muscle groups.

In this book Jim Kepner gives himself the formidable task of gathering the patient together into a whole human being within the theoretical perspective of Gestalt therapy and its actual practice. After all, Gestalt therapy, with its roots in field theory of Lewin and its emphasis on wholeness-giving principles of figure–ground formation, should be ideally equipped to build a broad integrated view of the whole person.

PROCESS INTERVENTION

What do I do, as a Gestalt therapist, when sitting with someone? What do I take in? What model do I construct inside me to manage a meaningful intervention?

I see, for one thing. I see a man sitting before me, leaning forward, talking passionately, his chest turned inward. I see this dark-eyed, delicately-formed man trying to make sense of his experience as best he can.

I can hear: his smoker's voice, his vocal chords straining in the upper ranges. I can hear his chest straining. I can hear his breath.

I can choose to smell and to touch him.

I am aware of his language, his boy-child fantasies, his nervous habit of repeating favorite words. I am aware that, at that moment at least, he is fully invested in being right here with me. I am aware that there are two of us here with an army of other characters "standing" behind each of us (our parents, uncles, aunts, teachers, friends), egging us on, criticizing, making pronouncements and demands, praising, asking questions, and so on.

I can focus, if I wish, on his "illness," his pain and discomfort. Or I can focus on his resourcefulness, his competence, his good looks. Or I can keep all of that in mind.

The sheer quantity of data confronting me—if I see and hear and smell and touch and analyze and ponder this person—is overwhelming. Thank God, my client likes to think things out. Perhaps I'll join him there. Thinking clearly is something I can give.

But the moment I respond to his words alone, I don't see him as clearly: my vision of him is filtered by his concept of himself or diagnostic pondering about him. It is as if both of us become two little black boxes attached to a vocal apparatus. One's eyes become glazed with insights. I join the client's linguistic perspective, landing myself in the tracks of his train, getting hitched in like a horse to the wagon of his perceptions. In the meantime what happens to his chest? What happens to his mother and father "standing" behind him? What happens to the "us" in the room? How can we manage all that without becoming scattered or confused?

I can construct a picture of his person that can include all of him in this moment. I begin to ask myself: What is his theme? What is his story line? What data are useful in making a meaningful picture of this man's being here with me?

When I integrate his story, his voice and language, his way of leaning toward me, the strain in his neck and his desperate staring at me, what strikes me is a kind of pleading, as if he is begging me. Within this theme I look at him again, and I begin to highlight some things that I observed randomly just a moment ago: his arms moving toward me, his voice asking for something, his whole head tilting forward on its thin neck. In my reverie I see a baby bird with its mouth open, begging its mother for a worm. Where is mom? If there is a beggar, where are the characters who had a lot but refused to give to him?

METAPHOR

He is saying something about asking his boss to let him "come here once a week at 3 p.m." So I say to him, "Ron, I experience you begging me as you talk," and I have suddenly organized a myriad of seemingly disconnected data together. He responds by remembering his mother begging his father not to travel so much. He stops suddenly and asks a question. He then grows quiet. He looks sad. His eyes moisten. I see all of this and, after some preparatory work, ask him to position himself in this room as if he were a real beggar. He considers the idea for a moment and decides to try it.

The moment he begins to move out of his chair, his knees bend and he moves stiffly, like an 80-year-old man. "There may be a beggar inside me, although I generally act proud—reminds me of Uncle Melvin. Melvin looked as if he had always been old. That's a little bit how I feel now. I feel I don't have, I'll never have, I won't deserve it even if I get it . . . I am doomed to plead and never feel entitled!"

After some experimentation with being Uncle Melvin, he stops. Sitting on the floor, he begins to cry quietly. "I lost my pride," he whispers. Soon his belly is constricting with spasms of deeper wailing. I sit down next to him while he experiences the mourning of a lost part of himself. Much later, in the next session, he tells me once again how his body has felt as a beggar, and I wonder aloud how he might look as the "prideful one" passing by and not bothering to toss a nickel to himself. What would happen to his shoulders and chest and knees and pelvis?

What kind of vision is able to organize itself around another's wholeness? It is a vision of process. It is a vision of the metaphors we experience of that person which he can't see himself because he is busy with his earnest commitment to his story.

How do we find this process intervention? We have to go away from him, tear ourselves away from the things he sees, and yet stay with him at the same time. We have to get into our hardness—where he can't reach us, where we can construct uncompromisingly a fresh image of this vision in front of us.

In momentarily "turning away" from our client, we make it most possible to join him at a "kernel place," a "seed place" where his awareness has not yet traveled. This time we join him with a metaphor.

Where does the metaphor of a beggar come from? Is the beggar all his? Of course not: he is the beggar I saw in the alley in old Jerusalem, he is the beggar I read about in a novel, he is the beggar inside my childhood where, during the war, I dared to step forward to beg for chunks of moldy bread.

I tell him about his beggar, as an expert beggar whose chest still wants to collapse, whose shoulders want to draw in to protect my heart, whose knees want to collapse into the pose of an ancient Jewish man.

Existentially we are both beggars at this moment. I, the "senior beggar," welcoming him into an old fraternity, and he, the "junior beggar," who appeared to have temporarily escaped his misery by placing himself in the world of a corporate manager-trainee.

If we construct a "process picture" of him, made of his words, his voice, his physical choreography, his way of gazing sadly, then that picture, that idea, that metaphor will "pull for" seeing a part of his wholeness. The metaphor, in this case, will organize his experience into an eye-opening insight that will depart from his own ego-syntonic small *Weltanshaung* and thrust him into an inner place where he once lived and where his whole body and soul seemed to be living. For example, he remembers a scene in his childhood when he begged his father to take him along to work—he visualizes his father wearing a dark winter overcoat, turning away from him and walking out alone into the cold Russian morning.

The story he tells is an old story for him. If you engage him there—literally there in his lively past—you will join his cast of characters. If you stand aside and look at him again and again with the fresh wonderment of a child, you might see the beggar, the murderer, the wise old man, or a trickster, or a young child asking for candy. Your own story line, evolving from the experiences of your inner life as well as his lively image, will create a play that may reorient his view of himself.

BUILDING THE PROCESS-SELF

There is no way we can do body process Gestalt therapy without having created for ourselves a rich and layered picture of our own lives. Process body work can only come from a therapist who is living his/her process.

A long time ago, Carl Rogers constructed a model of process awareness in which one of the central concepts was congruence: congruence between what is expressed, for example, and what is experienced within. Congruence between doing and being. Congruence between feeling and thinking.

The therapist's own therapy requires her/him to live fully. The good therapist is a well-lived teacher. All this living, this richness, comes back into the consultation room and we work on congruence between what was experienced and what is actually felt.

So metaphors, and the sense of what is thematic for the other, do not come out of the air. They come out of the thickness of one's literate being—out of one's inner sense of poetry, vividness of imagery, lively encounter with the world, sheer curiosity, and the courage to make something extraordinary out of the simple or to make something simple out of the seeming complexity of another person's expression. The metaphor then comes out of this inner "blood learning" that is finally ripe enough to put into language and come out of one's mouth—plainly, simply, boldly—without pretense or pompousness.

Rilke said something about "blood learning".

> For the sake of a single verse, one must see many cities, men and things, one must know the animals, one must feel how the birds fly and know the gesture with which the little flowers open in the morning. One must be able to think back to roads in unknown regions, to unexpected meetings and to partings one had long seen coming; to days of childhood that are still unexplained, to parents whom one had to hurt when they brought one some joy and one did not grasp it (it was a joy for someone else); to childhood illnesses that so strangely begin with such a number of profound and grave transformations, to days in rooms withdrawn and quiet and to mornings by the sea, to the sea itself, to seas, to nights of travel that rushed along on high and flew with all the stars—and it is not yet enough if one

may think of all this. One must have memories of many nights of love, none of which was like the others, of the screams of women in labor, and of light, white, sleeping women in childbed, closing again. But one must also have been beside the dying, must have sat beside the dead in the room with the open window and the fitful noises. And still it is not yet enough to have memories. One must be able to forget them when they are many and one must have the great patience to wait until they come again. For it is not yet the memories themselves. Not till they have turned to blood within us, to glance and gesture, nameless and no longer to be distinguished from ourselves—not till then can it happen that in a most rare hour the first word of a verse arises in their midst and goes forth from them.°

We let "blood-learned" intervention land on or, better yet, stand under our client's awareness. We let it "tickle" him/her. So, eventually, s/he can sense it in her/his bones and joints, muscles and tendons, eyeballs and tear ducts, mouth and saliva.

It is this kind of intervention which Jim Kepner describes so well—organizing our thinking so clearly around all the circumstances that make this integrated work possible.

Comparing Perls' work to Reich, Jacobson and Alexander, Kepner shows how Gestalt therapy alone approaches the patient's sensation and awareness, not bypassing resistances but incorporating body work with the patient's awareness and sense of choice.

Kepner's work, as most classical Gestalt therapy, is based on awareness. The phenomenology of his therapy session works thus: The client starts with his/her awareness of self, including sensory experience of the physical self. When attended to, the physical side changes and, at the same time, awareness changes: "When I inflate my chest, I feel big and tough." The client has it within his/her own volition to deflate his/her chest and experience some vulnerability or remorse, or to inflate the chest and experience pride and strength. Muscular-skeletal change and postural stance change with increased awareness and sense of one's own choices, complexity, and richness. These changes are whole, involving the total organism, and appear to last for many years.

Change in character structure does not come about from the charismatic directives of the therapist as to how to breathe, stand, or walk, but from the client's own awareness-directed experimentation. Both from my own therapy with the author, as well as from reading this concise volume, I am left with the clear sense of Kepner's enormous respect for the client's moment-to-moment process and for the client's integrity and dignity as a human being. The therapist and client are a team, work-

°Rilke, Rainer Maria (1949). *The notebooks of Malte Laurids Brigge.* New York: W. W. Norton, 1949.

ing together to explore, understand, and experiment with the client's unfolding experience.

Dr. Kepner supports resistance as an integral part of self in that he gives it the "somatic voice" needed for the client to learn something very important, specifically as an expression of self that is allowed to emerge consciously, choicefully, deliberately. Resistance is seen as a disowned part of the body-self that needs to be brought to awareness and reintegrated into the person's total functioning. On the basis of his understanding and treatment of resistance alone, I see the author's work as a major contribution to psychotherapy, and to Gestalt therapy in particular.

This book is the first major, comprehensive effort to integrate the so-called cognitive-awareness therapies with the various body process and body manipulation therapies. The author presents Gestalt therapy in its broadest range: how it views the whole organism and how it treats the therapist–client relationship—as guiding, touching, and experimenting in an atmosphere of intimate contact.

Broadly conceived and crisply executed, this work does not promise anything that it doesn't deliver. Without drama, exaggeration, or fanfare, Kepner gives detailed clinical examples of all principles and techniques discussed. Although he does not use the often-heard word "creative," he nevertheless shows how and in what ways creativity operates in treating another human being.

The Gestalt Institute of Cleveland and its professional staff are pleased and proud to present this beautifully written book to the reader.

Joseph C. Zinker, Ph.D.

Acknowledgments

A number of people deserve my special thanks for the help they gave in the formation of this book:

Joseph Zinker, whose mentoring, therapizing, cajoling, tears, and abiding love have allowed me to recognize my depths and appreciate my limits. His faith in the value of my vision has helped me to have that faith as well.

The faculty, staff, and students of the Gestalt Institute of Cleveland, who have given me a forum for the development of my ideas and have supported my learning.

Robert Hall, Richard Heckler, Allysa Hall, and Catherine Flaxman of the Lomi School, who gave me the base from which my current work has developed.

Ansel Woldt, Ed.D, and Kent State University for the grant of a University Fellowship (on Ansel's recommendation), which allowed me to develop the original manuscript for this volume.

My colleagues Tom Cutolo, Jody Telfair-Richards, Jeffrey Schaler, Rene Royak-Schaler, and Warren Grossman for their special spirit, friendship, and encouragement.

My parents and family for their continued interest in, and support for, literary pursuits.

Shirley Loffer, for her superb editorial assistance, advice on the craft of writing, steady improvement of my spelling, and help in distilling the raw material of the manuscript into a cohesive text.

Finally, and most important, I thank my wife, Mary Ann Kraus, for her love and caring through the highs and lows of writing. She has remained always committed to my treading the "path of heart."

The Author

James I. Kepner is a psychologist in private practice in Cleveland, Ohio, where he is also on the professional staff of the Gestalt Institute of Cleveland. He is the chairperson of the training program Working with Physical Process at the Gestalt Institute of Cleveland. He received his B.A. degree (1976) magna cum laude in psychology from Cleveland State University, where he also received his M.A. degree (1978) in clinical community psychology. He received his Ph.D. degree (1982) in counseling psychology from Kent State University.

Kepner's professional interests include teaching of Gestalt therapy and training psychotherapists in body-oriented methods. His special interests are treatment of adult survivors of childhood abuse and application of body-oriented therapy to chronic disease states. He is currently developing a manuscript, *Healing Tasks,* based on his model for treating abuse survivors.

Kepner was granted a university fellowship by Kent State to develop much of the theoretical material now in *Body Process.*

BODY
PROCESS

Introduction:
Body Process
and Psychotherapy

Mainstream psychotherapy commonly defines the therapeutic process as working with and correcting mental events and conditions. Tools of the trade have consistently emphasized the "psycho" aspect of therapy—verbalizations, thoughts, ideas, dreams, and the like. Even emotion is viewed as a mental event. Whether the goal is "reduction of psychological conflict" or "improvement of self-image" or "restructuring cognitions," our theories and methods have traditionally attached little importance to body phenomena in the context of psychotherapy. At its root this is a reflection of the extreme emphasis on intellect and reason in our culture at large. The world view of psychotherapy, after all, is limited by the world view of the culture in which it is embedded.

This one-sided emphasis on the cognitive side of human nature, while understandable from the cultural perspective, has always been curious to me given the bodily nature of much that people bring to us on entering therapy. Such problems as obesity, psychosomatic distress, emotional deadness, chronic tension, lack of emotional expressiveness, headaches, sexual problems, and bodily violation resulting from physical and sexual abuse all involve the fundamental fact that our existence is an embodied existence. What happens to us as persons happens to us in physical ways as much as in psychological ways. We live not only through our thinking and imagining, but also through moving, posturing, sensing, expressing. How, then, can we ignore the fundamental physical

1

nature of the person in a profession where the aim is to heal the self, the whole person?

Yet a shift is taking place. It is increasingly common for mainstream psychotherapists of varying professional and theoretical backgrounds to take into account body phenomena as part of the significant data of therapy, even if their methods present no cohesive way of understanding such phenomena. I have noticed this shift over the course of a number of years of conducting training workshops for therapists in understanding and utilizing body process in therapy. Students now see as reasonable what years ago took much convincing on my part: that the client's posture, movements, and bodily experience are relevant to therapy.

In recent years two new influences seem to have increased the interest in body phenomena in psychotherapy. One has been the interest in body arts and therapies in the humanistic psychology and human potential movements, including a resurgence of Reichian-oriented therapies, the body emphasis in Gestalt therapy, and the body arts such as Hatha yoga, martial arts, the Feldenkrais and Alexander techniques, and Rolfing (structural integration). A second influence has been the understanding of nonverbal behavior as communication. This supposedly new influence[*] has been utilized by psychotherapies such as Eriksonian hypnosis and modern communications schools of therapy (e.g., couples' communication).

Within this recent surge of interest in body phenomena, there are significant differences in the ways in which body process is understood in the context of psychotherapy. These differences are reflected in four viewpoints: (1) therapies, such as psychoanalysis and cognitive therapy, which give little attention to body phenomena other than as symptoms of "underlying" mental problems (i.e., as epiphenomena of the mind/cognition); (2) body arts, such as those mentioned above, which work only with body processes, much as psychoanalysis works only with mental processes; (3) communication and behavioral schools of therapy, which see body phenomena primarily as a set of signals to be monitored or as behaviors to be modified; (4) depth body therapies, such as the Gestalt and Reichian schools, which see the body as intrinsic to the self and the person as a whole.

It is the aim of this book to present and elucidate one particular "depth" approach to understanding and working with body phenomena in psychotherapy. The intent is to demonstrate a framework within

---

[*]It is often forgotten that Wilhelm Reich called attention to the importance of body phenomena in his *Character Analysis* (1945/1972) during the early days of psychoanalysis.

which practitioners of different persuasions can better appreciate body processes in the context of the whole person, rather than as isolated events. I will describe how the body is intrinsic to the *self,* and as such is significantly related to our emotional life and enduring life themes, and is the physical foundation of our existence in the world.

For those therapists who see their work as predominantly mental in nature, I hope to demonstrate how attending to body process can make their therapeutic work with emotion and thinking more powerful by including bodily sensation, awareness, expression, and movement. For practitioners of body arts, I hope this book will highlight the importance of the body posture and experience in emotional and psychological functioning. For therapists with a communications perspective, I hope to show that the meaning of body process rests not only in the communication of information, but also in its fundamental, existential expression of self. And for those therapists who already are familiar with depth body-oriented work, I hope that this book will provide a cohesive viewpoint that will firmly ground body-oriented interventions in the client's awareness and sense of self.

The material in this book has been forged out of my own frustrations with the existing integrations of body approaches and therapy. The overriding theoretical structure is derived from that of Gestalt therapy, particularly as described by Perls (1947/1969) and Perls et al. (1951), and as taught at the Gestalt Institute of Cleveland where I have been both student and faculty member. Although the focus here is specifically on a body approach and is not intended as a thorough explanation of Gestalt therapy, readers unfamiliar with the Gestalt approach should find an adequate introduction to its principles in this text. Those who wish more in-depth knowledge of Gestalt therapy should consult the literature referenced throughout the book. I view this work as an extension of the existing view of Gestalt therapy, and not as a "new" school of therapy.

Writers about psychotherapy are given the dual task of presenting clear and detailed case descriptions in order to illustrate the application of ideas, while still protecting the confidentiality and privacy of their clients. I have attempted to respect both by significantly altering details of the case material so as to disguise the participants without distorting the clinical picture. In many places, composites from a number of different cases are used and dialogue is not verbatim.

Part I
Basic Principles

Chapter 1

Self and Embodiment

It seems odd to many people when I suggest that attending to body experience, their own or that of others, can be important in solving problems of daily living: coping with tension, forging relationships, understanding feelings. It may seem odder still to suggest that body experience has relevance to even deeper problems of self, such as identity confusion, emotional conflicts, or a sense of fragmentation. We normally consider "body" to be something other than "self," and thus irrelevant to the "I" that is struggling with the problems of living a full and meaningful life.

People who are feeling the kind of distress that prompts them to seek help are often intent on getting rid of some uncomfortable body experience. They want to be relieved of the pounding heart and gasping breath that go with anxiety. They want the rushes of anger and the sensations of dread to disappear. They want the discomfort of tense muscles and the constant headaches to be taken away.

In addition to bodily symptoms and discomforts, clients are often at odds with their existence as physical beings. They may think of themselves as ugly or inadequate. They may find that attending to their body experience feels "wrong," too sexual or animalistic. To experience their bodies may have been so associated with pain, sickness, or violation that their bodies have become something to avoid. Thus initially to ask them to attend to this aspect of experience seems counter to the problems for which they are seeking help.

6

Most therapists also approach therapy from such a disassociated state, although for slightly different reasons. The theories and methods we are taught place the focus of change on mental constructs: conflicts, cognitions, interactional loops, and structures of the mind. Body phenomena are considered only as symptoms to be diagnosed, behaviors to be modified, communications to be understood, or as symbols for underlying processes.

Added to this is the therapist's degree of contact with his or her own body experience. We frequently feel the same discomfort with our body experience as do our clients. We are products of educational systems and training programs where the intellect is seen as the only relevant tool for dealing with human problems. This is apparent in the work context of the therapist: sitting immobile for hours, barely breathing, listening to and responding from the intellect.

The psychotherapeutic context, however, is not the only factor undermining the linkage of body and self. Our language encourages the distinction between body and "I." We have no single word that allows us to say "I-body." At the most we might say "my body" in much the same way we might refer to "my car," implying that one's body is property, but certainly not *self*. Our language supports the notion that our body is an object: something that happens to me, rather than the "me that is happening."

Given this commonly disassociative experience of the body, it is no wonder that suggestions to consider one's body as self and body experience as experience of oneself are met with consternation. What do I mean to suggest such a thing?

BODY EXPERIENCE AS EXPERIENCE OF SELF

In keeping with the experiential focus of this book, I offer an experiment to focus you on your own body experience and the link between your sense of self and sense of body.

Just as you are sitting, without intentionally altering your body posture or position, begin to attend to your body experience. What are your first sensations? What tensions do you feel? Where? How are you breathing: fast, slow, deep? What is your posture? Are you "holding yourself up" or allowing the chair to support you? Are you slouched or loose or straight or rigid? How does that sitting posture affect your breathing?

So far you have just begun the process of attending to your body experience. Many people tell me that they don't feel anything when they first focus on their body. If this is true for you, then this lack of feeling is itself an important statement about your sense of "self." But most people will have some sensation of their body processes; if you stay with attending to your body patiently enough, the details will become richer and fuller.

> As you continue to attend to your body experience, make statements, silently or aloud, starting, for example, with: "Right now I notice that my breathing feels tight and shallow." "Right now I notice warmth in my belly." Take your time. Let the statements help you to focus on your body experience at this moment.

You may notice that some sensations stand out more than others. You may be more aware of your breathing or of your posture, or perhaps of tension in your neck or legs. In Gestalt terms these sensations are figures that stand out against the general background of your body experience. A figure, something outstanding in your awareness, begins to draw attention and gain energy if it has importance for your self.

> Now try changing the "I notice . . . " to "I am . . . ," so as to experiment with connecting your "I" to your body experience. For example, change "I notice tension in my shoulders" to "I am tensing my shoulders." Change "I notice weakness in my arms," to "I am weak in my arms." Continue this for five or six statements.

What happens when you shift to the use of the term "I" in reference to your body experience? Some people protest the implication of ownership: "I do not tense my shoulders, they are just like that." If you felt this urge to protest, then I would ask: Who is tensing your shoulder if not you? Tension is something you do to yourself in response to something. But you may not yet experience your tension clearly enough to feel that it is you who is producing it. Let us return to the body experiment to see if we can bring an even fuller sense of "I" to your body process.

> Focus your attention on the two or three sensations of tension that stand out most for you. Taking one at a time, how would you des-

cribe the character of this tension? Does it feel like compressing? Holding on? Tightening? Binding? Bracing? It might help you to consciously exaggerate the tension so as to get a clearer sense of the character of the tension.

Using the words that describe the character of the tensions (they may be different tensions), let me suggest an additional experiment. Assume, for the sake of our experiment, that your body is your "self." If, for example, the character of one of the tensions on which you focused was that of "compression," use that word to make a two-part statement about yourself: "I am compressing myself, and this is my existence." Or, "I am containing myself, and this is my existence."

Repeat the statements a couple of times to fully appreciate their meaning to you. Feel the impact of considering your bodily state to be descriptive of your existential state.

If you have been doing the experiment and not simply reading about it, one or two of your statements may have become meaningful to you. Perhaps you were able to express something directly that previously you had only vaguely experienced. You might have experienced the "click" of recognition between your physical experience and your sense of present life or some past situation.

Or perhaps you had a difficult time finding anything meaningful within your body experience. You stopped halfway through the experiment, or noticed "nothing" about your body, or felt only "trivial" sensations. In the context of the experiment I would ask you to make statements about your difficulties in the same way that I asked you to make statements about your body experience:

"I don't feel comfortable attending to my body, and this is my existence."

"I don't feel much of myself, and this is my existence."

"My body is trivial to me, and this is my existence."

Your resistance, discomfort, or sense of meaninglessness is just as much a statement of your relationship to bodily self as any other statement.

EMBODIMENT

The experiment has given you experiential grounding in a basic premise of the Gestalt approach to body therapy: the self or "I" is an embodied self as well as a thoughtful one. We exist, love, work, and meet our constantly changing needs through our physical being and interactions in the world. Experience of our body is experience of our self, just as our thinking, imagery, and ideas are part of our self.

When we make our body experience an "it" instead of "I," we make ourselves less than we are. We become diminished. The more we have removed our identity from our body experience, the more things "seem to happen" to us. We feel out of control, dissociated, fragmented. We lose contact with the primary ground of human experience—our corporeal reality. This, of course, is a common description of the difficulties we are called upon to treat as therapists. But it is also not too different from the malaise of our society at large: fragmented, cut off from our feelings, desensitized, and out of control. Could this social phenomenon have roots in our relationship to our body?

Over the course of this book, I will describe how our bodily being is intrinsic to our relationship to our world, and forms a base for our contact with our environment—our physical and especially our human environment—so that we may meet our needs and grow. Working with people as they embody themselves helps us, as therapists, to concretize our abstract notions of self, existence, and being, and adds to our appreciation of the whole person.

SELF AS INTEGRATOR OF EXPERIENCE

Since I will use the term "self" frequently throughout this book, it would be useful to describe in more detail how I am using this concept. The concept of the self is a complex and confusing one in the literature of Gestalt therapy, but central to our orientation. The complexity of the notion is attributable to its status as an elusive and ephemeral part of the organism, and the confusion results from the use of the term in a number of different ways. Gestalt therapy views the self not as a thing, a static structure, but as a fluid process. The self is not a frozen set of characteristics ("I am this and only this"). In health the self is various and flexible in its capabilities and qualities, depending on the particular demands of the organism and environment. The self has no nature of its own except in contact with or in relation to the environment. It has been described as the system of contacts or interactions with the environment. In this sense the self can be seen as the integrator of experience.

The self has available what are called contact functions, that is, *specialized actions and capabilities*. In this view it would be accurate to say that the self is nothing else *but* the system of contact functions. The self and contact functions are one and the same to the Gestalt view. The self has been described as a "system of excitement, orientation, manipulation, and various identifications and alienations . . . " (Perls, et al., 1951, p. 315). These general categories of contact functions describe the basic ways in which we interact with our environment to satisfy our needs and adjust to environmental changes. Through excitement we feel our needs. Through orientation we organize ourselves to meet these needs in relation to our environment. Through manipulation we act in the service of our needs. Through identification we take into our organism (make "I") what can be assimilated, and through alienation we reject (make "not-I") what is foreign to our nature and so cannot be assimilated.

Full and adaptive functioning is dependent on contact functions being fully available to the organism to meet the changing requirements of interaction in the environment. When contact functions become unavailable to awareness, the organism no longer can adapt fluidly to its world. Those aspects of one's functioning that are disowned—that is, not *experienced* as self—are not fully available for contact with the environment. The more limited one's capabilities for contact, the more one's experience of self and of the environment becomes fragmentary, disorganized, and subject to resistance.

Based on this definition of self, my aim is to show the importance of the bodily basis of our contact functions and how psychological ill health is related to our loss of these functions through estrangement from our bodily being. Part I of this book is devoted to understanding how that which is intrinsically a part of the self, the body, becomes alienated and treated as not-self, and the clinical stance for healing this split. Part II presents a detailed theoretical and clinical description of the bodily nature of the contact functions of excitement (sensation), orientation (figure formation and mobilization), manipulation (action), identification (contact), and alienation (withdrawal and assimilation).

Chapter 2

The Body and the Disowned Self

> The description of psychological health and disease is a simple one. It is a matter of the identifications and alienations of the self: If a man identifies with his forming self, does not inhibit his own creative excitement and reaching toward the coming solution; and conversely, if he alienates what is not organically his own and therefore cannot be vitally interesting, but rather disrupts the figure/background, then he is psychologically healthy . . . But on the contrary, if he alienates himself and because of false identifications tries to conquer his own spontaneity, then he creates his life dull, confused, and painful. (Perls et al., 1951, p. 235)

Most of us do not identify or experience our body as "self." We feel ourselves often to be living *in* our body, or out of touch with our physical being altogether. In the view of Gestalt therapy noted in the quote above, psychological disease occurs when a person alienates what is organically his or hers and so disrupts functioning. How is it that we come to be alienated from (or to alienate) our physical being and identify only with ourselves as mental and noncorporeal beings?

ADJUSTMENT TO A DIFFICULT ENVIRONMENT

In the Gestalt model of human development, growth and the formation of self come about through contact (interaction) with the environment. Through this contact we seek and find that which we require for our survival and development, assimilate those novel experiences that can be used for growth and change, and alienate (reject) that which cannot be assimilated (Perls, 1947/1969). In the course of this process of contact, growth, and development, aspects or qualities of our self may become problematic in a particular physical or social environment. For example, a child's expression of the need for love is met with rejection, aggression with punishment, vulnerability with cruelty, curiosity with defensiveness or impoverished surroundings.

Human beings are resilient as well as persistent, and single instances of rejection or punishment rarely damage the person. We do not require a perfect environment for growth but only, to paraphrase Winnicott (1960), one that is "just good enough" for healthy development. However, there are responses from the environment that have a less than salutary effect. A frequently repeated response, such as constant and regular criticism and discouragement from others, can have a major impact on the developing person. Singular events, in which a child's natural impulses are met with a major threat of withdrawal of nurturance, can also have a profound effect, such as when an infant's cries for hunger evoke a look of hatred from an overburdened parent. Additionally, double binds, such as when a parent punishes a child's natural sexual play as "dirty and disgusting" while surreptitiously acting coquettish and seductive towards the child, can also have a critical effect on the forming self.

Conditions such as these demand that the person cope with a conflict between the need for survival and qualities of the developing self. Just as unassimilable aspects of the environment are alienated (rejected from the organism), aspects of the self that the environment rejects become alienated. Qualities of the self—the impulse towards curiosity, the want for love, the capacity for vulnerability, sexual feelings—are alienated or, in the common clinical usage, disowned° from self.

Disowning intrinsic aspects of one's self, be they needs, capacities, or behaviors, is something like deciding you don't want a particular room in your house but cannot get rid of it because its existence is essential to the integrity of the rest of the building: all you can do is board it up and pretend it does not exist. We can relegate such parts of ourselves to the boarded-up dark of unawareness, but they continue to exist even while

---

°I use the term "disowned" instead of the more technically accurate term "alienated" largely because the latter term carries too much of a negative connotation in current usage, e.g., "alienated youth." "Disowned" more accurately captures the subjective experience of "this is not *me.*"

we pretend that such qualities are "not important." I can prevent myself from behaving in emotional ways, and I can remove emotionality from my image of myself, but I cannot truly excise my emotions from my being. They (no longer "I") function out of my sight, but continue to function nonetheless.

What happens to the disowned aspects of our organism—the feelings, needs, and expressions, the movements and images? How are they kept out of sight and unaware? In what arena do such self functions, now not-self, operate?

SPLITTING THE "I" FROM THE BODY

To a large degree, we maintain the existence of disowned aspects of self through their linkage with body functions and processes. By making the body-self an "it," and relegating the "I" or identified-self to the mind, our body in a sense *becomes* the disowned self. We split our organism into an "I," which consists of thinking and verbalization, and an "it," which consists of feeling and nonverbal expression. We then experience much of that which comes in the form of body experience as alienated from self and thus irrational, and most of that which comes in the form of thinking and verbal expression as rational and therefore acceptable to our self-image. The fusion of the disowned self with the body results from the fact that many of the organismic functions we must disown are rooted in our physical nature. Thus, to disown those aspects or functions of the self requires that we disown the bodily aspects of self that are involved.

The work of maintaining this split and keeping the disowned self out of our awareness is aided by the bodily nature of repression itself. To the Gestalt therapist, repression is not merely a "mental" mechanism. We can keep our disowned self out of our awareness by physically preventing the movements intrinsic to those parts, such as tensing to prevent the movements of reaching out to others and thereby maintaining the identified-self characteristic of independence. We can physically dull and deaden the bodily sensations (by tensing against them) that are part of feelings of love, anger, and compassion.

The language of the self provides another means of maintaining disownership and lack of awareness. The vocabulary of the identified-self becomes predominantly verbal, while the vocabulary of the body-self is kinesthetic. Like an unused language that is gradually forgotten, the expression of the body-self comes to "make no sense." It is without words, is little reinforced socially, and is difficult to talk about. Is it any wonder that the communications of our disowned self, the language of the body, seem irrational and without meaning? Additionally, the unity of our experience is destroyed when the feelings and motor components (bodily aspects) of both past and present experiences are split from the verbal and imagistic aspects of experience. Without their intrinsic unity as wholes, memories are difficult to recall, or to the Gestalt way of thinking, recreate, and present contact is disturbed. This is like cutting out parts of a picture until its essential form is no longer recognizable.

As I have noted, the identification between the body and the disowned aspects of self comes about because much of what we need to disown, to divorce from our sense of self, either has a strong physical component or is in itself predominantly a physical process. The body-oriented therapist recognizes just how much of our existence is grounded in the somatic and physical, despite the common perception that the real "me" is actually mental. Let us take a look at what aspects of our somatic self might need to be disowned.

The Feeling Self

It is common to think of "feelings" as mental events, but Webster's gives us a clue as to the close link between kinesthetic processes and feeling by defining feeling as "an emotional *sensation*"[italics mine]. In looking at the person from a holistic standpoint, we must recognize that much of our feeling life involves somatic experience.° Feelings of sadness involve sensations of warm heaviness in the chest, tension in the diaphragm, constriction of the throat, and watery eyes. Feelings of excitement include sensations of upward lifting of the chest, tremulousness in the belly, and tingling and flowing sensations in the limbs. † You can experiment with this by vividly imagining a situation that involves some strong feeling, such as longing for an absent loved one, the pleasure of doing something you really delight in, or an argument with

---

°For purposes of discussion, I am separating the *experience* of feeling as sensation (discussed here) from the *expression* of feeling into the environment (discussed in the next section). They are both part of the same phenomenon we commonly label emotion, but for the sake of clarity I am abstracting and discussing them separately.
† In Gestalt therapy we would say that the existential event called "feeling" is actually a whole involving body sensations, mental events such as images and thinking (self-verbalization), movements, and the environment; but clearly a significant part of this whole are the physical sensations.

your boss. Pay careful attention to your sensations and body responses. What are the physical components of your feelings?

If there is conflict about a feeling—the sadness is overwhelming (i.e., there is not sufficient organismic or environmental support) or you are told that "We Jones's don't indulge in such feelings" (you risk rejection from people significant to your welfare)—then you are put in a position of having to divorce your feelings from normal contact. To remove a contact function is to disown it from self. In the case of feelings, this frequently means divorcing oneself from the bodily sensations of feeling. In trying out the small experiment above, did you have any difficulty? You may not have been able to distinguish any sensations. Or you might have been aware of sensations with some feelings and not with others. This might reflect such a loss of contact with your body, a disownership of body-self with respect to feelings.‡

The Moving Self

Muscular action is an intrinsic part of any interchange with our environment. It is through movement that we express feeling, manipulate and shape the environment, relate and react to others, create and modulate boundaries, and defend our organismic integrity.

The word *emotion* comes from the Latin *e* (out) and *movere* (to move): to move outwards. The visceral and sensory experience of feeling becomes movement out towards or into the environment. The feeling of sadness becomes the act of crying when we allow the sensations to develop naturally into the contractions of the breathing musculature, vocal sobs, and facial expressions of grief. The feeling of longing, when allowed to develop into movement, includes reaching out physically for the loved one. It is only through movement, in fact, that feeling has full meaning. Only by moving can we connect the need the feeling manifests to the environment where needs can be completed.

There are conditions under which one's feeling, the sensory aspect of affect, must be disowned or suppressed. Similarly, the expression of feeling in emotion, showing one's feeling, may be difficult. If reaching out is criticized or rejected, it becomes a risk to show one's need for love, and the musculature of the arms and chest (over the heart) tenses to counter reaching out. If even small expressions of anger are reacted against, then the movements of anger must be prevented. If "big boys

‡How this occurs and is maintained (the resistance of desensitization) will be discussed in detail in a later chapter.

don't cry" or a child is stuck with the role of being "the strong one," the ability to soften into vulnerability and allow oneself to sob must be countered muscularly. Eventually such movements become alien and threatening to one's sense of self, disowned and no longer accessible as a contact function.

Movement is not only a function of affect; it is a function of any interaction with the environment. If we examine the organismic functions that movement serves and understand something of the environment to which the organism must adjust itself, it soon becomes obvious that in this adjustment the motor faculties will be affected.

As needs come to be motorically expressed in the environment (needs to relate and react, to define boundaries and defend one's integrity, to reach out and obtain nurturance), accommodation to environmental demands may require that such needs not be expressed and the motoric expression must be given up.

The expression of curiosity, for example, cannot take place without motoric manipulation of the environment. Yet a parent who fears losing a child's dependency will tend to limit the child's activity and movement away from the parent. Such movement becomes alien and threatening to the child because it threatens the parent, the source for satisfaction of other essential needs, and the ownership of many body movements is damaged. Since we cannot give up what is intrinsic to us, we can only disown the movements involved.[*]

The Painful Self

Growing up involves among other things, a series of painful bumps against the hard edges of the world: table edges, hot stoves, rough pavement, and the limits of adults' tolerance. None of these things in themselves do any damage to self-development, as long as they can be assimilated properly into ongoing functioning. Mother kisses the hurt, thereby helping the child to "heal" by moderating an otherwise overwhelming experience. Falls and bumps can be responded to by recognizing that one needs to pay more attention or learn a new motor skill. Parents' anger can be responded to by learning to recognize the signs and conditions that lead to its arousal. Such situations are assimilable because the child can adapt and learn to cope without sacrificing any part of his or her essential integrity, that is, what is required for functioning.

[*]Chapter 10, "Action and Body Process," discusses in more detail the processes by which movement is disowned.

Other pains are more compromising: either their severity and constancy demand a major response to adapt, or the pain is intended to restrict functioning. The most obvious examples are cases of physical abuse: severe beatings, demeaning punishments, constant threats of physical harm, manipulation of and intrusion into one's body by others. One client was rarely beaten but constantly threatened, and so his posture came to assume the attitude of someone ready to duck to the side from a blow. Another underwent repeated beatings from her father and could only cope with the pain by dissociating herself from her body. Others have been forced to stand for hours on end facing a corner until their legs could no longer support them, or thrust into dark closets to endure the emotional pain of loneliness and terror. The less severe pain but humiliating discomfort of bodily intrusion is similar: enemas, manipulation of toilet functions, and other bodily intrusions by adults.

In all of these situations of unbearable and constant pain or threat of pain we can see how the aspect of self being damaged is somatic in nature. The child responds to such hurts by shrinking away from the contact surface of skin and muscle. With repeated hurt, the child shrinks even further away from the source of pain, divorcing the sense of self from his or her body, disowning the location of pain to help reduce the damage. The result, which I see so often in people who come to me for body-oriented work, is heartrending. They desperately seek love and relationship but are so detached from their body surface that they cannot bridge the gap between their self, so deeply pulled into their body core, and the other with whom they want to connect because the medium of connection, the body, is no longer identified as self. Instead they seek abusive relationships that confirm and reinforce the need to disown their body and maintain their protection against pain and hurt.

Creating an environment where clients can risk coming back into their body is a labor of love and caring by the therapist. As each layer of body-self is recontacted, old emotional wounds must be reopened so the disowned experiences can be brought to the present where true healing can take place. Facing the outpouring of emotional "pus" as the person reconnects with his or her body is an emotionally trying task for both client and therapist. In addition, persons with such hurtful experience of human contact will constantly test the limits of the therapist's caring, frequently projecting the characteristics of their early abusers onto the therapist. Not infrequently the therapist may justify such projection by reacting out of his or her own hurt when such suspicious and testy clients so constantly reject the therapist's displays of caring and help.

Another situation that supports disownership of bodily aspects of self because of pain is that involving disease or painful medical treatment. One young woman had had surgery from the age of three months to 18 years at a rate of an operation each year to correct a birth defect. Her parents and family coped admirably, and did everything they could to minimize the impact of the operations on her life and help her to master the difficult but necessary treatments. Even with such remarkable help, pain is pain, and many of the ways in which she coped with pain involved detaching herself from her body. As our work reconnected her to her body, she began to recognize how much her disownership of her body minimized her feeling life, and how her stance of "I can take anything" prevented her from feeling and acting on needs for comfort and support.

The Sexual Self

Our sexuality, like other aspects of our body-self, can be either an integrated aspect of our functioning or disowned. If one's sexual nature is denied or distorted, then contact with one's body, particularly the erogenous areas and also the fact of one's physicality itself, become denied or distorted, and disowned as self. Freud has pointed out the important effect of parental emotional seduction on sexuality in his descriptions of the Oedipus and Electra conflicts. Reich later elaborated on this in his comments on the effect of societal moral strictures on psychosexual development and character. The implicitly sexual emotional seduction between the parent and child and the moral condemnation of natural sexual urges create fear, revulsion, and anxiety about one's bodily being.

Under such conditions the *self* that is sexual is soon disowned as "the body" (no longer "I" but rather "the," an object). How can something that is "dirty" or "disgusting" (in the case of moral strictures about sexuality) or arouses fear of rejection or castration (in the case of parent–child seduction) be part of my "self"? To accept it would mean that I am dirty or disgusting, or that my feelings must continue to produce fear. Instead the aspects of my organism, my bodily nature and sexual organs, must be disowned. It is now "my body" (not me) that has sexual urges, or my spouse to whom I must "do my duty" when my own sexual nature is rendered unimportant or nonexistent.

Even more devastating is the effect of incest and sexual molestation. How can sexuality remain a function of the self if one's own organs are at the service of another person's wants? How can one "own" one's body when it is invaded and intruded upon by another? One client said: "For all the times I was sexually abused there was always a part of me that they never even touched ... I kept that part of me sealed away from what they were doing to my body." She could keep a part of her safe from sexual intrusion by separating the aspects of her self to which such intrusion occurred, her bodily self, from that which she experienced as "self."

But it is not only intrusion into one's body that damages the connection of bodily function to self. There is also disownership created out of the tremendous emotional confusion about bodily sensations, urges, and impulses. The parent, who is just as confused regarding feelings and acts of love and nurturance versus feelings and acts of sexuality, creates such confusion in the child. In the family "currency," little distinction is made between sexuality and affection, the result being that family members don't know how to ask for love without asking for or promising sexuality.

Frequently there is denial of the existence of sexual abuse in the family. The abused child has no support for his or her experience of reality (the abuse) from the nonabusing parent, and often is coerced to withhold the truth by the abusing parent. When the truth of the violation is denied, the solution is to detach from the body and "its" reality. The clinical evidence of depersonalization and disembodiment in clients with a history of sexual abuse demonstrates this. I have seen a number of cases where adults who had no previous awareness of any history of sexual abuse began to recover such memories in conjunction with therapeutic work to reown their body experiences.

In addition the child may also feel pleasure despite being coerced into the act. This might be actual sexual pleasure in the older child, or the pleasure of "making Daddy feel better." This puts the child in even more conflict since, having felt pleasure, he or she may actually feel responsible for what occurred, and have great difficulty recognizing that it was also hated and feared. The victim of sexual abuse disowns his or her body, not only because of the direct effects of sexual imposition, but also because of the conflicting and unreconcilable feelings that are brought about by the situation itself and the victim's own natural responses. Reconciling one's anger at being violated with one's love for the abusing parent, the pleasure of sexuality with the pain of violation, the helplessness of imposition with the power over the parent's needs, the self-value derived from the alliance with the parent and the self-loathing derived from submission to the parent, forces one into denial and disownership of the body "in which" they occur.

One client, a woman who was repeatedly sexually abused as a child, often had sexual feelings towards people with whom she had filial wants and needs. Teachers, superiors, nurturant friends, and other "parent-like" people in her life would evoke sexual feelings and fantasies because such feelings were never discriminated from one another in her family. Since such feelings always brought violation of her body and an image of herself as dirty and evil, she learned to divorce herself from her body so that she did not have to experience her sexual self. She also made herself fat so that others were less likely to respond to her in a sexual way. At times such feelings were strong enough to break through anyway and, as they were disowned and therefore alien and terrifying, she would try to cope by becoming psychotic. She divorced herself not only from her body, but from the reality that was evoking her feelings.

THE RANGE OF EXPERIENCE

The disowning of one's body ranges from mild distancing of one's identity from specific body feelings, to a more pervasive and severe disownership characterized by conflict about many bodily feelings and actions, to depersonalization and even more severe distortion, and finally, to psychotic disembodiment. The degree to which body process is disowned has an important relationship to the severity of pathology and the degree of contact with reality, as noted in Figure 2-1.

The more contact functions disowned, the narrower is the range of behavior available for action within the environment. The "I" becomes more rigid and constrained, with fewer areas of legitimate operation, as more of the self's capacities (feelings and actions) are rendered alien and thus unusable.

At the disowned extreme, we find the disembodiment seen frequently in psychosis, where the person has divorced himself or herself almost entirely from the feelings of the body and exists in fantasy. Somewhat less severe are conditions where perception of the body is distorted or "at a distance," as in depersonalization. This is seen in anorexia nervosa, where there is a severe distortion of perception of the body; in neurotic crisis, where body feeling exists but is experienced in a detached manner; and in borderline disorders, where significant

Highly
Owned

Highly
Disowned

Some aspects of body
disowned ("normal")

Distortion/depersonalization
(severe neurosis, anorexia,
borderline experience)

Somatic
materialism

Conflict w/feelings
and physical nature
(neurosis, somatic
symptoms)

Disembodiment
(psychosis)

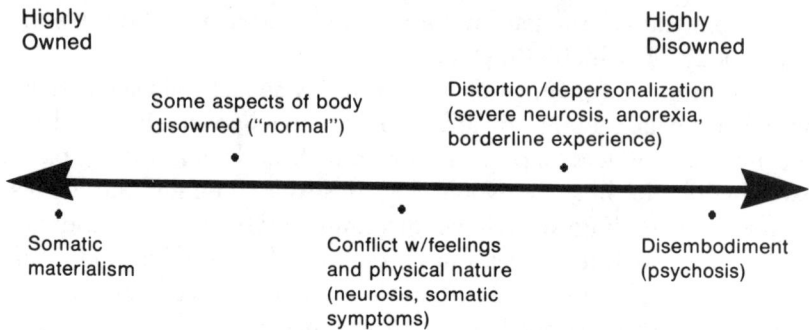

Figure 2–1. Continuum of disownership of the body.

"chunks" of the body-self have been lost to awareness, thus creating a sense of fragmentation and periodic breakdown as the person struggles for unity.

The neurotic has more capacity for contact with the body-self but has significant conflict over particular feelings and actions. The disownership of these particular body processes results in depression when they are strongly withheld from contact, in anxiety as such contact functions threaten to occur, and in psychosomatic symptoms when they come to partial but distorted expression. In crisis, however, the neurotic must resort to more severe means to cope with such contact functions, and may depersonalize temporarily. When not stressed the neurotic appears "normal" in that the needs, feelings, and actions that are problematic are not being evoked. The person is "in control."

Midway between the "normal" and the neurotic is the "modal," or most usual degree of body identification. The body is experienced, but frequently not fully as "I." We see this in the way in which many people treat the body as if it were a machine—exercising it, pampering it, racing it, flogging it with work—it and not I. The disownership is subtle and frequently general in form. The "modal" is mildly distanced from his or her body experience and so has mildly dulled all feeling and experience.

The "normal" person experiences some disownership of body experience, but to a lesser degree, and more of the self is available to awareness. Important somatic experience and behavior can be fully identified with as self, and there are possibilities for ownership of aspects of the body-self that have been disowned as a function of previous creative adjustments. I hesitated to use the term "normal" since it is somewhat contrary to the spirit of Gestalt therapy, but it seemed better than "optimal," which assumes a standard or absolute ideal. My point is that the desirable degree of ownership is, at least in part, a function *also* of the context. There is no "best in all circumstances" degree of body ownership. The desirable is a matter of the best creative adjustment that can be obtained in a given situation.

On the extreme left is somatic materialism, a situation I have come across now and then with persons who have become so focused on their physical reality that they ignore other aspects of their being. The self is *only* a body-self that does not include other aspects of self, such as a cognitive or imagistic or spiritual self. This is a case of the body becoming a fixed figure, displacing all else from awareness. Rabid devotees of body therapies can be victims of this stance.

Metaphorically we can look at the self as consisting of both land (the "I") and water (disowned aspects of the self). Healthy functioning requires that the proportion of land to water is balanced, and that it is possible to obtain nourishment from the sea—that is, to have some possibility of commerce with less familiar aspects of the self. The problems of living have eroded some people to such a degree that much of what was land has become water. These people are like islands with little left that they can own as "I." Frequently the possibility of having commerce with the sea, or even acknowledging that the water exists, is so frightening that it is preferable to turn one's gaze inward and pretend that one isn't on an island after all. When one's body, as well as much of one's cognition and imagery, has become the unknown and forbidden water, where else can one go but into fantasy? Less extreme on the continuum, the interchange between disowned and owned aspects of self takes the forms of symptoms, frequently somatic in nature.

The case of a client I will call Thomas may help to illustrate this. Thomas came to me suffering from chronic muscular pains and severe tension. Despite a lack of organic disease, his posture was more distorted than that of almost any person I had seen. It contained many elements in opposition: thick and upwardly thrusting legs, narrow waist, frozen pelvis, collapsed and concave chest, overdeveloped and upwardly raised shoulders, sagging head and neck. He was literally tied in knots, and the pain of these opposing forces had reached major proportions during the two years prior to our consultation. He had tried a number of somatic approaches, all with only temporary palliative effects.

Thomas' pain and distortion had no apparent rational significance. He was a bright man with a good job, a lovely family, a solid upper-middle-class life. There were times he didn't like his job, but isn't that true of everyone? He saw himself as having met many of his life goals, and certainly as being moderately successful. Why, then, all of these pains and tensions?

We used direct body work to begin to put Thomas in touch with his body process. He had little awareness of his body, other than of pain and discomfort, and had no sense of his feelings or his needs. Our initial work simply focused on increasing his awareness of his body process beyond that of pain and tension. As his awareness and ownership of his body increased, I began to help him connect words to his body experience. Through statements such as "I am tied in knots" and "I feel full of opposing forces," Thomas began to entertain the notion that there were more parts of himself than he was aware of on the surface, and that his body had something to tell him about those parts.

Gradually we were able to bring into view a very different sense of Thomas. Loosening his chest and opening up his breathing put him in touch with a tremendous sense of emptiness, yet this "wanting heart" conflicted with his image of his "happy marriage." Work with his back and legs brought out clearly aggressive movements—kicking, pushing, striking out—yet he had to hold back these movements because he could never be "like that." As the energy began to flow through his arms and connect to his heart, he became aware of a great need to give to others and touch them with his caring. However, he had to control this impulse because his family could not accept it, and he did not feel he was worthy or likable enough to have anything desirable to give.

Each body symptom was both the expression through movement and feeling of an unrecognized aspect of his being *and* his holding onto that expression because of its conflict with his life situation and definition of himself. As we related this emerging picture to his life situation, a number of things became apparent. Thomas was frequently passive and withdrawn, and had great difficulty saying "no" at work. This resulted in his taking on work that was not rightfully his and having to smother his anger at this. He was similarly nonconfrontative in his relationship with his wife, which resulted in an appearance of domestic calm behind which seethed a storehouse of resentments. He felt his relationship with his wife to be dry, with little passion or affection, and he felt afraid to reach out and give for fear she would reject his offers.

Thomas had little sense of his capacity for life—the strength of his hands in touch, the warmth of his heart, the humanity expressed in his eyes, and the power of his musculature in anger and his pelvis in sexuality. Without the physical rooting of these capacities in his body, he had no support, and so feared trying new things and pushing his own limits and those of his relationships with others.

Over time he began to allow himself more expression, through body movement and verbalization, of his aggression and power, of his deep feelings of sadness, of his wants to reach out, of his long–denied sexual desire. From this he could begin to re-own these denied aspects of his being. This, of course, was no simple matter. Recovering these parts of himself brought new abilities and a fuller sense of himself, but also demanded that he confront painful choices and take risks that were difficult and frightening: risks that threatened the status quo of his life—his marriage, his work, his sense of self. Recovering what he had disowned did not necessarily make his life easier, although he was less tense and in less pain from this tension. But it did make his life *fuller* in the range of his feelings, including painful feelings, and gave him more possibilities and choices. He no longer needed to be helplessly stuck between forces he did not know or know how to express. As Perls and colleagues (Perls et al., 1951) put it:

> But growing, the self risks—risks it with suffering if it has long avoided risking it and therefore must destroy many prejudices, introjects, attachments to the fixed past, securities, plans and ambitions; risks it with excitement if it can accept living in the present (pg. 368).

BODY PROCESS AND POLARITIES OF THE SELF

Although we describe the self in Gestalt therapy as having no particular character in and of itself, it is clear that when the self is in action, people seem to act according to specific qualities or stances: Mom holds me softly and Dad holds me firmly. It is also apparent that when people describe themselves by using verbal or imagistic symbols, they tend to ascribe to themselves a set of qualities or charateristics: "I am strong and tough" or "I see myself like a beggar in a palace." Implicit in each description is an opposing quality or characteristic. For example, the polarity of strong and tough might be weak and soft; the polarity of the beggar might be the king.

It is in the form of polarities, sets of qualities or images in opposition, that the self organizes and defines its action and describes those functions that are owned (identifications) and those that have become alienated or disowned. Zinker (1977) presents us with a picture of the polarities.

Figure 2-2 describes a complex set of polarities available to one's functioning and sense of self. We are each capable of hardness and softness, clumsiness and grace, kindness and cruelty. We all have qualities

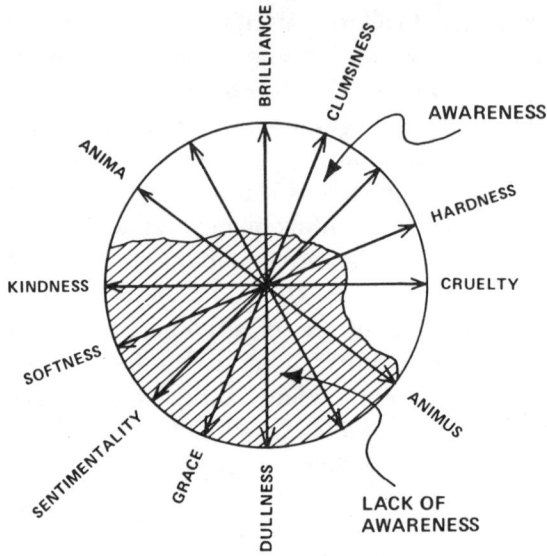

Figure 2-2. Polarities and awareness of polarities in problematic functioning.

(Adapted from Zinker 1977 by permission of author).

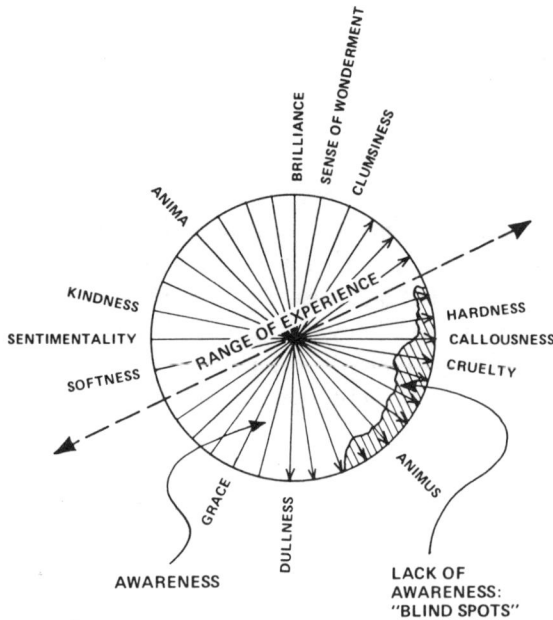

Figure 2-3. Polarities and awareness of polarities in healthy functioning.

(Adapted from Zinker 1977 by permission of author).

we can characterize as "female" or anima, and as "male" or animus. In the Gestalt theoretical view, the healthy person has awareness and capacity for ownership of a relatively wide range of these aspects of his or her self-functioning, and can accept aspects that may not be desirable but that nevertheless exist. "The healthy person may not always approve of all his polarities, but the fact he is willing to suffer their awareness is a significant aspect of his inner strength" (Zinker, 1977, p. 200).

Figure 2-2 describes a person whose disownership and lack of awareness of a large range of contact functions have limited the person's behavior and self-image to a small range. This person not only has lost much of the potential range of experience and behavior, but also no longer can recognize important needs that may be intrinsic to the disowned polarities and must work hard to keep such needs from expression in awareness and action.

Those polar qualities we identify with and can allow ourselves to act from, form what we might call the "self-image" (description of the polarities of which we are aware), while those qualities we have alienated come to be represented as the disowned self, what Jung has called "the shadow" self.

So far this description of polarities has focused on their verbal and imagist symbolization. Such polarities are part of our physical process and behavior as well. Consider the polarity of hard and soft. If I make contact with my environment in a hard way, then I literally must harden parts of my body, perhaps my heart or my posture; when I make contact from my capacity for softness, I literally soften my muscles, my heart, my gaze. You might test this by vividly picturing a situation in which there is a person toward whom you take a "hard attitude," and pay attention to how you alter your body tension or stance. Now try this with a person or situation toward whom or which you feel soft and warm, and notice how you shape and express yourself physically.

Each polarity of the self is rooted in our bodily feeling and behavior as well as in our imagery and verbal symbolization. In exploring the conflict one client was feeling about a relationship, I noticed her curiously collapsed and sunken posture. As she experimented with this posture, she became aware of feeling aged and bitter. In contrast she felt young and optimistic when she assumed the opposite picture, sitting upright and uncollapsed. Given each of these postures voice as well as physical expression, I asked her to make comments about her love relationship. Her "young woman," the most owned and aware polarity, was optimistic about the relationship and wanted to go full speed ahead. Her "old woman" reminded her of the bitter disappointments she had previously experienced in love, and was cautious and pessimistic about the relationship. She preferred not to listen to her "old woman" because such feelings seemed to leave no option for love in her life. But as soon as she would ignore that part of herself, her posture would collapse and she would lose energy for the relationship.

Assuming that each polarity had something worthy to say, I asked her what she would communicate to her lover from her "old woman" side. She replied that she would tell her lover she wanted to go more slowly, and that she had some specific concerns about their interactions which she wanted to discuss and work out. With only her optimistic "young woman" polarity available to her aware functioning, this woman was unable to recognize some important concerns that interfered with her relationship. Disowned from her self, her "old woman" remained apparent in her bodily expression and had impact on her functioning.

INTEGRATION OF BODY AND SELF

Healing the split between mind and body (an example of classic polarity) involves bringing into awareness the disowned aspects of self so that the full range of needs, feelings, and behaviors can be appreciated and allowed to affect the forming of figures. When a greater qualitative range of contact functions is available, each contact takes place out of the spontaneous union of our organismic forces rather than from a partial sense of self. Bringing these disowned parts of self into awareness requires that we bring out the bodily nature of our polarities so that, in re-owning, we do not merely increase the range of our self-*image*, but also the range of our active *being*. What use is it to accept the importance and reality of my capacity for softness if I am unable to physically soften my musculature? How much have I really owned my strength and toughness if my posture is rickety and unstable? The contribution of body-oriented work to the process of change in psychotherapy is to "flesh out" our words and images with sensations, movement, and the concreteness of our bodily existence.

Chapter 3

Approaching the "Person as a Whole"

This then, which is one and simple by nature, man's wickednesse divideth, and while he endeavoureth to obtaine part of that which hath no partes, he neither getteth a part, which is none, nor the whole, which he seeketh not after. (Boethius, 1963, p. 72)

The separation of body from self, and by extension the separation of body and mind, is an adaptation to distressing life events that are experienced physically. The person is a whole, but has come to experience him or her self as if in parts. In this fragmenting of oneself into parts, the "I" is usually identified with mental functioning (producing thoughts, images, words, etc.) and those aspects of one's body experience that have been problematic and distressing are experienced as "outside" oneself. Dis-ease is the result of this splitting of the self into parts and the misidentification of a part as the whole. It can only be cured by a therapy that views the person as a whole and does not itself identify the problem as occurring in a part. The therapeutic method must integrate the client's experience into a whole by the recovery and reownership of the disowned aspects of the self, particularly the bodily aspects of self.

Two problems are apparent for the therapist interested in working within a holistic framework. First, traditional therapeutic models view body and mind as distinct entities, with the self or "I" usually identified with mental functioning. One either treats the mind through verbal therapy, or the body through physical therapy. In both viewpoint and method these models collude with the splitting of the person into parts, and so cannot heal the division that has resulted in the condition we hope to cure.

Second, persons enter therapy with varying "distances" between their sense of self and their body process, as well as with differing degrees of access to their body experience. Therapists are challenged with understanding what it means to approach the person as a whole, with determining what is necessary to recover that which has been fragmented into parts and disowned, and with supporting the integration of these parts into a whole, functioning person.

ORIENTATIONS TOWARD THE PERSON

Psychotherapy has traditionally aimed at affecting the mind as separate from the body, with a resulting emphasis on a predominantly verbal methodology, and has not in general claimed to be holistic. Body-oriented psychotherapy, having been formed through amalgamation and combination of the varied and often disparate approaches that found favor in the human potential movement, has often given at least lip service to the notion of holism. Today we are faced with the task of sorting out this plethora of influences on philosophy and method.

A recent compendium (Kogan, 1980) describes at least 15 different approaches roughly labeled as "body works," some of which are clearly psychotherapeutic in intent and others of which are more accurately described as physical therapies, their major intent being to affect bodily health. On the one hand are the apparently psychophysical approaches, such as Reichian therapy (Reich, 1942, 1945/1972; Baker, 1967), neo-Reichian therapies (Lowen, 1958; Kelly, 1976; Keleman, 1979, 1985), and Gestalt therapy (Perls, 1947/1969; Perls et al., 1951); on the other hand there are the predominantly physical therapies such as Rolfing (Rolf, 1977), the Feldenkrais method (Feldenkrais, 1972), and the Alexander technique (Alexander, 1971).

Add to this the practice of combining methods, such as Darbonne's (1976) joining of Rolfing, bioenergetics and Gestalt therapy, or Rubenfeld's (1984) combination of Alexander technique, Feldenkrais method, and Gestalt therapy, and Mehl's (1981) joining of hypnosis and applied kinesiology.

All of these methods claim to be holistic and are often seen as such because, at minimum, they seem to have a basic belief that the processes generally referred to as body and those referred to as mind are in some way connected. But to speak of a person as composed of connected parts is not necessarily the same as to speak of the person as a whole; nor does the use of conjoint verbal and physical intervention necessarily create an integrated therapy. What is really meant by a holistic approach and what makes a therapy an integrated psychophysical approach?

This chapter will discuss the problems and pitfalls in understanding and working with persons as unitary wholes, rather than as consisting of separate but interrelated parts. It will outline the developmental process of holistic intervention that respects the parts of the person in their own right, while emphasizing the way in which these parts form the person as a whole.

THE PERSON AS PARTS*

Nineteenth century science viewed the universe as a collection of related but essentially separate parts and particles, each of which could be studied and understood separately (Bohm, 1980). Most systems of psychotherapy and body therapy are extrapolated from this notion and view the person as consisting of an amalgamation of parts. In this view the whole is *equal* to the sum of its parts. If a person is the summation of separate parts, then it follows that each of the parts can be separated from the whole and treated as distinct, additive units. †

This psychotherapeutic model views the person as consisting of two main classes of parts—a body, which is made up of organs and cells and so on; and a mind, which is made up of a conscious and unconscious, or a self and ego (depending on the particular "theory of mind" to which one ascribes)—which collectively comprise the person. In most cases the "self" or "I" is identified with the mind, which is contained within the body. These parts are viewed as separate and unintegrated domains,

---

*The author expresses his thanks to William Kohner (private conversation) for his noting the distinction between layered and integrated forms of work, which was essential to formulating this chapter.

†The formal term in science and philosophy for this view is reductionism—proposing that the whole can be understood by reducing it to its constituent parts, understanding the functioning of these parts, then reassembling them into the whole.

although they may causally affect one another. For example, bodily events such as physical trauma or disease may affect the mind by causing depression, or mental conflicts may affect the body by causing high blood pressure. Psychosomatic or somatopsychic phenomena are seen as a function of a causal relationship between two essentially distinct, separate domains.

There are essentially three main branches of the "person as parts" world view: monism, dualism, and parallelism. Each results, because of its belief system, in a different therapeutic approach. In the monistic view, mind is nothing more than the product of electrophysical chemistry in the brain; that is, a person is equivalent to the functioning of his or her organs, and problems can be traced to and treated by healing the particular organs involved. This view has led to the modern chemotherapy approach to treatment (biological psychiatry) and will not be discussed here because this approach sees no purpose in psychotherapy for what it considers medical problems.

In dualism the domains of mind and body are entirely separate from one another, and each requires treatment in its own right; verbal therapy for mental problems and physical therapy for bodily distress. In some dualistic approaches, these two separate domains are admitted to have some effect on one another, but correct treatment in the domain where the "real problem" lies is thought to be the most desirable approach. I define the treatment approach that arises from a dualistic model as a *singular* approach.

In the parallelistic model, the domains of body and mind are seen as separate yet linked together, such that one inevitably affects the other. Depending on the extent to which one sees each part to be related, problems in one domain will be a function of dysfunction in the other, and change in one area will have impact on the other. In parallelism, for example, psychological stress is seen as affecting the body by increasing physiological arousal, somatic problems may represent emotional conflicts, or bodily distress may cause mental depression. If the person is a set of related but separate parts, then each part may be treated separately, but with the understanding that changes in one area may affect the other by nature of their intrinsic relationship. I have called this treatment approach an *alternating* method.

Singular Approaches

Mainstream therapies, whether psychotherapy or physical therapy, have traditionally maintained a singular approach to the person, either in philosophy, in method, or both. Psychological therapies such as psychoanalysis (Freud, 1938), client–centered (Rogers, 1951), and rational emotive (Ellis, 1962; Ellis & Harper, 1968) utilize interventions that are almost exclusively verbal. Practitioners identify the point of change as mental processes or structures. To the extent that body processes are seen as related to psychological processes, as in psychosomatic problems (physical events caused by the mind), the physical process is often seen as an epi-phenomenon—related to but separate from the underlying mental events.

Just as singular in form are numerous body therapies, such as structural integration (Rolf, 1977), the Alexander technique (Alexander, 1971), and the Feldenkrais technique (Feldenkrais, 1972). These and other somatic approaches acknowledge the contribution of psychological processes to the formation of body tension and postural imbalances. However, there is no formal methodology for working with or explicitly linking psychological processes to the somatic work. Like the traditional psychological approaches, these somatic approaches treat the physical as essentially separate from the mental.

So long as one believes that the person consists of separate and unitary parts, and that only one aspect of the person is the problem, a singular approach seems correct. When the body is hurting, you treat it through somatic method and minimize emphasis on psychological concerns; when the mind is disturbed, you treat it with verbal means and assume the conjoint physical problems will be alleviated when the mental problems are cured.

If one looks at the person from a holistic standpoint, the singular approach presents some philosophical and methodological dilemmas. The first problem is that a singular approach, since it addresses only one aspect of the person, a part of a whole, encourages compartmentalization and splitting of the self. The source of the organismic imbalance, that important parts of the person have been rendered unavailable to functioning, is maintained rather than healed. Even when a psychotherapy verbally addresses a somatic phenomenon, such as through interpretation of a somatic symptom as a psychological conflict, the lack of somatic methodology (direct work with the body) leaves the person with a sense of distinct parts linearly connected: the mental conflict *causes* the physical symptoms, rather than a unitary organismic dilemma having various manifestations. Burton and Heller (1964) aptly describe this dilemma in a discussion of the body and psychoanalysis:

> The body in psychoanalysis ultimately became a container of complexes at best, and an interference to the analysis of those complexes, at worst. It got in the way of the analysis and, if it suffered pain, it was to be referred else-

where, or the pain was to be itself a subject for analysis. Thus today we often have, if we may be forgiven the metaphor, the analysis of the complex without the encumbrance of the body . . . The penalty for such reification is often the reduction of the complex, but the continued ill health of the patient. The body not being a part of the treatment, it does not subscribe to the cure . . . and neither the psyche nor the body alone is satisfactory for the integration of modern man. (p. 125)

When there is no explicit method of linking psychological and physical issues and experiences, it is easy for the client to compartmentalize the body and mind segments, just as the therapist does in the way of understanding the client.

Some singular approaches go so far as to assume an interdependence, although not a true holism, of body and mind. This assumption arises from a belief in the mutual connection between structure and function. For example, from a psychological standpoint, if you alter the psychological process (conflict or defense), you alter the somatic structure that depends on it. From the somatic standpoint, if you alter the structure (body), you alter the function (psychological) that depends on it. This structure/function premise is quite explicit in many of the somatic therapies (Rolf, 1977; Barlow, 1973; Feldenkrais, 1972; Feitus, 1978), and is implied in the way in which most singular approaches to psychotherapy understand and address somatic complaints.

A commonly used example of the structure/function interdependence in these somatic therapies is that of posture and mental attitude of a depressed person. If you alter the sagging and slumped posture, the client will feel less depressed—function follows structure. If the cure for depression was simply to teach a client better posture, there would be little need for any type of therapy. A depressed person cannot *maintain* an undepressed attitude, physical or mental, until the depressing parts of the self are made apparent and the feelings being depressed are released and worked through. Similarly, the psychodynamic exploration of the conflicts and repressions inherent in a client's depression does not always alter the shallow breathing and sagging posture that is an essential aspect, in a holistic view, of the depression. The client will find it easy to slip back into the emotional pattern because the physical pattern still exists and will tend to shape perception and feeling.

I do not wish to imply that there is no relationship between body structure and organismic functioning. Indeed, without that relationship there would be no reason for a book claiming to explore the importance of body phenomena in therapy. Most psychotherapists have watched a client resolve some critical dilemma and have seen the client's posture, breathing, and demeanor spontaneously change. Similarly, many somatic therapists have witnessed the integration of a postural imbalance lifting a client's mental outlook and attitude. My point is not that these things do not occur, but that such change is based not on a causal connection of part to part (body to mind or mind to body), but on the fact that these aspects of the person are of the same whole. If conditions support integration of these parts, then a shift of the whole can occur. But if conditions do not support integration of the whole, then structure-to-function or function-to-structure change will not occur or will be short-lived. Singular approaches have no way of bridging the experience gap between parts, nor of treating the structure/function relationship *as a whole* so as to prevent isolation of the parts. A singular approach tends to look at the relationship between structure and function as linear and unidirectional.

It is not uncommon for individuals who have been through various body therapies to have shown little corresponding change in their emotional life. Frequently they are unable to maintain their postural and muscular organization changes because they have not examined the place of these physical aspects in their emotional lives. Similarly, there are people who have participated in extensive psychotherapy and yet whose habitual body attitudes prevent insight from becoming embodied in their behavior and interactions.

Alternating Approaches

One alternative to the dilemma of singular approaches has been to honor the relevance of the somatic and psychological aspects of the person by alternating physical and mental therapy methods. Anyone who has experienced the wonder of bodily change and release in somatic arts knows their value. Similarly, the resolution of long withheld emotional conflicts or a change in the perception of oneself resulting from psychotherapeutic work can affirm the importance of this mode of growth. Doesn't it make sense, then, to find ways to combine these two methods and so be able to work toward a true integration of the person? This has been the natural direction for many psychotherapists who learned somatic approaches and somatic practitioners who learned therapy skills.

One way of combining mental and physical work is to *alternate* between each type of intervention. This view is often characterized by the word "and," as in bioenergetics *and* Gestalt therapy *and* Rolfing (Darbonne, 1976), Rolfing *and* fantasy therapy (Schutz & Turner, 1977), or Feldenkrais technique *and* psychotherapy. The therapist works alternately with verbal therapy and then a body-oriented approach in an attempt to address both the mental and physical elements of the client's experience and functioning.

Such alternation may occur within a single therapy session or in completely different sessions, and even with different therapists. In alternating work there is no concurrence of methods: they take place at different times and there is no attempt to simultaneously work with body process *and* psychological process as a unit. Each form stands alone. As Darbonne (1976) comments in his article on combining Rolfing and Gestalt therapy, "During any actual rolfing session I do not interrupt the rolfing in order to do psychotherapy" (p. 611).

The problem with alternating therapeutic approaches is that, since there remains a clear separation between somatic and psychological work, the sense of a split may be reinforced. There is physical work and there is psychological work and, although they are seen as related, they are still viewed and worked with as if they are separate. The continuity between mental and physical processes cannot be fully reflected when the working method only looks at one aspect of the person at a time. The *present sense of unity* of one's being is difficult to experience when body work occurs at one time and psychological work occurs at another time.

As before, this does not mean that integration (the sense of self as a whole) does not occur through an alternating approach (for examples see the descriptions in Schutz & Turner, 1977). However, integration is dependent on certain capacities of the client that therapists cannot automatically assume. The processes of disownership and the resulting compartmentalizing and splitting of the various parts of self often undermine the transfer from one mode of intervention to another. With clients who are not overly separated from their bodies or cognitive processes, this carryover may occur. With others the sense of separateness and disunity will be reinforced rather than healed by alternating from one mode of work to another, because no *bridging function* is intrinsic to the method. Additionally, since the therapies being used may not necessarily be philosophically and methodologically consistent with each other, the client may have conflicting experiences.

Layered Approaches: Bridging the Parts

A *layered* approach involves the concurrent use of a body approach, say, the Feldenkrais technique or Rolfing, and psychotherapeutic method. This approach is not clearly delineated in the literature, but is apparent when observing the actual work of some body-oriented psychotherapists. Layered work occupies an intermediate place between working with the "person as parts" and the "person as a whole."

Layering appears at first to be unified. The therapist may initiate a dialogue with the client and develop it in a way consistent with Gestalt therapy work on polarities; for example, a conversation between parts of the self. Simultaneously, the therapist works on the client's body alignment and muscular tensions to encourage their release. The work is elegant in the way of a duet; two parallel but different voices form a common melody line. The physical and psychological methods remain separate voices, although working together. To the untrained eye, the work appears to be integrated, and at times it may become so, but to the more sophisticated eye, it is apparent that a clear delineation between somatic and psychological processes remains.

Despite the elegance of the duet, layered work continues to treat the person as separate components. As in the alternating approach, the slight gap between methods disrupts the true continuity between physical and mental processes. It is possible to perform simultaneous physical and mental work that has no common theme and is not intertwined in the client's experience—much as you can have your hair cut while talking about the weather. Concurrence of methods does not guarantee concurrence of *experience*. There can be a subtle slippage between the client's sense of body-self and thinking-self that discourages the integration of the self as a whole.

As mentioned earlier, the capacity to compartmentalize the body work and psychological work also lends to the maintenance of the split of the self. We frequently experience our body as an object, rather than self. Thus anything that happens to one's body, while it is consciously felt and experienced, is often easily divorced from one's *self*. Layered work does not address this splitting process and the projection of the body as an object, and so has no way of bridging the gap between the layers of work.

Another potential problem with a layered approach is that the physical and psychological methods may be derived from different theoretical and philosophical sources. For example, client-centered (Rogers, 1951) and transactional analysis (Berne, 1964) therapies do not include an explicit understanding of body phenomena in their theory and method. The use of these approaches with a body method would make it likely that the layers of physical and psychological work would remain parallel and unintegrated. There is no explicit understanding of the importance or link of body phenomenon to emotional processes, which means that methodologically they have no clear way of bringing the layers of work together.

Worse, a layered approach does not rule out the use of two methods that are philosophically or theoretically in conflict. For example, Gestalt therapy and Rolfing have very different views on the nature of tension as resistance.* The same is true of Reichian and Gestalt therapies, which are often used in combination (usually with the Reichian technique being the body component and Gestalt technique being the verbal component), but whose views of the person are strikingly different.†

To layer two incompatible approaches means that either (1) the therapist must ignore the differences between them and so put the client in a bind experientially, for example, the difference between the Reichian view of breaking down resistance versus Gestalt therapy's stance of valuing the resistance; or (2) the therapist must fundamentally alter one of the two approaches being layered so that it is no longer true to its origin. Thus one may legitimately *alternate* Rolfing and Gestalt therapy, but if one performs them *together,* one is either not remaining true to the theory and spirit of Rolfing, or not remaining true to the theory and spirit of Gestalt therapy, or both. A truly integrated approach looks for holism in both its methodology, and its view of the person.

THE PERSON AS A WHOLE

A holistic view is based on the principle that the whole is greater than, or different from, the sum of its parts. The whole is not merely the result of an accretion of parts, but rather has an intrinsic unity of its own, a particular structure and integration of its parts. For example, a word on this page is made up of parts called letters that can stand alone, but the word formed by the letters is a whole in and of itself that is essentially different from the letters. It has specific order and form. Similarly, the next greater whole of the sentence in which the words take place is not merely an additive effect of a number of words, but acquires meaning because of its particular structure. The same words could be used to make up a new sentence with an entirely different meaning, an entirely new whole, with each resulting whole being more than the sum of its parts.

*These differences are discussed in Chapter 5.

†Because of the frequent confusion as to these differences, an appendix is included that compares critical assumptions of Reichian and Gestalt therapies.

In the human sphere, the principle of holism challenges us to see the person in a different light from that which our culture and science have emphasized. From a traditional dualistic perspective, we define "the person" as a set of parts collected together: a body, which itself is a collection of parts, containing a mind, which is also a collection of parts (for example, ego, id, superego, or self-concept, persona, etc.). Like a set of nesting Chinese boxes, the body contains the mind, which contains the self, and so on.

To view the person as a whole greater than the sum of its parts is to view the person as all of the parts: body, mind, thinking, feeling, imaging, moving, and so on; but not the same as any one of the parts. It is the integrated functioning of the various aspects of the whole in time and space that is the person. In this view to treat one aspect of the person exclusively or identify a part as the cause of the problem is to artificially fragment what is in reality a functioning unity.

An Integrated Approach

An integrated approach to the person attempts to look at any process (such as a conflict, a life theme, a physical symptom) as part of a larger whole, which *includes* somatic and the psychological aspects. Any psychological issue (e.g., a conflict between parts of the self, an emotional trauma, an unfinished interaction) is part of a larger gestalt that includes the physical expression of that dilemma (e.g., pattern of tension, way of holding the body, breathing inhibitions). Any somatic symptom, such as a chronic tension or postural distortion, is an expression of a larger whole, which includes a psychological dilemma and is part of its expression. Note the use of the word "includes" and the phrase "a part of, " rather than "caused by" or "causing." The classical psychosomatic view in psychotherapy is that the mental conflict causes the physical symptoms. The integrated view looks at both as parts of a *unitary* expression of the self or, in Gestalt therapy terms, the organism.

In terms of method, an integrated approach aims to *bring together* all aspects of the person so that the person can experience him or herself as a unitary organism, rather than a mixture of parts. From this standpoint, therapeutic technique should not split the person by attending to one aspect of the person as if it is intrinsically different or separate from the other.

More specifically, in an integrated therapy:

–The psychological process being verbalized—for example, conflicts or beliefs—are explicitly connected to their bodily expressions.

–Physical processes, such as posture, muscular holding, and somatic disturbances, are seen as meaningful expressions of the person.

–Both physical and psychological processes are looked at as aspects of the same whole (the person/organism) and the divisions into parts both within and across each domain is the issue of therapeutic concern. Therapeutic technique strives to restore the sense of the self as a whole and reassert the mutual identity of the parts.

Let us describe some examples. Take the case of a client who has a great deal of discomfort about sexuality. A singular-approach therapist might look at the rigidity of superego controls or another at the client's illogical beliefs regarding sex. A somatic therapist might focus on loosening the tensions in the client's pelvic area. In an integrated therapy, however, the pelvic tensions and holding against movement and breathing *and* the beliefs and conflicts within the personality are seen as identical. Sexual conflict includes *both* the physical tensions and the mental conflict. In integrated therapeutic work, the two are linked together and treated as a functional whole, with the concern being the way in which such conflict has become experienced as one between self and body, that is, indicating a disownership of bodily aspects of self.

Likewise, a physical symptom, such as shoulder tension, is part of a whole that includes its psychological context. For example, such tension may hold back the arms so that the client does not yield to the impulse to push someone away and set boundaries. The therapeutic work must not merely get rid of the tension in the shoulders, but it must also link the tension to the belief, "I must not assert my want to push away," and work through the unfinished situation that gives rise to the client's tension and fear, freeing the person's arms for aggressive movement.

By link I mean not only an intellectual understanding or interpretation, but the *experience in the present moment* of the mutual identity, the wholeness, of the shoulder tension and fear of assertion. To neglect the tension and only work with the belief also neglects the whole and leaves the client's experience separated and disconnected.

INTEGRATION AS A DEVELOPMENTAL PROCESS

It is probably apparent to the reader that, although perhaps desirable philosophically, the conditions necessary for integrated work frequently do not exist for most people entering into individual therapy. As emphasized earlier in this book, the starting situation for most of us, clients and therapists alike, is an experience of our being fragmented or identified with various parts to such a degree that the notion of oneself as a whole, and thus the possibility of integrated work, is unlikely at the onset of therapy. It is precisely this experiencing of oneself as parts that has initiated the person's seeking of therapy. Thus, although our viewpoint is that the person is a whole, this is far from our starting point in therapy in terms of the person's experience of his or her self.

Even a holistic approach must start with the existing condition of the experience of self as consisting of parts, and work to develop awareness of the parts, of how they are maintained as split off from the whole, and to integrate the person's experience into a sense of self as a whole.

Wholeness cannot be mandated by the therapist or by theoretical supposition, nor can it be explained or "taught" as concepts or ideas are taught (Perls et al., 1951).

> What we are arguing, then, is not that these conceptions, Body, Mind . . . are ordinary errors that may be corrected by rival hypotheses and verification; nor, again, that they are semantical misnomers. Rather, they are given in immediate experience of a certain kind and can lose their urgency and evidential weight only if the conditions of that experience are changed. (p. 266)

Therapy is a developmental process in which we must create the conditions necessary for *moving toward* the experience of wholeness. In this way, we can look at integrative work as the culmination of a developmental sequence, rather than as per se, the starting point of therapy.

A certain groundwork must exist for such a high level of organismic integration to be possible. What is the point at which integrated work can legitimately occur? Additionally, if we are not to fit the client to the therapy but rather to fit the therapy to the client, how do we account for differences in individual needs and development? Integrated work may be seen as the ultimate goal of a holistic therapy, but it would be contrary to the respect for clients *as they are* to force them toward the goal of the therapist (integration) if that need is not apparent to the client. Integrated therapeutic work requires a number of conditions for it to be possible and relevant:

1. *A sufficient degree of body awareness.* Without adequate awareness of the body, the client is missing an essential part of the data that make up the unified whole for which we are aiming. The degree to which many of us have blocked out much of our body sensation is quite

evident to any therapist who uses a body approach to therapy. Some limited capacity for awareness of our body sensation must exist before integrated work is possible.

2. *A sufficient degree of awareness of the relationship of one's self to current life issues and problems.* Without some sense of the relevance of psychological issues to one's life, integration has no foundation. For example, if I have no sense of the major issues I am confronting, of the relevance of my personal history to my present functioning and my present functioning to who I am as a person, then there is nothing to connect with my body process. I must recognize that my recurrent life problems don't just happen *to* me, but have something to do with the way I am and how I relate to my world.

3. *A basic trust in the relatedness of bodily process and psychological issues.* As awareness of body and psychological functioning develops, the compartmentalization of the two must begin to be bridged. A basic trust that the two are connected must exist to propel the client toward higher-level integration. While some people entering therapy may already experience some degree of relatedness, for the most part this trust is rarely a given. It is built out of small linkages accumulated over time in the course of therapeutic experiments; that is, out of the client *experiencing* the bridging of the gap between physical process and psychological process.

From the general principle that the person is a whole, and that therapy is the process of developing the conditions for experiencing oneself as a whole, we can now see alternating, layered, and integrated approaches as stages of a developmental process rather than as separate and distinct methods. In this way the therapist can utilize singular, alternating, or layered work to form the building blocks toward integration, that is, as appropriate to particular stages of development, rather than in opposition to integration (assuming that the methods being alternated or layered are compatible with each other in theory, philosophy, and application).

Similarly, the therapist can keep the philosophy and ultimate direction of integrated work as the most fundamental principle, while not losing sight of the client as he or she is. In this way our stance remains appreciative of each individual's integrity and creative adjustment to difficult life circumstances, rather than critical of them for their lack of integration. With these principles in mind, both our philosophy and our method can allow us to perceive and approach others and ourselves as whole beings, with nothing left out.

The Working Process

The whole is greater than the sum of its parts, but it nonetheless *consists* of parts.*

For integration to take place, the parts need to be accessible to the self (the integrating function of the organism). Most people entering therapy identify with one part to the exclusion of other parts, with significant areas of unawareness and scotoma for various aspects of themselves (particularly an unawareness of their body process), or they enter therapy with some disowned aspect of their process that is "causing trouble" which they demand be fixed. All of these possibilities indicate that therapy does not start from a place where integrated work is possible.

One woman was referred by her physician for assistance with her back pain, for which he could find no clinical indications of disease. She entered therapy, as it were, "bringing her back" to me. Her attitude toward her bodily distress was, "Make this thing stop hurting *me* and disrupting *my* life," indicating the degree to which she experienced her back pain as outside of her self. She had no contact with her back pain as *her* hurting and, indeed, had little awareness of her body, except the pain she experienced. She described her life as quite fine, and reported no significant life distress that she was aware of—other than her back pain, which had virtually taken over her life energy and focus.

Earlier in my career, and even now at times when fatigue fosters my expediency, I might have tried to explain to this woman the notion of her body symptoms as statements of the self or have told her that there must be more going on in her life than was apparent. But my task is not to get her to accede to my belief system about the unity of body and self, but to support the development of her capacity to experience her symptoms as a part of her self as a whole.

I began by seriously considering her distress, by accepting "her back" as our starting point, and by recognizing the relevance of her sense of separation from this part of her. I worked directly with her back: through teaching her breathing work; through the use of touch to teach her to relax and release spasmic muscles; and through work to develop her awareness of her body and what she did that affected her bodily state (e.g., what increased her pain, what decreased her pain,

---

*Here the understanding of holism that Gestalt therapy derives from Gestalt experimental psychology differs from the undifferentiated holism described by Boethius in the quotation at the beginning of this chapter. The Gestalt view considers the question of part versus whole to be a matter of one's perception rather than an issue of objective truth or falsity.

what encouraged tension, what encouraged relaxation). The initial phase of this developmental work appeared singular in nature; our work was very body focused, with little of emotional or psychological import emerging. But her awareness was developing and her back pain was becoming a more differentiated experience: something that changed over time and varied in relation to life events, and something she was beginning to affect with her awareness.

As her awareness developed, I began to ask her to make statements about her experience of her back as we worked: to change "My back hurts" to "I am hurting," and "My spine feels under pressure" to "I am under pressure" (see Chapter 8). This layered work helped to create a bridge between her body process and her sense of self. We began to talk about the things in her life about which she felt hurt, and the ways in which she pressured herself or experienced pressures from others. We spent several sessions alternating body work with verbal discussion of her life situation: her marriage, her family, and the ways in which these situations were hurtful to her.

Later in our work, sessions took on a more integrated character in that body-oriented work with her back merged naturally into expressive movement related to her life themes. For example, she became aware of holding onto a "hot spot" in her back; experiments with "letting go of her hotness" evolved into angry verbalizations directed toward her husband. Similarly, our discussions of her life issues merged with her body expression and feeling. For example, as we discussed her difficulty in standing up for her own needs in confrontations with her mother-in-law, I asked her to stand up in the therapy room and experiment with ways in which she supported herself posturally (i.e., her stance) as she expressed those things she wanted to say to her mother-in-law. Her back pain became clearly related to giving into the pressure of her mother-in-law to conform to family standards.

If we reflect on the starting point for this woman in terms of the three criteria for integrated work, it should be apparent that her degree of body awareness, awareness of life issues, and trust in the relatedness of her body to her life process all made the possibility of integration unavailable to her. Yet I did not criticize her for being unintegrated; rather I accepted her sense of herself as she was, trusting our work and our relationship to develop the awareness and ownership of her parts, such that she could discover the higher-order integration she required to experience herself herself as a whole being.

This case history describes work that is both lengthy and intensive because of the nature of the person and her developmental needs. With other persons the intensive body-oriented therapy described would not be the focus to as great a degree, because the problems they bring to therapy are not as clearly of a bodily nature.

For example, a man who was trying to make a decision as to whether he should divorce his wife brought in a different focus. Our starting point involved taking the time to elucidate and appreciate the nature of the decision for him and the context in which it occurred. During one session I noted that he attempted to approach this major life decision through exclusively logical and intellectual means. What other sources of information did he need to make such a decision? Noting a lack of information from "other parts of him" below his head, I began to work with him on enlivening his body sensation through breathing and movement so as to see what his heart had to say about this decision—his gut, his hands, and his genitals. With more of him available to our work, he could bring all his parts to bear on this decision and understand the nature of his indecision—different parts of him had different responses to the question of his marriage. In this case body-focused experiments were interspersed (a form of alternating work) during our "talk therapy," and created a base for more integrative work on the problem at hand.

With still a different person, long-term development in one sphere may be required before there is a context for alternating body and verbal work. For example, I frequently see people who begin therapy with a problem with differentiating self from others. They cannot distinguish between another's experience of them and their own experience; they have difficulty perceiving their own wants and needs; they have difficulty acting with assertion; they may be highly enmeshed in their families, with little sense of their self as a distinct entity; they lose all sense of self when engaged in an intimate relationship. With such problems our initial work is focused on developing a sense of self. I worked with one woman for a year and a half, once a week, mostly through verbal means, to sort her out from her family and friends. We occasionally used small experiments in attending to her body experience to support her experience of her body boundaries and feelings. But it was only after she had a more differentiated sense of self as distinct from others that more extensive body-oriented work, and later integrative work, made sense to her. Without some broad sense of self, there is no context for appreciating one's body-self.

The illustration (Figure 3-1) expresses this developmental process and shows the utility of each modality within a holistic framework. Singular work develops awareness of parts that have been outside awareness and thus unavailable to the person's integrative function.

| Singular | Alternating | Layered | Integrated |

Mind

Mind

Mind   Person

Body

Body

Body

Body

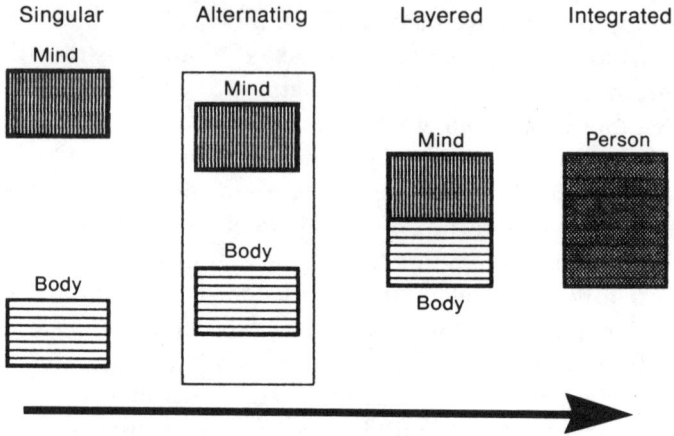

Figure 3–1. Schematic of therapy modalities as part of a development towards an integrated whole.

Alternating work develops a sense of complementary physical and mental processes and brings them within the same boundary, if not together simultaneously. Each aspect of the person is respected in its own right, while acknowledging their "coexistence." Layered work allows for the bridging of parts of the self that have been split off from each other and is the first approximation of integration. Integrated work uses this groundwork to bridge the final gap, so that the person experiences and appreciates the whole formed by what was previously experienced as separate, or not experienced clearly at all.

Chapter 4

Structure and Process—The Organization of Body and Self

We all have remarkably similar basic biological equipment and are all subject to the same laws of mechanics and physics that govern postural distribution and movement. I will call this given structure and mechanics of body functioning our *biological body structure.*°

All humans, with some variation among racial groups and individuals, are born with the same biological structure dictated by the evolutionary adaptations of our species. But if we carefully observe people from a body point of view, we notice something striking: there are many variations in the ways in which people posture themselves, move, and breathe. It is these variations in body structure among individuals—the characteristic tensions, postures, stances, movements, and expressions of the body parts—that are of interest to us as students of human nature.

The beach or local swimming pool is a good place to observe variations in body expressions. We see one man who stands as if he has the weight of the world upon him. His shoulders roll forward over his chest, his head and neck slump forward, his upper back is humped, and his chest is collapsed and compressed. Another person draws her head into her collar bones like a turtle withdrawing into its shell. Her neck is shortened, her shoulders are thrust up around her ears, and her lips are

°Rolf (1977) superbly describes the basic movement mechanics and ideal postural organization of biological structure in our species.

47

tightened into a grimace. A third person stands with arms akimbo, legs splayed and belly hanging, jaw jutting forward—looking for all the world like a sergeant on a parade ground rather than a father watching his children splash and play.

The posturing and body expressions I have decribed are not a matter of conscious choice. The "turtle"° cannot snap out of her muscular shell. The burdened "Atlas" cannot easily straighten his slumped and hunched posture. Often such postures and tensions are not noticed by the individual, although the pain and discomfort that result may be. Despite the fact that we know these variations are not a natural or necessary part of the mechanical structure of the body, it seems as if they are built into the individual's body, an inherent part of the bodily structure.

I refer to these individual variations of the body as the adaptive body structure. Whereas the biological body structure is our common genetic base formed through biological growth and maturation, our adaptive body structure is formed out of our adaptation to our life history and experience *as persons*.† These adaptations are many and varied, and their cumulative effect profoundly affects our physical being in the world.

Adaptive body structure is characterized as postures, stances, and tensions that are:

1. consistently and persistently used over time.
2. either frozen into the musculature so that the structure is continually visible, or preprogrammed muscular responses that channel energy and movement into a stylized movement pattern.
3. automatic and involuntary (under most circumstances).
4. not easily or comfortably modified merely by trying to stand or move differently (i.e., behavioral change).

Most of the body-oriented therapies have grown out of trying to understand and modify the nature of such chronic structural tensions. The classic formulations have attempted to typologize the variations in body structure and relate these body types to character and childhood trauma (Lowen, 1958; Reich, 1945/1972) and temperament (Sheldon, Stevens and Turner, 1940). The approach of Gestalt therapy differs from body typology approaches in its experiential and phenomenological emphasis. The following presents a formulation of the nature and origin of adaptive body structure from the perspective of Gestalt therapy.

°These labels are used as metaphorical descriptions and are not intended to define character types.

†Keleman (1979) refers to this as our "shaping" of ourselves.

THE NATURE AND ORIGINS OF ADAPTIVE BODY STRUCTURE

Rolf (1977) has called the variations from biological structure "randomizations." By this she means they are often random with respect to good mechanical organization of the body in relation to the earth's gravitational field. But my belief is that the individual variations in body structure, despite the apparent randomness of their gravitational organization, are not random, but are full of meaning and significance. A person's body structure is a total of the person's organismic adaptations to life and becomes meaningful when seen in this context.

The context in which our individual variations in body structure must be seen is that of our adaptation and creative adjustment to our personal life experience. We each have a unique family history, set of life experiences, and sense of self, all of which we adapt and respond to not merely by shaping our thinking and attitudes, but also by shaping the way in which we embody ourselves—how we physically respond, move, stand, sit, and so on. Just as the patterns of family interaction, behavior, or sense of self become persistent, so too does the way in which we shape our bodily nature until it is so habitual that it seems a part of our bones and fiber.

Recall how you have responded physically to a situation of danger, threat, or fear. The natural processes of defensive posturing—holding your breath, hunching your shoulders, turning aside to avoid the danger—form a part of how you adapt yourself to this environmental change. Imagine what it would be like to live in a situation of constant threat or danger. These processes, which are easy enough to alter after a momentary startle, become a constant reaction. Your held inhalation (startle), hunched protective shoulders, and askance position may become a part of your stance and harden into your muscles. What was a momentary and flexible *process* of adjustment becomes a constant and fixed *structure* of your body posture.

Organismic processes of adaptation and adjustment become fixed body structures when they are used habitually—either because the environment constantly requires the same response, or because we come to fix our sense of self, allowing ourselves little flexibility. An example of the former is a family situation in which constant threat of punishment or criticism requires constant physical readiness to retreat or defend. An example of the latter is a young boy's attempt to define and feel his self as tough and to obviate his sense of weakness by hardening his chest and pectoral muscles and assuming a rigid posture. These become part of the adaptive body structure: the way we shape ourselves and have been shaped by our life experience.°

For the inexperienced it is often exceedingly difficult to distinguish between biological body structure, the genetic given, and adaptive body structure resulting from life experience. In training workshops my students frequently have a difficult time seeing that individual variations in posture and muscular development are something the person has developed. They frequently "geneticize" such variations, attributing them to familial similarities: "My father hunches his shoulders the same as I do." Or they normalize such variations: "But I've always had a stiff chest" or "I've never been able to inhale much." This results in part from inexperience, but in even greater part because, by normalizing or geneticizing adaptive body structure, we can maintain our lack of awareness of the meaning of our bodily nature and the disowned parts of the self to which these structures relate. Experienced body-oriented therapists know that much of what appears fixed and given about a person's body is actually quite plastic and changeable under the right conditions. If such seemingly fixed structures can be altered, then perhaps they have been shaped and altered in the first place from the more balanced and flexible body structure we all have in common.

The examples of body structure given earlier will help illustrate what I mean by adaptive structure. The "turtle's" chronic withdrawal into herself and protection of her head have become a frozen structure rather than a temporary process of adaptation to a difficult situation. Regardless of the relevance of the protective process during the time in her life when it was necessary, the structural continuation of her avoidance now leaves her with no other option. The process or act of avoidance has become a built-in stance, and her ability to move out into the world is delimited by her physical structure. An adaptive process becomes a fixed structure.

The drill sergeant, like the turtle, has institutionalized and frozen certain organismic processes into his body structure. His aggression and stubborness have become chronic structural attitudes towards his world. No matter what the situation, his body structure supports only certain behaviors because his patterns of muscular tension are habitually structured. Like a railroad car, he can slide along only one track. The aggression and stubborn resistance that is useful at times for anyone is ready all of the time for this man. It is likely that his structure also prevents him from softening and opening himself, and so limits his sensing and ex-

°See Dychtwald (1977), Keleman (1985), and Kurtz and Prestera (1976) for diagrams of some of the most common variations in adaptive body structure.

pression of warmer and more contactful feelings. His adaptive structure forces him to perceive and behave one dimensionally.

But merely to call them habit does not sufficiently explain the meaning of these adaptive body structures. We must ask how these processes become so habitual and predominant as to become structural. Earlier I discussed the notion of the unity of body and self, and pointed out that when parts of the self are disowned, it is frequently the bodily aspects of the contact functions that are alienated from one's sense of self. It is the process of disowning one's body self—the inhibition of certain movements, the desensitization of bodily feeling, the removal of "I" from body experience, the unfinished physical expression of self—that becomes structured into the body over time. In this sense one's adaptive body structure has implicit in it the disowned contact function, the disowned movement or feeling, and the process by which it is disowned, i.e., the tension that blocks it from awareness and expression. The self has been split into parts and is in conflict with itself. The emotional conflicts that are most important to the individual, and thus are persistent, inevitably become structurally manifest in the body.

Let us return to the example of the drill sergeant. He shows himself as tough and aggressive, as is evident in his posture, movement, and stance towards the world. Where is his capacity for vulnerability and softness expressed? His braced and stiffened chest, his set jaw and hardened face allow no alternative stance. His muscles are set in place and he has no control over their positioning. It may be that he identifies with his tough side and calls that "me." He would see no point in being soft and vulnerable, and might even see such vulnerability as dangerous. His body structure expresses what he can own about the nature of his self, with the opposite polarity of softness and vulnerability literally unavailable to him.

Or he may see himself as warm and soft, and would be surprised if you pointed out the incongruence of his body structure with his self-description. He may be troubled that others always react to him fearfully when he feels friendly, unaware of how he physically presents himself or what that relates to in his life. In this instance it is the nature of his body structure that is the ego-alien and disowned polarity of the self, and the rigidity of his structure prevents him from feeling, owning, and knowing the part of himself that is aggressive and hard. That stance is so much a part of him that he does not feel it; it is "normal" and yet disconnected from his sense of self.

Another common origin of adaptive body structure is adaptation to and compensation for physical trauma, disease, or genetic defect. For example, one man with whom I was working stood with his right shoulder two inches higher than his left and his neck twisted and shortened on his right side. This was so frozen into his musculature that he could not balance the position of his shoulders and neck without strain. As we explored the nature of these structures through touch, it soon became apparent that he was also extraordinarily sensitive to intrusion in his right shoulder and neck. He had been very athletic in his youth, and had received a number of injuries. Over time he was able to experience how his positioning of his shoulder and neck emerged from a severe fall and blow to that area of his body, and the resulting pain, fear, and injury. His continued unaware structuring of his body to protect this vulnerable area from further insult became less necessary as our work allowed him to express the unfinished feelings from the event. With each integration he could allow himself to straighten his neck and drop his shoulder more.

We react in similar organismic fashion to adapt to the bodily and emotional trauma of disease, surgery, and other injury. These events require not only mechanical adjustment to protect a painful body area or to compensate for limitation of movement, but also emotional adaptation that involves bodily tension and feeling. The physical adjustments to the limitation of movement due to a disease such as polio, and the unfinished emotional reactions to the disease such as fear and mourning for the lost bodily wholeness, become part of the individual's posture, movement, and breathing—the adaptive body structure.

STRUCTURE, PROCESS, AND THE THERAPEUTIC TASK

Given this view of body structure and the self, the therapeutic approach to working with structure takes on a new meaning. The task is to *help change frozen or automatic body structures to active organismic processes, and to facilitate the integration of the underlying split of the self.* Thus the aim is not to remove structures, but to transmute them into the processes they represent, and to integrate that which has been disowned or unassimilated into the self.

Gestalt therapy is distinguished from many therapeutic orientations by its emphasis on holism, the unity of the organism, and its focus on the experimental and phenomenological. These distinctions also apply to a Gestalt approach to body process and body structure.

The emphasis on holism implies that mere physical change in the body is not enough. The Gestalt practitioner, in working with body structure, is equally focused on improving the physical support and range of movement *and* exploring the meaning and feelings involved in the maintenance of that structure. The goal is not merely physical change, but change of the person as a whole. It is my experience that *body work which focuses on physical change and deemphasizes emotion and meaning is as one-sided and unintegrated as psychotherapy that ignores body processes.*

The Gestalt focus on the experiential and phenomenological brings to body work an emphasis on how the client experiences his or her physical being rather than how the therapist analyzes the client's body structure. The Gestalt body therapist is interested in finding ways for the client to experience the body more fully and to define the meaning of these experiences for himself or herself, rather than in interpreting the client's body and experience.

Out of this emphasis comes the basic unit of work in Gestalt therapy, called the experiment. An experiment is an activity designed to heighten a person's awareness by focusing experience or bringing into the foreground an aspect of experience that is vague. The exercises, manipulations, stretches, and movements used by the therapist are aimed at increasing the client's experience of his or her body and increasing choices, rather than changing the client in a way predetermined by the therapist. Rather than saying, "You need to bring your chest up, try this exercise," I might say, "I notice your chest is collapsed. What changes in your experience of yourself if you raise your chest? What do you feel if you collapse it more?" My interest is not in "changing" the client's chest. The purpose of the experiment is for the *client to experience* the meaning of his or her chest structure.

This gives the general philosophy and orientation of a Gestalt approach to body structure. But what do we actually do? The following provides a general framework for experiment with body structure. Keep in mind that not all of the stages are so straightforward in actual practice as they may seem here.

Awareness of "What Is"

Most structures that are important to a person's way of being are not a matter of conscious choice; at least the person is unaware of the meaning of a particular posture or tension. The obvious first step is to help the client become more aware of what he or she is doing physically by bringing the experience of body into the foreground of experience. (This is what I call the process of "resensitizing," which will be discussed in more detail in Chapter 7.)

In this initial stage of work, the aim is not to push for the meaning or significance of the posture or tension, but simply to sense more clearly "what is" so that the meaning can emerge naturally out of clear sensation. I may do this by simply having the person physically exaggerate the structure. I may also use direct contact (manipulation of the muscle structure), movements, or stretches to revitalize and enliven specific parts of the body.

Heightening "what is" initiates a process of re-ownership. When I can consciously "do" this posture or tension, it becomes more "mine," less separate and alien. I begin to identify with my body structure.

The Emergence of Body Process from Body Structure

As ownership and identity with the structure increases, the client begins to get a sense of the process or meaning behind the posture or tension. For example, I was working with John, whose rib cage and chest were chronically stiff and structurally fixed in a hyperinflated position. He had no awareness of holding his chest up or of its meaning for him.

We worked initially to open up and resensitize him to his shoulders and chest through touch and stretching of his tense muscles. When I began to focus on his breathing, I noticed that his structural inability to allow his chest to drop prevented full exhalation. Does this mean he cannot "let go"? Is this part of a frozen startle response (catching one's breath)? Is he bracing himself in pride? Rather than impose my interpretation on him, I suggested an experiment to heighten his own experience of what he did with his chest and how it affected his breathing.

For the experiment I asked him to consciously exhale fully while I encouraged fuller exhalation by pushing down on his chest. Initially he found this difficult to do. It was as if he literally did not know how to exhale by dropping his chest. Gradually he began to take over more of the work from my hands and to re-own the act of exhaling. When I asked him to tell me his experience of the experiment, he reported that he felt very energetic and excited. As we continued to experiment with pushing out his exhalation and his excitement increased, he also began to feel anxious. We explored the process of him energizing himself through breathing and controlling his energy through tensing his chest, and his related beliefs about "getting too excited," which he reacted to with anxiety.

Experimenting with the experience and behavior of a body structure brings out the active process behind the static structure and makes the client more aware of the conflict at its root. There are a number of alternatives at this stage of work. One approach is to emphasize the opposite of the structure. This is essentially what I did with John by having him drop his chronically raised chest. This approach explores the least aware polarity, and therefore may be experienced as frightening and high risk. It must be used carefully in an atmosphere of support so that the client does not feel suddenly thrust into a part of the self with which the client cannot cope or admit to awareness.

Another approach is to emphasize the structure itself. I might have John hyperinflate his chest or inflate while pushing against my hand on his chest. His experience would have been focused on that part of himself he uses to avoid the energized and scary feelings. He might, for example, have reported that inflating his chest made him feel tough and big, or that it made him feel as if he had created a wall with his chest. This approach generally feels less alarming because it explores and supports the more acceptable and protective side of the self.

Regardless of which approach is used first, both sides need to be explored and developed. Unlike body therapies that try to break through resistance and self-protectiveness, the Gestalt approach aims to integrate parts of the self rather than make one part dominate over the other. Rather than say to John, "Stop holding on to your inhalation, you are breathing wrong and you shouldn't do that," I would say, "Both your holding of your inhalation and your feelings that come with full breathing are important parts of you, so let's see how these two needs can find a fuller expression so that we can understand your dilemma."

One way of fleshing out this dilemma is to have the client physically alternate between the structure and its opposite. I would ask John to alternate between exhaling while letting his chest drop fully and inhaling while pressing his chest up against my hand. This would not be a mere mechanical shifting back and forth, but a continuous exploration of John's experience of the alternating processes. I would also pay attention to what else emerges during the experiment. What changes in skin color, facial expression, or breathing pace occur? How does John physically organize himself to perform this shift? All of these observations can be used to facilitate John's experience of his polarities and find what is meaningful for him.

Development of Theme from Structure

Theme emerges as the meaning of a structure and its underlying process becomes clear. A theme to explore for John might evolve out of the question, "What do you fear when you become energized?" It might develop that, as he continues to breathe fully, he feels anger or the desire to hit someone, and feeling his anger is frightening for him. The theme might be phrased as "controlling my energy so I don't get too angry." Or John might begin to feel sadness as he exhales, and then respond by stiffening his chest to wall off this feeling. The theme here might be stated as "walling off sadness." The theme is a way of capturing and stating the essence of experience, what is most meaningful and important about John's here-and-now experience.[*]

Statement of theme is not seen as curative in itself, as interpretation or reflection is considered in other therapies. It is intended to organize the direction and flow of work. In developing the theme further, we would be interested in the nature and process of John's fears, and with supporting the expression and integration of the polarities involved.

The theme emerges out of awareness of body structure and thus is explicitly tied to body experience, movement, and physical expression. In body-focused therapy, theme development will generally maintain an explicit physical connection, how the theme is *embodied.* Problems in contact and intrapsychic conflict are not only things we think and feel; they are also things we feel and do. In developing a theme, it is essential to continuously pay attention to its psychological meaning and verbal expression, as well as to its representation in posture, movement, and other body phenomena. This prevents verbal therapeutic work from becoming overly abstract and maintains the principles of an integrated and holistic therapy.

To the development of theme from body phenomena and the physical experiments to transmute body structure into lively process, we add the use of verbal dialogue. While at certain times focusing purely on physical process can be appropriate (particularly for those who are already highly verbal), eventually the polarities manifest in the body must be given words or we merely continue to dichotomize body and mind. This prevents the conflict from being isolated to physical tension and body experience and moves the conflict and feelings into the realm of the ego, which includes words and abstractions.

Body structure can be seen as a frozen conversation or dialogue between conflicting parts of the self. The conversation has been frozen only because one part has gained dominance, and a balance of power, fragile or taxing though it might be, has been achieved. What was once an active power struggle between individual and environment, then be-

[*]Use of theme in Gestalt therapy is detailed in Polster and Polster (1973) and Zinker (1977).

tween parts of the self, has become institutionalized in physical behavior and structure. The aim is not merely to physically express the feelings and behaviors of each side, or to reverse the balance of power from one polarity (aspect of the self) to the other, but to resolve the conflict and allow all aspects of the self to exist and function for the total organism.

One way to begin this process is by verbalizing the meaning of the bodily expression as one actively engages the behavior. With John this might be having him experiment with stating, "I am walling myself away from you" or "I am a wall," as he actively inflates and stiffens his chest. Approaching his conflict from the other side, he would say, "I am sad" or "I feel my sadness," as he softens his chest and allows his breathing to deepen.

Further work may use dialogue between the two parts of the self or with the introjected figures that were part of the original adaptation. With John we might develop a dialogue between his image of those who originally rejected his feelings (the parent he had to wall his sadness from) and his feeling self. The dialogue would be explicitly tied to body experience and expression through the use of movement, posturing, and the support of breath and sensation through my use of touch.

As change and balance occur and the ego-alien becomes more tolerated and acceptable to the self, new ways of contacting the environment and fulfilling needs without the tension and distortion of conflict must be developed and practiced. It is not enough to express the unexpressed and change one's internal state. The distorted structure developed as an adaptation to the environment and continues in response to the environment. It is important to reestablish a more flexible adaptation to the environment.

The use of experiment stresses the importance of doing something new and different in the here and now. John and I would experiment to find new ways of being, first with me, and later with others in his day-to-day world. John first needs to be able to be *both* soft and walled in relation to me in the safety of the consulting room. He needs to practice these fully in my presence and in relation to contact with me. Then his "softness" and his "wall" must be capable of conscious and full expression (both verbal and physical) in his interpersonal contact with others. Through this he can allow himself flexibility and begin to learn to discriminate between environments where feelings are appropriate and safe to express and environments where he needs to wall and protect himself.

John may also need to find more active and less constrictive ways to protect his feelings. We may experiment with John stopping someone verbally *before* his feelings are hurt, or with acting tough through words so that he does not have to toughen his body. In this way John learns to respect the need to protect his feelings while finding more flexible and adaptive (less harmful to himself and others) ways of accomplishing this.

The goal is not to invalidate or get rid of the defense, but to make it more functional and discriminative so that the other side of himself can also find expression when the environment is supportive and appropriate. For John always to be tough and walled is no longer adaptive to his present life or he would not have sought to change. Yet there will always be times when he will need to protect his feelings from "the slings and arrows of outrageous fortune." It is possible to find ways to live feeling fully, judicious in our expression of feeling, and aware of the differences between environments that support our feeling and expression and those that do not.

Chapter 5

Resistance and Body Process

> In the usual character-analysis, the resistances are 'at-
> tacked,' the 'defenses' are dissolved, and so forth. But
> on the contrary, if the awareness is creative, then these
> very resistances and defenses—they are really counter-
> attacks and aggressions against the self—are taken as
> active expressions of vitality, however neurotic they
> may be in the total picture. (Perls et al., 1951, p.
> 248)

In all psychotherapies—be they behavioral, analytic, or systems,
physical or verbal—sooner or later the phenomenon of resistance is con-
fronted. Despite the genuine desire for change expressed by the client
and the most intelligent analysis and well-chosen skills of the therapist,
progress in therapy begins to falter. The client knows what he or she
"should" do or wants to do and yet cannot. The therapist can see a direction for positive growth, but is unable to move the client in that direction. The client, whether an individual or group, couple or family, seems
to undermine the therapist's efforts to help and persists in behavior that
is apparently unhealthy.

Resistance is not only a phenomenon of psychotherapy. When you
believe you need to be more (or less) assertive but simply cannot, when
you know that you should do your homework but just cannot seem to get
to it—this is resistance. When a friend constantly arrives late at meet-
ings with a genuine disclaimer, "No matter how hard I seem to try, I just

can't get anywhere on time"—this is also resistance. In relation to body processes, many people have been told to sit up straight or to stand tall throughout their school years, and yet cannot seem to maintain "correct" posture despite the best of intentions—this too is resistance. Resistance is any change we know we want to or should make but cannot seem to accomplish. Something is in the way, resisting that change.°

The particular way in which a therapy explains resistance phenomena is critical to the therapist's intervention in such processes. Body-oriented approaches are no exception: the way in which bodily manifestations of resistance are identified, defined, and understood is critical to the therapist's way of working with such body phenomena.

In verbally-oriented therapies, resistance frequently manifests indirectly, such as through lateness or missed appointments or the failure to carry through on homework. In more direct forms of resistance the therapist's interventions seem to lack impact: the client's responses to interventions are consistently negative, certain topics are avoided, and so on.

All of these occur in body-oriented therapy as well, with an added dimension. Since much of the body-oriented therapist's work is aimed at reducing chronic musculature tension and postural disturbances, a frequent form of resistance is seen when tension does not yield to the therapist's efforts. Tense musculature does not loosen in response to therapeutic work. It may temporarily loosen during a session, but will return to its original tense state once the session is over. Apparent changes in muscular patterns do not result in related changes in posture and movement, such as when the release of musculature that holds the shoulders curled forward does not result in the shoulders uncurling and shifting back.

What is the meaning of such phenomena? In the following, I briefly discuss some of the alternative views of resistance phenomena as a contrast to the Gestalt approach to resistance.

VIEWS OF THE NATURE OF RESISTANCE

The "Common Sense" View of Resistance

Psychoanalyst Bertram P. Karon (1976) notes that, "According to common sense, there are only two possibilities; either we do not know

°It is important to distinguish true resistance from mere ignorance; sometimes what seems to be resistance is simply a lack of knowledge or skills.

what to do, or we know what to do and do it" (p. 203). If we know the right thing to do, then we should do it! The common sense approach is frequently used by friends, family, and well-meaning co-workers, and with similar frustrating effects, by some psychotherapies and somatic approaches. In the common sense view, resistance to change is considered to be: anti-self (alien to the "I"), weakness (lack of will), irrational, or force of habit.

Resistance is viewed as anti-self because the goal of change is deemed the best thing for the person, so anything contrary to that goal must be against the best considered aims of the person. It is considered weakness because, as many relatives and friends note, if you really wanted to change, you would be able to; hence inability implies a lack of will on your part. It is irrational because, obviously, your logical choice is to change, and yet you cannot despite all of your reason telling you it is the right thing. It is viewed as force of habit because if you are persistent enough, you will replace it with a new habit.

Somatic approaches often approach resistance from a common sense point of view. Although not so naive as to accuse the resistant client of being weak-willed, somatic approaches are prone to labeling resistance phenomena either as irrational or as mere force of habit.

When resistance is labeled as irrational, the therapist refuses to acknowledge its manifestations, confident that the correct and rational thing is being done, even if the client is in pain or avoidant. Clients (and therapists) are urged to ignore or tolerate the pain as best they can, knowing that the goal somehow justifies the means.

An example of this approach to resistance is described by Rolf, the founder of structural integration, or Rolfing. Rolfing is a somatic approach that treats tense, rigid musculature by the application of physical pressure by the practitioner. It is frequently quite painful. Rolf describes a client (Feitus, 1978) who reacted angrily toward a Rolfer, accusing him of hurting him during work in the groin area. Rolf discounts the client's reaction as "a projected, irrational response" (p. 150), and tells the Rolfer, "You're not there to spend time investigating the sources and means by which this projection has been released," and urges the Rolfer to ignore the resistance in order to accomplish the required intervention.

This view minimizes the client's experience. Certainly the Rolfer was not intending to hurt the man, only to do him a particular kind of good, but he caused pain nonetheless. To react with anger to pain is a natural organismic response. How can this be construed as an irrational response? Must the client repress the natural, and I would say healthy, response to pain simply to comply with the Rolfer's emphasis on the goal? What happens to the client's sense of hurt and desire for self-protection? It does not simply disappear; one cannot entirely get rid of a valid and legitimate organismic response. The result is a further alienation from the identified self of natural impulses.

Other somatic approaches view resistance as strong habit. These methods emphasize retraining body habits through control of old "bad" habits, substitution of new "good" habits, and constant practice of the new and more desired habits so as to prevent return to the old "bad" habits. I call such approaches mastery approaches because the emphasis is on mastering the body by the ego (will). In this case the "I" remains distinct from the body and shapes "it" through altering behavior, that is, through changing habits.

Unless the change of habit comes about by addressing its reason for existence, it can only be mastered, not undone. The new habits may "feel better" because they are mechanically better organized for movement. Clients may also feel better because they now have mastery over what had previously been experienced as victimizing and controlling. But what has happened to the original impulse the habit or structure contained?

Let us take a hypothetical (although quite common) case where a woman has controlled her feelings of sadness over the death of a parent by tightening and compressing her chest. She felt that she must be strong for the remaining parent and not "fall apart." Over time she has split her holding off from her self and merely experiences tension and discomfort, which she wants to get rid of. If she is taught new ways to hold herself or stylized ways to move and breathe that are patterned after a model of "correct" posture and biomechanical functioning, she may feel more comfortable and have some relief from the pain. However, her way of coping with sadness has become divorced from the physical process on which it is based. Nothing has been done to release the held feeling or to alter the neurotic belief that "I must always be strong" and "Falling apart is horrible."

If the conflict identified with the body process is not clarified and worked through, the old habit will return. We do not so easily get rid of parts of ourselves merely by unlearning them. Worse, however, is the possibility of so overlearning the new, good habit that the original conflict becomes inaccessible beneath a thick layer of secondary repression. I have seen this repeatedly in devotees of various training arts, such as dance, athletics (particularly weight lifting), and the martial arts. Such people have often so assiduously worked to counter their bad habits that the original feelings and expressions are driven far below the surface. These clients have to spend much time undoing their overlearned "good" habits before they can restore contact with the self-expressions that led to the tensions and distorted postural holdings.

Psychoanalysis and Resistance

Freud brought the understanding of resistance beyond the common sense approach. To continue with Karon's (1976) earlier comment:

> There is a difference between a psychoanalytic therapy and a common sense approach. According to common sense, there are only two possibilities; either we do not know what to do, or we know what to do and do it. Any real therapist knows that there is a third possibility—knowing what one should do, but being incapable of doing it. Here is where most of the time in psychotherapy is spent, finding out why it is that the patient cannot do what he believes makes sense. (p. 203–204)

The addition of this third possibility was one of the major contributions of psychoanalysis to the art and science of psychotherapy. Resistance, far from being irrational or the result of weakness or merely habit, had a meaning and function of its own in the life and economy of the person. This meant that the therapist, rather than ignoring or denigrating the resistance, looked on it with curiosity.

Freud considered resistance as one of the two "facts" that psychoanalysis "endeavors to explain" (Freud, 1938/1966, p. 939). His prototype was the resistance of forgetting, since psychoanalysis requires the remembering of one's past, which he called the defense of repression. In psychoanalysis resistance is seen as the operation of a defense in the context of therapy: "What serves as a defense for the patient in his neurosis is directly observed by the therapist . . . as resistance. A defense operating against the efforts of therapy is termed resistance" (Colby, 1951, p. 95).

In this view resistance is the functioning of defenses against internal drives that threaten the personality structure. Such defenses are by definition unconscious in their operation because they defend the person from conscious recognition of problematic impulses. Since the aim of analysis is to reconstruct the past and make conscious what is unconscious, resistance must be "overcome," as Brill has put it in his introduction to Freud's work (1938/1966), through its interpretation as a defense and the exposure of the underlying impulse.

Psychoanalysis considers defenses the means by which the psyche maintains equilibrium in the face of internal conflict between drives and the external evocation of that conflict. In this sense it is viewed as a mechanism or tool used by the person. This distinction between the person and the defense allows the analyst to see resistance as functional in the psychic integrity of the person, but as something that is not essential to the self given proper conditions. Thus the analyst sees resistance as necessary to the psychic economy of the person and yet must undermine its presence so that the work of reconstruction can take place. This distinction will be important in my discussion of the Gestalt view of resistance later.

The Reichian View of Resistance

Wilhelm Reich extended the psychoanalytic notion of resistance into his notion of character and character armor (Reich, 1945/1972). Reich also saw resistance in therapy as the operation of a defense. He saw this defense as identical to the person's character, what he called the characteristic defenses or "armor." Reich believed that the character armor was the same as the body armor (chronic physical tensions). The characteristic way of being for the person, including physical tensions, posture, and mannerisms, constituted the defense against disagreeable memories, especially those that the analyst was trying to bring to consciousness. (See the appendix for a more detailed description of Reichian therapy and how it compares to Gestalt therapy.)

In his view it is only by dissolving this character armor, in the form of its bodily manifestation, that one can contend with resistance to the analytic work of reconstructing and resolving conflicts from the past. Character analytic work (work on the character resistances) functions by vigorous comment on and interpretation of characteristic mannerisms, and physical work to break down and loosen up the defensive body armor. Resistance, whether in the form of muscular tension or character style and manner, is considered a secondary phenomena that covers the "true" self. Resistance is seen as necessary but only minimally desirable, since the goal is to restore access to the true self (Lowen, 1983), which has been repressed and distorted by parental needs and socialization.°

The understanding of resistance as a defense was a major advance for psychotherapy. But this explanation also created problems of its own. In particular the more vigorously a resistance was attacked by the therapist, the more tenacious it became. This occurred whether the resistance being attacked was a cognitive defense (as in psychoanalysis),

---

°In his later work, Reich clearly turned away from the pure drive theory of psychoanalysis, believing that the central conflict in neurosis was between internal drives and social forces rather than of internal drives with each other (Reich, 1945/1962). See Miller (1984) on drive theory in classical psychoanalysis.

a character mannerism, or an unyielding body tension (as for Reich). From the therapist's standpoint, such defenses interfere with the aim of therapy, and ultimately the health of the patient, and so must be eliminated before progress in the central task of therapy can be accomplished.

Approaching resistance from the client's standpoint, however, gives us a clue to the dilemma inherent in this approach to resistance. From the point of view of the client's psychic economy, we might substitute the term "protection" for "defense." By resisting the therapist, the client is protecting himself or herself from a perceived harm. It is difficult to argue with the natural impulse to protect oneself from harm. The therapist who attacks or overcomes resistance is thus put in the position of having to overcome a natural and valid response. What organism could be expected to give up protection of its integrity, even when this is supposed to be "good for it"?

Even where the client fully agrees with the aims of the therapist and looks on his or her own resistance as undesirable, the therapist and client are merely colluding to circumvent the natural protective functions of the organism. Such a task will frequently be blocked, as the needs for survival and self integrity generally outweigh pressures for change.

Gestalt Therapy and Resistance

The view of resistance by Gestalt therapy is closely related to its predecessors and yet has some important differences. Like psychoanalysis and Reichian approaches, Gestalt therapy goes beyond the common sense approach and asserts that resistance has meaning and must be worked with therapeutically. Gestalt therapy also considers resistance to have an important function in maintaining the balance and integrity of the organism.

An important difference in viewpoint is that resistance is not considered a mechanism or tool of the self; it is seen as the self *itself* in action. There is nothing behind the resistance that is in substance different from the resistance itself, no "true self" different from the resistance. Both the defense and the defended are self. To the Gestalt therapist, to break down or eliminate resistance would be the same as breaking down and eliminating a capacity of the self. Resistance, in this view, is an expression of self.

The opening quotation to this chapter notes that resistances, in Gestalt therapy, are taken as "active expressions of vitality" despite the fact that, in thwarting the conscious intention to change, resistances seem pathological in terms of the "total picture."

If we are not to get rid of them, how do we work with resistances to the benefit of the therapeutic process? While resistances are expressions of the self, they are frequently not fully owned and aware expressions and so occur automatically and in a truncated or partial form. This means that these expressions, given their operation outside awareness, are not expressions of choice. They do not allow the person to adapt to environments and organismic needs that are different from those under which they were learned. Given their truncated and partial form, they are not full expressions, and so the organism cannot serve all its needs fully.

Let me contrast the Gestalt view of resistance with the others presented using the example given by Rolf earlier. The Rolfer, following Rolf's common sense belief that the man's anger at being hurt is irrational, must convince the person either to inhibit or to bypass the emotional response so that the work can continue and so result in a "new place" for the client's physical structure. An analytic approach to this resistance might be to interpret the man's anger and pain as a transference reaction; the client is projecting his feelings towards a castrating parental figure onto the Rolfer who is causing pain in his groin area. A Reichian approach to the tension and resistance in this client's groin might use breathing and touch to encourage the man to release his anger so as to break down the restraining body armor and thereby evoke the original natural sexual feeling of his pelvis.

In contrast, from a Gestalt perspective, both the tension in the client's groin and his anger towards the therapist are expressions of the self (the organism). A Gestalt therapist might choose to encourage the man's expression of anger at being hurt in a clearer and more direct way, suggesting he experiment with phrasing relevant to his life experience: "I won't let you hurt me here, just like I didn't let Mom hurt me . . . "

Another choice, certainly not exclusive of the foregoing, might be to back up a few steps when such a strong reaction is encountered and look at the tension itself in terms of the client's self-expression. The therapist would ask, "What movement or posturing is he creating through his pelvic tension, and how can we bring this into fuller expression?" The client would then be asked to emphasize the tension, perhaps by pushing against the therapist's hands or encouraging the implicit movement that the tension only partially expresses. The goal is to allow the client's full ownership and expression of the nature of the tensing.

A similar phenomenon occurred with one of my own clients. Over the course of our work, it became apparent that she could not allow tension in her left shoulder to release, although she could let go of her right shoulder fairly easily. In the early days of my own work, I might have simply redoubled my efforts to effect release, ignoring the pain and discomfort I was causing. Having a different appreciation of the meaning of resistance, I slowed down our work, taking the time to build a clearer picture of the nature of her persistent holding of her shoulder. One time I asked her to intentionally push back against my hands with her shoulder. This clearly had a mobilizing effect for her—her breathing, facial expression, and bodily stance quickly supported her pushing. I asked her to say "no" to me while she pushed, and she began to smile. The theme of her difficulty with acknowledging her need to protect her boundaries became an important one in our subsequent work. Here it can be seen how her resistance to letting go of her shoulder tension was in itself an expression of a previously restrained function: the act of saying "No."

Another example of this approach to resistance took place while working with a man, a mild-mannered and scholarly individual. I began by working with him to release some of the structural narrowness and tension of his chest. As I supported him to breathe more fully and to release his chest, tension appeared in his legs. With each release of tension in one area, he would become tense in some other body area. It was apparent that the existence of his tension was important enough to his functioning that he was finding ways to maintain it, despite my attempts to help him release it! In my early days of practice, I might have seen this resistance as undesirable and insisted that he learn to inhibit this transfer of tension. In this case, however, I focused on how we could utilize this "conservation of tension."

Rather than encouraging him to relax and let go, we began to experiment with converting his tension into action by him pushing back at me. We discovered that this resulted both in release of his chest tension and in less displacement into other body areas. This confirmed my hypothesis that when he translated his tension into action, there was no need to conserve it. I then asked him to stand, a position appropriate for more active work, and began to develop this pushing-back process, with me pushing against his chest and asking him to use his breathing to push back. I encouraged him to convert each tension that became apparent into a fuller, more direct action. As I noticed tension in his jaw, I would ask him to exaggerate it into a grimace; as he began to tense his arms, I asked him to find some way to use his arms to engage with me; as he tightened his throat, I asked him to add sounds to his exhalation.

The result was a lively and delightfully aggressive engagement between us—a vocal and vigorous tussle. In the processing time after our experiment, he noted how he had not wrestled another man since early childhood. Being the skinny and weak younger brother in a family full of boys, he had learned to restrain his aggression and withdrew into books and studies, avoiding the humiliation of getting trounced. Our wrestling gave him an opportunity to feel his strength without being overwhelmed by another, and allowed him to put his energy into action rather than continue to engage it against himself.

Had I approached his displacement of tension as something to get rid of or inhibit, or interpreted it as a resistance to yielding his heart to his father, or as his armor against orgasm, we would not have been able to discover the function such tension served *in its own terms.* Certainly his tension could be looked at as a defense against his aggression, in the analytic view, and indeed it served as such. But it was not merely a defense; the tension was itself the *expression* of his aggression, albeit in a more indirect, retroflected form. By trusting the validity of his tension and finding ways to develop and expand it, we were able to make more apparent its meaning to his functioning. Further, we were able to bring the resistance fully to the service of the organism, that is, fully aware, owned, and expressed.

So far I have been speaking of resistance and body phenomena in a very specific and technical sense. I have commented that, according to the view of Gestalt therapy, we can look at resistance as *self* (or, more accurately, as a function of self) and an expression of one's intrinsic being. When viewed in this way, particular physical manifestations of resistance can be reframed as expressions. This allows the emphasis of therapy to shift from surmounting resistance to bringing out expressions.

SOMATIC PROCESS: MESSAGES FROM THE DISOWNED SELF

To truly understand the meaning of resistance, we need to place it within the context of the whole person. Resistance is not merely expression of self; it is a particular kind of expression, or rather the expression of a particular aspect of self. To understand resistance, including such complex forms as somatic and emotional symptoms, it is important to understand the relationship between the self, the body, and the organism as a whole. The traditional understanding of resistance and somatic symptoms comes about because we identify "self" with a limited and narrow set of characteristics, and so feel other parts of our self to be foreign and alien to our goals.

Imagine a situation in which one person must communicate an important message to another. If the person who must hear the message is receptive to the communication and the communicator can send a clear message in language that is mutually understood, the important information will be conveyed. If, on the other hand, the person who must receive the message wishes to have nothing to do with the sender, in fact would like to deny the very existence of the sender, and the sender can only communicate in a relatively unknown language, then important information will be difficult to convey. Given the gap between sender and receiver, the sender has virtually to hit the receiver over the head merely to get the receiver to attend to the communication!

This is analogous to much of our seemingly irrational body process. In a previous chapter I described how we alienate our body from our sense of self, so that body process and our disowned contact functions become identical. Since these aspects continue to have relevance to our functioning, despite the fact that we disown them, they are constantly seeking expression. Like the unattended message sender, our disowned body-self can only communicate nonverbally about important things to a "receiver" (the owned self), who would rather pretend that the sender is unimportant and not worth listening to. Is it any wonder that our body-self frequently has to do something drastic—migraines, disabling back pains, impotence, ulcers—to get our attention?

Like Perls' formulation of dreams as "existential messages" or communications between parts of the self (Perls, 1969), much of our "inexplicable" body processes can be usefully viewed as existential messages from disowned parts of self. The therapist is faced with the task of helping the client make the messages from the body intelligible, and resolving the unfinished situation that required the person to alienate that aspect of the self, and thereby restore the gaps in the organism. The following are the tasks of the therapist:

1. To work with the body to restore contact with body processes.

2. To develop a verbal vocabulary to describe body experience and clarify the meaning of movements, sensations, and other nonverbal processes.

3. To establish a relationship (dialogue) between the split-off parts of the self.

4. To work through unfinished situations so that the disowned functions are assimilated back into the self, the range of possible responses is expanded, and a new creative adjustment is possible.

I will illustrate with a clinical example. I had been working with one man for several sessions on restoring a sense of connection to his body. He was born in Italy but was educated and had now settled in the United States. He was strongly motivated to achieve and much of our body-oriented work had been focused on recognizing the identification of his tension with the high degree to which he pressured himself.

During one session we were working in his abdominal muscles and discovered that he seemed to have little awareness and sensation in this area. As I used touch to enliven and loosen his stomach muscles, I asked him to verbalize his experience. He reported that his stomach felt very distant. Coupling his report with his obvious lack of awareness of this area, I suggested he make this into the statement, "I have lost touch with you, stomach, I feel so distant from you," and to say this to his belly area and pay attention to any response it elicited.

As he spoke the words, he appeared profoundly moved, and when I commented on this he began to cry. He told me that the response to his statement was in Italian, his native tongue. When he "heard" this response, he immediately felt the appropriateness of the situation, since this language reflected a culture that was strongly rooted in the visceral and emotional center of the belly and lived life "from the guts." In recognizing how alienated he was from his guts and passion, he felt a deep sadness. To be accepted into the mainstream of U.S. society, he had worked hard to eradicate many of his Italian characteristics. In so doing he also divorced himself from his passion, his sensuality, and his attention to pleasure. Here, at last, was the missing counterbalance to his relentless drive and constant work.

In our continued work we paid careful attention to the sensations, tensions, and responses from his belly. We worked to discover how tensions there could be mobilized into movements, and what those movements meant. We worked to understand the "vocabulary" of his sensations in his belly, and how this vocabulary allowed him to connect with his passionate nature. We used his belly sensations as a commentary on his life that would signal his overinvolvement with his striving for achievement to the exclusion of his other needs.

Chapter 6

The Therapeutic Use of Touch

The notion that touch can be used within the context of therapy has been around for many years. Mainstream therapists have utilized touch in the limited form of communicating support through hugging clients or holding their hands. There has always been controversy about such uses of touch, particularly in relation to countertransference: whose needs is the touch actually serving, the client's or the therapist's? This is still of concern today. Unless you are an orthodox analyst, however, the current standards for tactile contact between client and therapist allow for the social use of touch—a handshake, touching a client's shoulder or hand to communicate support, and under certain circumstances a brief hug to acknowledge an important event—with the ethical caveat that all sexual contact between client and therapist is prohibited.

Touch is not always a necessary, or even a desirable, part of working with the body in therapy. Much can be done of a physical nature in therapy without the use of touch: verbally directing the client's attention to his or her body process (e.g., breathing, posture, and subtle movements); instructing the client in various exercises, movements, or postures; asking the client to touch his or her own body as a means of focusing attention and supporting body experience. With persons who cannot tolerate the physical proximity of the therapist or for whom tactile contact is an exceedingly foreign and frightening modality, much body-oriented work can still be done using the above methods.

Yet touch is such a direct and definitive way of communicating "body to body," that it is foolish to omit it *a priori* from therapeutic methodology. Touch can be an effective tool for illuminating bodily experience. Through touch, a therapist can directly demonstrate the existence of bodily tension, position the client's posture to illustrate new possibilities, directly release muscular holding, encourage the client to fill his or her bodily space with awareness, assist movement, and so on. In this way touch is a means to an end, it is used to facilitate development of a client's body-self through sensation, awareness, movement, and posture.

Touch can also be an end in itself. Touching and being touched are a fundamental mode of human interaction. In the human interaction of therapy, touch can result in the emergence of unfinished business: one client may have experienced touch as hurtful or intrusive and so physically organized himself to expect this kind of tactile contact; another client may have experienced a paucity of tactile contact and so has physically adjusted herself to cope with feelings of loss and body hunger for touch. The use of touch by the therapist, in carefully gradated and respectful ways, can be used to evoke and work through this unfinished business with respect to a client's experience of touch.

The full potential of the psychotherapeutic use of touch emerged with various body approaches to growth and awareness. This was first evidenced in the work of Reich (1942, 1945/1972), whose use of touch in his efforts to help free the body armor were apparent, although not central, in his writings. His student Alexander Lowen (1958, 1975) has continued that tradition. As psychotherapists experienced events of emotional significance in Reichian work, during the hands-on physical work of Rolfing (Rolf 1977) and other deep-tissue massage approaches, in the gentler hands-on body approaches of the Alexander technique (Barlow, 1973; Alexander, 1971) or Feldenkrais functional integration (Feldenkrais, 1972; Rywerant, 1983), it became apparent that touch could have psychotherapeutic effects beyond those of simple support. The skilled use of touch could deeply affect the client's bodily being and sense of self: the recall of body memory, the release of long withheld emotions, the reorganizing of body structure and resulting change in the client's relationship to life.

Notwithstanding the emergence of such touch-oriented approaches and their results, the psychotherapeutic use of touch continues to be a controversial subject for mainstream therapists. The healing effects of touch have been similarly denied and misunderstood in western medicine, despite centuries of healing through touch traditions in eastern medicine (e.g., shiatsu and acupressure massage) and the more recent

Western traditions of osteopathic and chiropractic manipulation. Neglect of the relevance of touch results from a number of factors: cultural embarrassment about our physical being and oversexualization of body contact; denial and disownership of our body-self; and life history of violation of self boundaries.

Western religious and philosophical traditions split the person (soul) from the body, relegating all the "sinful" (in religion) or "irrational" (in philosophy) impulses to our physical being. To touch, then, becomes an act of the base impulses of the toucher's body towards the bad, evil, and implicitly sexual nature of the touched person. Traditionally touch in western culture has had an overriding sexual connotation, which I believe is due in large part to the disownership of our physical nature in our religious and philosophical thought. If the body is base, dirty, and sexual in nature, then how can touch (body contact) be construed as anything other than sexual?

The developmental disownership of our physical self discussed earlier also has a profound effect on our attitudes towards touch. If much of your body experience and impulses has been rendered alien to your sense of self, so too will the profoundly physical act of touch be seen as alien, even frightening or disgusting. You might fear that if you touch, you will be overwhelmed by unacceptable urges, or that the other person will misunderstand or criticize you (a projection of one's own self-critic). You may be so disconnected from and inexperienced with your touch process that you fear hurting the other person, or feel clumsy and ineffectual. You may consider the other person's body as disgusting or unworthy (again, a projection of feelings about your own body) and so be unable to reach out. Or you may hunger so much for physical contact, which is simultaneously unacceptable and disowned, that the prospect of satisfying that hunger is overwhelming.

The frequent violation of self boundaries through physical, sexual, emotional, and narcissistic abuses has recently become apparent. Alice Miller (1984) describes the devastating impact of such intrusion and use of children by adults on a child's emotional and psychological development. Such use may involve actual physical violation (sexual or physical abuse), or require the child to give up his or her own wants and feelings in order to serve the parent's needs for esteem (narcissistic abuse). Such abuse and use of the self in the service of other people's needs frequently involve direct violation of bodily integrity (as in sexual and physical abuse), or require the repression of natural protective responses, such as anger at the intrusion, movement to stop the intrusion, or the urge to escape (all of which occur in narcissistic abuse as well as sexual or physical abuse). Only by disowning the aspect of the self that experiences the violation or the response to violation can we cope with such a difficult environment. If the body is the part of the self that has been violated and the reality of the violation itself is denied, then touch threatens to rekindle awareness of having been violated and the need to protect one's boundaries. The initial fear of being touched experienced by clients in therapy and the fear of touching experienced by many therapists may be related to the potential for recreation of this history of violation and the subsequent surfacing of rage, sadness and other strong emotions.

These issues load the consideration of the use of touch in therapy for both the client and therapist. I came to my first experience of body-oriented work with both a longing for touch and a fear of being hurt by it. I was estranged from my physical nature and lived uncomfortably within my body as if in a strange and distorted shell. My initial experience as a client for body-work trainees, and later as a student myself of a body-oriented approach, certainly gave me more comfort in my body, but I still disowned much of my bodily nature and was unaware of the hurts I had suffered that were intrinsic to my disowned body-self. I felt compelled to connect to others through the direct medium of touch, and yet was still estranged from the power of my hands and the contact surface of my skin.

It was no accident, of course, that I was attracted to body-oriented forms of therapy. In my own development as a therapist, I have had to confront my own fears and limitations and embarrassment about my bodily being, and recognize through my clients' fears of touch my own history of hurt. As I have worked through these issues, I have gained more ownership over my own touch and more appreciation of the tragedy my clients have experienced in the violation and loss of their bodily nature.

If therapists are to understand the use of touch in therapy and so be able to create for their clients an atmosphere that makes the use of touch safe, comfortable, and natural, we must first examine our own nature and attitudes. We must come to understand how we embody the cultural, as well as personal, beliefs and attitudes that make touch forbidden or frightening. The understanding of one's self and biases is a prerequisite for any therapeutic application, but is even more essential for such intimate and directly contactful work as touch.

THE NATURE OF TOUCH IN THERAPY

Touch as a Human Event

The process of touch can be looked at in a number of ways, and each way has different things to say about its therapeutic nature. We can consider touch from the point of view of its *physics*. This view looks at touch as a physical (mechanical) process that has related physical (mechanical) effects on the body being touched. Within a physical model of touch, illustrated by traditional massage and physical therapy approaches such as Rolfing and chiropracty, a certain amount of physical energy and mechanical pressure is used by the toucher to "move" a certain amount of muscle or skeletal mass to a new position. Theoretically the effect of touch is a measurable function of the energy required to shift a particular part of the body, that is, to relax or release a muscle or adjust a skeletal imbalance.

This physical model, while accurately describing one aspect of touch and its effects, does not adequately explain all its phenomena. Anyone who has had a deep massage or good back rub knows that the resulting relaxation frequently disappears once you return to everyday living. What has happened to the muscles that have been released through physical manipulation?

Additionally practitioners of such approaches, as I once was, are well aware that often no amount of physical force will release a given muscular tension, leading the practitioner to accuse the person of "resisting" or "not helping enough." Contrarily the lightest laying on of hands may result in profound and pervasive bodily change. The physical model of touch can only attempt to explain these phenomena by tacking on quasimechanistic notions of "energy fields" or "energy blocks" to understand why mechanical force alone does not produce results. I am not arguing against the existence of energy fields or blocks, but that these explanations are frequently applied because the human and interactional nature of touch is ignored or misunderstood.

What is not included in a mechanistic view of touch is that, in addition to physical effects, touch is fundamentally a *human* process. It is the human aspects that enlarge the effects of touch beyond its physics and mechanics, and so enlarge the scope of things we must take into account as therapists when using touch as a tool for intervention. As a human process, touch must be taken into account as an interaction between living, feeling, conscious persons. The feelings and awareness of each person, their existential state, as well as the relationship between them, must be understood to fully comprehend the result of and response to touch. If we believe that the body is self, then when we touch another person, we are not touching "a body," but the very self of this person with our own self. In this way touch ceases to be a mechanical event and becomes a process of interaction and communication. Through touch we physically make statements about the nature of ourselves, our relationship with each other, and the world at large. It is an event with multiple levels of meaning rather than simple cause and effect.

Touch as Communication

As I have developed as a therapist and student of body therapies, I have organically integrated the use of touch into the philosophy and framework of my therapeutic approach. But to many therapists, particularly those whose therapeutic model does not include a rationale for using touch or those practitioners of body approaches whose physical model does not integrate the notion of psychological change into the notion of physical change through touch, the relevance of touch to therapy is less clear. What therapeutic purpose is served by using touch? Is touch used merely for comfort and support? Do we use touch to break down the body armor that is holding back emotional traumas? Are we using touch to retrain or reprogram neuromuscular habits, as a kind of behavior therapy of the body? Is touch used to shift misaligned postural structures, or do we give direct relief of tension and muscular holding?

As with any therapeutic intervention, the use of touch is guided by one's philosophy and view of human process. Within Gestalt therapy I see touch as a tool for developing client awareness and ownership of their bodily being and the way in which they make contact with their environment. Touch is a medium of communication between therapist and client, with the therapist transmitting his or her presence, observations, and experiments through the use of his or her hands, and the client transmitting his or her statements, experience, and responses to the therapist's contact through his or her bodily reactions and changes.

The use of touch as a communication process for developing awareness, ownership, and expanded capacity for contact is grounded in the notions of the unity of body and self, resistance, and the phenomenological (experiential) emphasis that are intrinsic to the philosophy of Gestalt therapy.

1. *The unity of body and self.* If we view the self and the body as an intrinsic unity, then any use of touch is geared not towards "changing habits" or "realigning body parts," but rather towards contacting the *person* as embodied. If we touch "the body" and not the *person,* and so make clients an object, then how can we expect them to reestablish ownership of their body-self?

2. *Resistance and touch.* If we view bodily resistance as a manifestation or expression of self, then touch is not used to break down resistance and armor (tension), since this would result in the breaking down and loss of an essential self function. Rather it is used to bring that resistance into aware, owned, and full expression. We use touch, then, to dis-

cover disowned resistance and encourage the use of such resistance in contactful action, that is, to bring it back into useful engagement with the environment.

3. *Phenomenological emphasis in touch.* In a Gestalt approach to the body, the goal of touch is what is *experienced* by the person being touched, rather than a production of predetermined change. Touch is used, then, in the form of experiment, either as a support for clients to explore some aspect of their bodily nature, or as an experiment in and of itself. In the former case, I might use touch to bring awareness to the way a client is holding and positioning his or her shoulders; in the latter case, I might explore such questions as: "What is it like to be touched?" or "How do you organize yourself to meet my touch?"

These principles come together in the actual moment in therapy when I move my hands towards contact with something about a client's bodily being that captures my own and my client's interest. I may use my hands to invite the person's awareness and breathing into a part of the body that seems deadened and lifeless. I may use my touch to emphasize and heighten the way in which a client is holding himself or herself or to explore with the client the movement the holding is preventing. My touch can be a fundamental nonverbal communication of my presence and caring when a client is making contact with profound and deep emotions.

Skilled touch can often communicate something about body process with a specificity, directness, and immediacy that would require lengthy verbal explanation. I can say "Notice the way you are tensing this particular muscle in your forehead" with a simple feather touch, or "Try emphasizing the way you are hunching your shoulders and compressing your breathing in your chest" by gently shaping the client's shoulders with my hands and pressing briefly on the chest. I can demonstrate the possibilities for movement, breathing, and release of tension by the way I move the client's limbs through space, using the movement to nonverbally point out places of constriction. I can create an environment through my touch that can allow the client to bring out parts of the self that have been held (literally) in abeyance for many years. We may explore what it is like to reject my touch—to recognize and express one's power and capacity to accept only that touch that one wants on one's own terms—and so undo the pattern of feeling obligated to accept what is done to oneself by others at their whims.

In this way a framework and attitude towards the usefulness of touch are established that are consistent with our understanding of therapy. When we add to the directness of touch the emphasis and meaning of verbalization, we expand the depth of intervention even more.

Table 6-1
Varieties of Touch

Quality of Touch	Therapeutic Uses/Communications
Feather touch	Reminder, says "Focus here"; generally is along path (direction) of muscle's relaxation.
Laying on hands	Contacting, perceiving, and affecting energy field.
Simple touch	Presence, "I am here."
Light stroking	Comforting, soothing.
Moving touch	Guiding energy and flow along a particular path.
Rocking	Loosens skeletal units; comforting; reminder of natural flow and pulsation.
Rubbing	Enlivening of surface; soothing when light.
Vibrating	Enlivening; reminder of holding; energizing.
Tapping	Enlivening, says "Sense this structure"; resilience.
Moving limbs	
(a) Fast	Loosening, letting free.
(b) Slow	Repatterning neuromusculature; freeing range, developing subtle awareness of body.
Deep stretching	
(a) Moving	Breaking through; lengthening.
(b) Steady	Opening, releasing, enlivening; point-pressure work.

VARIETIES OF TOUCH

I originally received training in the use of touch that emphasized hard and deep pressure aimed at manually stretching and releasing tense musculature. Over the years I shifted my approach to include softer and more delicate forms of touch, particularly as I integrated more sophisticated concepts of resistance and phenomenology into my work. But unlike practitioners who dichotomize touch through exclusive use of either hard pressure (Rolf, 1977) or soft touch (Rubenfeld, 1984), I see legitimate use of the full range of touch depending on the theme of work, the person with whom one is working, the timing of the intervention, and the therapeutic intent. Table 6-1 illustrates some of the different kinds of touch possible and their therapeutic effects.

This table is certainly not exhaustive, and I anticipate the possibility of adding to it in the future. I would caution that correct therapeutic use of touch requires training, particularly with the firmer or movement-oriented kinds of touch. Table 6-1 is intended for illustration purposes to give the reader a notion of the possibilities available, and is not meant as an instruction sheet.

Firm Versus Light

There is no "right" kind of touch to use. Firm touch is not better than light touch, nor light touch better than firm. If we look at the use of touch holistically, within the context of a particular person, a specific body area, in a particular time, and with a sense of the relation between two people, we can move away from a dichotomous model of the touch process. By paying attention to the response of the client to a particular kind of touch on a particular part of the body, you can learn what this person needs at this time.

Firm touch may be responded to by one person or in one body area as intrusive and hurtful, especially if the person has been hurt or abused by others. In this situation, firm touch essentially replicates the abuse the client has previously experienced. Insisting that the client bear with it because it will be ultimately "good for you" only encourages the client to introject what *other* people say is good, rather than to develop an awareness of what his or her own organism feels is good or bad.

Firm touch may also be experienced and responded to as invigorating or mobilizing. Firm touch is appropriate and useful when the person does not have to deny his or her response to the therapist's touch, but is supported in an emerging sense of self. Additionally the deep stretching and release that can occur from respectful deep-tissue work using firm but gentle touch can, when the timing is correct, provide its own unique insights for the client. It is the response of the person that determines the appropriateness of certain kinds of touch, not the ideology of the therapist.

The appropriateness of various kinds of touch must also be essentially related to an understanding of resistance and theme. An example of this occurred when I was demonstrating deep-tissue work for a student. The client had been feeling some tension and pain in her lower back and wanted some deep work to release her tension. During the initial work, I used slow, but deep, pressure to begin to focus her attention and foster some release. It soon became apparent that, although my firm touch was not arousing any countering response (i.e., any pushing back), neither was there any change in her muscular condition. I asked her periodically to relate what she was experiencing from our work, and at one point she noted that she was aware of holding her hip muscles to "take" the firm pressure in her back, which she anticipated would be painful. When I asked her why she felt that she had to tolerate something that felt too painful to bear, she replied that she should do so because it would be good for her—that is what one is supposed to do in body work.

By this time I had shifted my touch to a gentler and more supportive mode, layering our verbal exploration with contact on her back to keep her connected with this part of her as she was talking. I asked her, "If you were not to modify yourself to tolerate the way I have been touching you, but were to modify how I am to touch you to meet what *you* need, what would you ask me to do?" She hesitated, and then replied, "Your gentle touch now feels so soothing and right. That feels like what I really need." At this she began to cry softly, and I could feel release of her back muscles and hips as the student and I continued to contact her with gentle touch and rocking motions. Had I continued with firm-tissue work and disregarded her experience in order to "produce release," I would have fostered her introjection of *my* standards of what was right for her and not have helped her to validate a sense of her own needs. This would have forced underground her legitimate self-protection against the pain. I have learned through hard experience as both a client and a therapist that being overly attached to technique frequently results in missing the important point where change and growth can occur.

It is just as true, however, that light touch can avoid essential aspects of experience under certain circumstances. Light, gentle touch and movement of body parts emphasize the qualities of letting go, of being soothed and quieted, and the softer side of human experience. It does not promote mobilizing, resisting, and more aggressive action. One man I worked with was so flexible and yielding that no matter what kind of touch I used, it did not seem to have any impact. He yielded to everything so that there was no sense of contact for either him or myself. After recognizing his unique response to my touch, I suggested he experiment with pushing back against my firm touch. Our work progressed into an active tussle within which he began to play with the contrast between his yielding and his actively resisting. Without a firm body boundary, he was confluent and devoid of a capacity for separateness, power, and aggression. Soft touch would not have provided enough contrast. This man's lack of discriminating response to contact would be missed by a therapist who does not discriminate the kind of touch he or she uses in different situations.

Similarly, when the use of firm pressure arouses muscular resistance (tension) against that pressure, I am interested in bringing that resistance into active and owned movement. I might use firm touch to heighten the person's experience of resistance while actually encouraging the person to resist my touch in active ways. In this way we can discover the intrinsic movements and expressions that the tension demonstrates in partial form, develop ownership over the ways in which the person says "no" covertly, and experiment with more overt and emphatic expressions. The use of firm pressure then forms part of an experiment with resistance.

ETHICAL AND CLINICAL CONSIDERATIONS IN THE USE OF TOUCH

No discussion of the therapeutic use of touch would be complete without noting ethical and clinical considerations. If we consider the cultural and personal fears that people bring to touch, it is obvious that the therapist has a great responsibility for care in the use of touch. If we add to this the conditions of trust, safety, and intimacy that any psychotherapeutic relationship requires, ethical clarity on the part of the therapist is clearly essential.

Issues in Use of Touch

Body-oriented work in general, and work that uses touch as a tool for intervention in particular, places the client and therapist in a position of unusual closeness and intimacy. The client is literally in the therapist's hands. The physical distance between the client and therapist is much less than the usual social distance and requires the client to let down some of his or her reserve to allow the therapist in. The therapist is potentially in a position of greater power and influence and the client is potentially in a position of greater vulnerability and openness than in the average therapeutic encounter.

The depth and potency of body-oriented work that are responsible for its great impact therapeutically also increase the need for its responsible use. Body-oriented work has the potential to put us in direct contact with long disowned parts of the self: sensations of hurt, movements and sounds of anger, trauma, and helplessness of past experience. As these disowned parts of the self emerge, and before they are more fully integrated into the whole of the person, the therapist has a responsibility to respect the fragility of the moment and not violate the experience by interpretation or judgment.

The act of touch powerfully evokes a fundamental need for tactile contact, the "skin hunger" we all have. Some individuals, by reason of the early deprivation of such essential intimacy, are literally starved for such contact. Therapists are frequently attracted to doing body-oriented work out of a need to assuage their own touch-starved inner child. If the therapist is unaware of this need, he or she may act out his or her own needs for comforting touch and be unable to distinguish the client's needs.

In addition, such intimate contact is often habitually associated with sexual contact, so that both the client and the therapist may be feeling sexual arousal merely as a result of their proximity. For the client this means that he or she may be feeling some confusion about how to react to the therapist's touch, some guilt for feeling aroused by an authority figure, and more vulnerable to violation or encroachment by the therapist. The therapist's feelings may blur the line between intervention and indulgence, particularly if there is conflict or confusion about his or her own sexuality.

Body-oriented therapy also has the capacity to work in a direct way with the muscular blocks to sexual feeling and movement. Experiments may use movements that are sexually related, such as moving the pelvis, deep rhythmic breathing, or release of tension in the buttocks, abdomen, or pelvic areas. This unique capacity also brings with it the potential for confusion of roles and boundaries.

These issues increase the importance of a number of boundaries in body- and touch-oriented therapy. One is the professional and personal boundary of the therapist. A second is the boundary of the client and an understanding of boundaries in the therapeutic process.

The Therapist's Boundaries

The first, and I hope most obvious, boundary that must be clear is that the therapist under no circumstances engages in a sexual relationship with or intentional sexual stimulation of the client. This is basic professional ethics for all therapy professions, but my reasons for setting this boundary so clearly are not based merely on professional code. Rules and regulations alone are not sufficient to help us understand why these boundaries are so essential to our work.

Trust and intimacy cannot exist, as it must exist for psychotherapy in general and body–oriented therapy in particular, unless there is complete safety from personal or bodily violation. The violation of one's personal integrity, be it from direct physical or sexual abuse or from having one's existence used to fulfill another's narcissistic needs, is one of the core life experiences clients invariably bring to therapy. It is my view that the very disownership of one's body-self comes about in order to cope with such violation. If the client is to re-own his or her body experience and work through the pain and rage of such infringements on bodily integrity, then the therapeutic relationship must be free of infringement. It is only by so clearly bounding sexual contact that the client has the full space to bring out, experience, and explore his or her own sexual feelings, hurts, and confusions.

In addition to this therapeutic rule, it behooves therapists to be as clear as possible about their own needs and feelings so that these do not leak unknowingly into the therapeutic process. As Gestalt therapists we believe very strongly in the validity of the "use of self" in therapy. By this we mean that the therapist's moment-to-moment experience has an important contribution to make to the therapeutic process. But by "use of self" we do not mean the use of the client *for* oneself. It is impossible to know the difference without having tread the path of self-knowledge through one's own therapy with a therapist who can maintain his or her own integrity and respect the client's. This is why I believe it is essential for anyone doing body-oriented therapy, using touch or not, to have undergone similar work as a client.

Working Contract

In the use of touch in therapy, it must always be clear that the client has the right to say "no" at any point. This is part of the fundamental contract for our working relationship. I spend a considerable amount of time with clients who are unfamiliar with body-oriented work explaining the rationale of such work, particularly touch work, and making clear to them my values about their right to stop, alter, or otherwise influence any work that we do together. With clients who come to me already familiar with body-oriented work, a detailed understanding of body work may be redundant, but a clear statement about my values concerning their role is still essential. Where a client raises objections to body- or touch-oriented work, this in itself is grist for the therapeutic mill.

Clinical Considerations in the Use of Touch

I am frequently asked in training workshops to delineate the appropriate diagnostic categories for using body-oriented or touch intervention. It is my firm belief and experience that some form of body-oriented intervention is appropriate for *all* kinds of clients, the exact nature depending on the particular person at a particular time. For example, grounding in breathing is extremely useful to establish better reality contact in severely disturbed clients if used carefully, but more active expressive body work is clearly inappropriate.

In relation to touch-oriented work, however, I see some more definite limitations on the basis of clinical considerations. Unless there exists a strong bond and close trust between client and therapist, I believe it is inappropriate to use touch with clients with severe pathology, for example, schizophrenic or paranoid disorders, or whose ego strength is extremely fragile. Such a client's life history invariably includes so much violation and intrusion by others, particularly parental figures, that the potential for similar intrusion by the therapist can result in hostile or decompensating (fragmenting) responses by the client. It is not that fragmenting or hostility is in itself "sick" or undesirable. Indeed, these resistances are no more than the person's strategies for coping with intrusion and harm from others, albeit at great personal cost. However, if there is minimal bonding and trust between the client and therapist, the client will be unable to distinguish nonharmful from harmful touch and to work through unfinished business with the original sources of harmful intrusion. The use of touch will only worsen the disorder.

Where such a strong relationship does exist, or the client has enough intellectual understanding of the use of touch and sufficient ego strength to tolerate closeness, touch can be used effectively even with clients suffering from severe problems such as psychotic, borderline, and other severe personality disorders. Norman S. Don (1980) describes in detail such a case and its successful outcome. His description, in addition to my own experience, suggests that the additional prerequisite for such highly intensive and emotional work is a great capacity on the part of the therapist to deal with primitive and powerful emotions, such as rage, intense suffering, and deep emptiness, without panic or fear. It is easy for the therapist, out of his or her own discomfort with such feelings, to suppress their expression by the client and so push further underground what the clients themselves have disowned. Again, there is no substitute for having been through one's own therapy so as to be thoroughly familiar with such feelings in oneself before attempting to work with them in others. Also, the importance of support from one's colleagues is essential to keeping clear with such intensely involving clients (Kernberg, 1975).

Work with touch can, like body-oriented work in general, be thought of on a continuum. Just as I can use attention to body process or breathing without doing any major experiment such as movement or vigorous exercise, so too I can use touch in a brief and unobtrusive way that does not involve extensive hands-on application. For example, in observing a characteristic facial tension, I may say, "I am noticing that you hold your facial muscles in a particular way. May I show you where I mean?" If the client assents, I may get up from my chair, gently and briefly use my hands to demonstrate what I am seeing, and then sit down again. This simple and unintrusive work gradually makes more extensive use of touch possible by making it familiar in a safe and graded way. In this way touch is used peripherally to support and develop other kinds of work with the body before becoming the center of the work.

And, of course, there are many clients with whom I may never do any form of touching because the goals and issues with which they are dealing do not require it. They simply are not coming for that kind of work and their focus instead is on acquiring some coherence and structure to their lives or in reckoning with some important life changes. In these cases my knowledge and awareness of body process enrich my background and understanding, while other concerns become the foreground of our work.

Part II

Body Phenomena and the Cycle of Experience

Introduction to Part II

In the first part of this book, I have shown the relationship between body process and the self, and given the reader an understanding of my general orientation and therapeutic stance. These chapters, however, do not provide an articulated framework for therapeutic work or for understanding the whole functioning person. The second part of this book details the importance of our body process in our organismic functioning, especially as it relates to therapeutic intervention.

SELF-REGULATION AND THE CYCLE OF EXPERIENCE

The model I shall present will describe the Gestalt view of organismic functioning and the relationship of body processes to this functioning. This "functioning" can be basically described as the organization of figure/ground. I will illustrate the bodily basis of this functioning and its interruption, the basis of emotional distress and dis–ease. I will also describe how body-oriented interventions may be meaningfully used within the therapeutic context to affect the body structures and processes that interrupt full functioning.

Gestalt therapy is founded on a theory of process. In Gestalt therapy, the most pervasive aspect of our functioning is our interaction with, or "contacting in," the environment so as to find completion for our needs. This process of organism/environment interaction comes about through the formation of figures of interest that compel us to find completion in the environment through our behavior. The result is the achievement of self-regulation, a balance of the organism/environment field. For example, as I sit here writing, I notice some discomfort. The words on the page, which were capturing my interest, fade into the background as I focus on this discomfort. I recognize that I have been sitting stiffly for a while and that I need to change my position. I shift my posture and stretch my back, and my discomfort recedes, so that I can once again attend to the task of writing. The emergence of a figure of interest, my uncomfortable back muscles, gained enough energy to outweigh writing; after attending to this discomfort, it receded into the background and a new interest emerged.

This process of compelling need (a figure of interest standing out against the background that organizes behavior), contact in the environment to complete the emerging need, the receding of the figure into the background (balance and completion), and the emergence of the next figure of interest is the most basic description of organismic process. In most contacts there are no apparent stages or defined phases within the experience cycle. Figures spontaneously emerge, organized behaviors arise, contact is made, and the next figure emerges in smooth transition. Observation has led us to understand that there are certain basic ingredients or necessary processes that form a sequence in contact. Although in many contact cycles there is nothing but flow, making it seem as if there are no particular punctuation points, it becomes apparent in more difficult contacts, such as when the environment makes us work to achieve satisfaction or when we interrupt the natural sequence of contacting and become stuck, that phases of the process can be elucidated.

This sequence is called variously the contact cycle, the cycle of experience, or the cycle of self-regulation. From the viewpoint of the organism/environment field, the cycle describes the sequence of interaction. From the viewpoint of phenomenology, the cycle outlines the particular "figure of the moment," or what one experiences as the foreground at particular points during a contact episode. From the point of view of the organism, the cycle is the sequence of behavior and experience that results in self-regulation.

The cycle can be seen as a generic map of any contact episode, that is, any sequence of perception and behavior geared towards the completion of an organism/environment interaction. The process of organis-

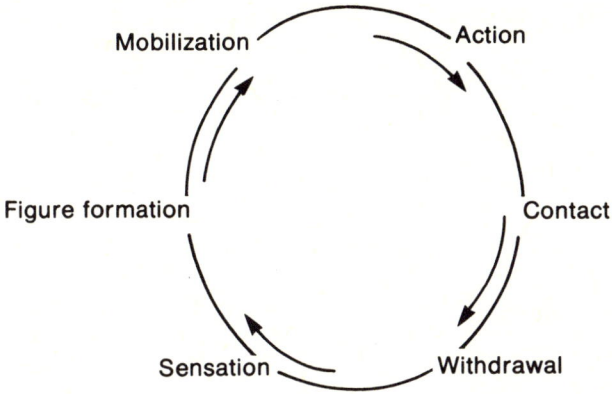

Figure II-1. The cycle of experience drawn as a circle.

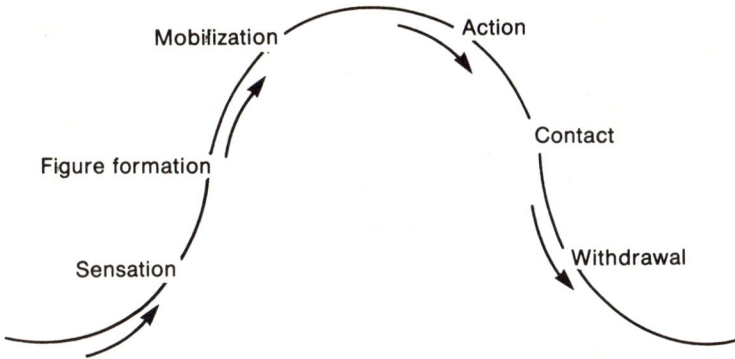

Figure II-2. Cycle of experience drawn as a wave.

mic self-regulation is similar, regardless of the particular content involved. Roughly the same process occurs in any experience cycle,
whether one is concerned with contacting food, contacting disowned
aspects of oneself, contacting other people, or contacting and working
through a major developmental life theme. The content may differ, and
the cycles may take place over different spans of time, but the phases of
each experience (organismic self-regulation) cycle are the same. These
phases for the above examples are illustrated in Figures II-1 and II-2.

The pattern of a wave or circle emphasizes the continuous nature of the process.°

Sensation is the raw data of experience, the background from which we begin to organize our functioning. In the foregoing example, the discomfort of my back emerged from the background of bodily discomfort and sensation. Figure formation is the pulling together of experience into a meaningful whole that can organize behavior—the recognition that I was stiff and needed to move. The figure is the combination of sensation, its meaning in terms of need, and its relationship to the environment. Mobilization is the surge of energy or interest that impels the figure into action—my readiness and "urge" to stretch. Action is the behavior or movement that brings one into contact—the act of stretching. Contact with my bodily needs and the pleasure and satisfaction of stretching is the completion of the figure, the actual meeting of the need so that withdrawal, the fading of that figure into the background, can occur.

These phases of the cycle are not, of course, as discrete and defined as they are represented in theory. Sensation does not end when figure formation starts, nor is sensation absent in action and contact. The point of this model is not to define "where everything belongs" so much as to describe what is necessary to good self-regulation and what is figural in one's experience at particular points in the cycle of experience. Each element is also a necessary prerequisite for later phases; that is, good sensation is a requirement of good figure formation, mobilization is required for strong and complete action, strong and complete action is a requirement for full and satisfying contact and completion to occur, and withdrawal from one contact is essential for a fresh new sensation to form into figure.

There are times when the flow of figure and completion in the environment cannot be smooth. Some environments do not support the easy completion of some needs because they have insufficient supplies to meet them. Or the behavior with which we meet our needs may evoke a hostile response. There are also times when we must delay the completion of needs and must be able to interrupt some experience

°This framework for describing organism/environment contact was briefly sketched in the last chapters in *Gestalt Therapy* by Perls et al. (1951) and is supposedly largely the work of Paul Goodman. This cursory description has been expanded, refined, and developed over the years as a teaching and diagnostic tool at the Gestalt Institute of Cleveland (GIC), and it is the GIC elaboration of this experience cycle on which I have based my own presentation of the relation of body process to the cycle of experience. The particular description I present here is, however, purely my own application of this model, and therefore should not be seen as necessarily representative of that developed by GIC.

cycles so that the pace and form of contact adjusts to the changing circumstances of the world and of our organism. In Gestalt therapy the capacity to temporarily interrupt or "resist" contact is useful and healthy as a creative adjustment to the vicissitudes of experience and environment.

Difficulty arises when the cycle is habitually interrupted in a way that is out of our awareness so that our needs cannot find resolution. This incompleteness is manifest as organismic disturbance and dis-ease. For instance, if I push myself to keep on writing and stoically ignore my bodily discomfort, my back will become painful. If I continue to resist recognizing the way in which I am pushing myself and am unwilling to stop writing so that I can give myself a truly good stretch, I will have to constrict my breathing and distort my posture to try to take the stress off my sore muscles. If I do this habitually, I will eventually have a "bad back," which I feel subject to and victimized by. Yet my bad back is simply my need for less drive and more self-care. This need must remain incomplete and nagging if I cannot allow myself to listen to it as important. It is the embodiment of my unfinished business, which comes from ignoring my initial need for movement. Similarly the interruption of other important needs results in unfinished business that is manifested as discomfort—pain, anxiety, depression, disease, and lack of spirit and wholeness.

Phases that are skipped over or blocked form the basis for poor organismic self-regulation. The cycle of experience may be seen as a template that allows us to locate where a person becomes stuck within the sequence of self-regulation. These points have been called *resistances to contact* and remain at the core of therapeutic work in Gestalt therapy.

Resistances are not exclusive to only one phase of the cycle, although they are most marked in particular phases. The reader should keep in mind that although, for example, desensitization is discussed here as particularly critical to the sensation phase of the cycle, it may also occur in other phases as well—such as during final contact when the sensory experience can be dulled by minimizing one's breathing.

Part II of this book looks at the bodily nature of the cycle of experience and interruptions, creative and otherwise. My aim is to illustrate the therapeutic principles derived from this view, through theoretical description and case material.

Chapter 7

Sensation and Body Process

Moral regulation must lead to the accumulation of unfinished situations in our system and to interruption of
the organismic circle. This interruption is achieved by
means of muscular contraction and the production of
anaesthesia. A person who has lost the 'feel' of himself... cannot expect his 'self regulation' (appetite) to
function properly... (Perls, 1947/1969, p. 45).

The experience cycle begins in sensation: bodily feeling, organic
drives and wants, images and thoughts, perceptions of the environment.
This is the raw datum of experience, undifferentiated until it is organized by an emerging and pressing need, but available as a pool of energy
and information about the current status and relation of the organism.

If you allow yourself to unfocus your attention for a moment and simply notice what occurs in your awareness, you may be able to glimpse
this emerging and pregnant pool of sensation. You may discover images
or feelings, bodily sensations or thoughts, all of which appear and disappear in your awareness. Do one or two of these begin to hold your attention more? An image might begin to unfold into a fuller scene or story. A
body sensation might take on prominence until you recognize that your
sitting position is uncomfortable. If you stay with this emerging sensory
background, eventually a clear and differentiated need and direction
for your behavior will emerge: you will shift your position.

Sensory background can be likened to the colors, forms, and shadings available to a painter. When a painter has a full range of colors, a clear sense of shading and light, and a repertoire of forms available, the final painting is the result of the full scope of the artist's experience and capacity. If we were to remove colors from the palette or prohibit certain forms from use, the final painting would become less a product of all of which the artist is capable and more a test of his or her ingenuity in working within given limitations. The more colors we remove from the palette, the more restricted is the final product.

Similarly when we have a full range of sensations accessible to awareness, the resulting figure (a meaningful sense of our needs that moves us towards contact) more accurately reflects the full scope of our organismic situation. If certain sensations are unavailable to our awareness, the resulting figure cannot as accurately reflect all of our needs. When large areas of sensory background are blotted out, there are significant blind spots about those areas of experience. Behavior and contact are based on guesses about our needs, or on our images of what we "should" need or want, rather than actual current experience.

For example, a young woman was seeing me because she was having difficulty settling on a career. She was constantly torn between her parents' urging about what she should do with her life and her own confusion and seeming lack of desire for any particular career direction. One of her difficulties was that she had no idea what it felt like in her body to *want something,* that is, to experience her organic response to something *she* desired as opposed to what her parents thought of as good. To create a space where she could begin to discover her own sense of attraction, we set up two chairs. While sitting in one chair, she could voice her parents' opinions about "proper" careers; the second chair was for her self, where she could state her own wants, urges, dislikes, and attractions to career choices. Each time her internalized parents interfered with her perceptions of her own wants, she shifted chairs, voiced "their" opinions, and then returned to her own space better able to attend to her own sensations.

SENSATION AND REALITY

In addition to the importance of our sensory background for a clear figure on which to base the cycle of experience, a capacity for full sensation is essential to our sense of reality. This has been called "grounding" in Gestalt therapy, because our sense of reality is based on our degree of contact with our sensory ground (background). When we have poor experience of our sensation, we become ungrounded, related neither to our personal realities nor to those of our environment. The common phrase, "He doesn't have his feet on the ground," points to the importance of physical contact with the world for our sense of reality, the need to be physically and literally *grounded.*

Sensory capacities can be divided into two categories in reference to our reality contact. There are the senses that are oriented toward our internal sense of self: proprioception (sense of location of body parts), kinesthesia (sense of movement), viscera sensations (fullness or emptiness of digestive organs, hunger, heartbeat), and various receptors of pressure, pain, and pleasure; as well as the "sensations" of thoughts and visual images. These senses tell us the current state of our organism, of our feeling, wants, and needs, and ground us in our personal reality. Without clear inner sensation, we lose touch with who we are and what we need.

There are also senses oriented towards our relationship with our environment: vision, hearing, taste, touch, and smell. It is through these senses that we are grounded in the reality of our environment and determine our relationship to it. Without clear external sensation, we lose touch with what is available, what we must contend with and adjust to, and how we must direct ourselves to fully experience and act on our sensations.

All of our experience and action in the world emerge from and are grounded in our sensory background. To alter Descartes, "I *sense,* therefore I am." This is a fundamental premise in Gestalt therapy. Without clear and available sensation, we lose touch with our needs, our present organismic state, our location in the world, and our relation to our environment. Without a clear feel of ourselves and a clear feel for our environment, we lose our base in the world. Without the information this base supplies, the meanings we create and actions we take are unrelated to our real needs, and often founded on guesses and estimations.

Bodily sensations are a primary means of grounding ourselves in the reality of self and environment. They are also the means by which we can limit, distort, or muddy our sense of self and environment.

DISTURBANCE OF THE SENSORY GROUND

The normal state of affairs for the average person is a rather dulled and diminished capacity for sensation. This is not something of which we are aware until we are given some sense of contrast—what could be possible if we were sensing more fully.

Let me ask you to experiment briefly with exploring the quality of your sensory ground. Slowly "scan" your body with your awareness, starting from the soles of your feet and moving up to the top of your head. Try it again even more slowly. As you do so, notice the quality of the sensations you feel. Do you find that you can feel some body areas clearly and others less so or not at all? Can you feel the depth of your body parts from skin to bone, or only the surface layer and very little of your "meat"? Do you have any sense of your organs, your heartbeat, the cavity of your torso? Do some areas feel numb? Can you perceive the back of your body more than the front, or vice versa? Do you tend to skip over some body areas with your awareness, as if they do not exist or are unimportant? Do some body areas feel alien, as if they do not belong to you?

It is likely that you found some body areas with which you do not have a clear or full sense of yourself. Perhaps you experienced blind spots, numbness, confusion, or vagueness. Following the premise of the book, that body is self, you could say that in those areas you are blind to yourself, or numb towards yourself, or confused and vague about certain aspects of yourself. These "unsensed" parts of the body relate to dis-owned self functions—alienated parts of the self.

Turning towards your sensory grounding in the environment, try another kind of experiment. If you turn your awareness towards your visual sense, you can experiment with the difference between gazing and seeing. Looking at the room you are in, allow yourself to alternate between focused, sharp seeing, and then light gazing, without sharply focusing on anything in particular. Notice the difference in your experience of the room and your location in it when you are in one mode versus the other. When your vision is sharply focused, you might notice that *you* feel more clearly connected to your environment, "I *see*." When your vision is vague and superficial, you might notice your sense of the environment and yourself to be dull and vague, "I see unclearly." The quality of our sensory grounding in the environment can have a significant effect on our sense of self and our relation to our world, and is something we can alter to make it (and ourselves) sharper or duller.

The Ungrounded Self

All of us have at least some areas of our sensory life we have limited our deadened, or what is called *desensitized*.* The range of desensitiza-

---

*This term is used here differently from the standard psychological nomenclature. There is a psychological technique called "systematic desensitization" (Wolpe, 1961), which is used to treat phobias. Under the assumption that a phobia is a conditioned overreaction to a stimulus, the client is intentionally taught to be less sensitive through

tion reaches from the severe disembodied state of psychosis to the more selective desensitization most of us use to respond to temporary discomforts. I find, for example, that I no longer feel the impact of the evening television news after seeing more than a week or so of wars, murders, rapes, and other horrors.

Most of us also limit certain areas of our experience. Perhaps you find that you have difficulty feeling sad on occasions when sadness is appropriate, as was true for me for many years. Or perhaps you don't experience the degree of sexual pleasure your friends describe (assuming they are not merely bragging). Some people only realize they are desensitized to certain feelings when another person comments on, or gives contrast to, their limitations of sensitivity. Moderate gaps in our sensory ground result in selective dead areas in our experience of our self and the world. Perhaps you experience a more general and chronic lack of aliveness and feeling for life. Life isn't bad, just dulled. Even occasional highs or lows seem to be not much, and little grips you or stands out in your experience.

As more of our feelings for life and connection with the environment becomes inaccessible, more of our sense of self, our experience of living, also becomes unavailable. We isolate our contact functions within a narrow range. One result is that we come to experience life with a sense of "business as usual." There are fewer highlights and contrasts, except when we force our experience through hedonism,° drugs, alcohol, or the seeking of danger, risk, and crisis to shock our deadened flesh into life. Those who flee their feelings through intellectualization and the disembodied life of pure thought are similar in nature, though not in kind, to those who must flog their bodies alive by severe and addictive physical exercise: both have lost touch with their bodily selves.

Greater degrees of desensitization result in a sense of disembodiment (clinically called depersonalization) when the desensitization is directed at one's sense of self, and feelings of disconnection from the world (clinically called dissociation) when organs of perception of the environment are desensitized. To one client I would suddenly appear to be far away from her whenever I began to get too close to her emotionally. By distorting her vision, she could keep me at a distance. It was only through patient and careful work with her eyes and seeing, com-

---

conscious relaxation. In Gestalt therapy the term desensitization refers to ways in which we render ourselves less sensitive to stimuli as a resistance to contact or defense mechanism, phobias being seen as retroflections as opposed to oversensitivities.

°Since desensitization dulls both pleasure *and* pain, in order to experience more pleasure without resensitizing and so exposing oneself to pain, one must seek out hedonistic experience to heighten pleasurable sensations and overcome a lack of aliveness and feelings.

bined with learning that she could control and tolerate emotional close-ness, that she could begin to feel herself more connected to her world. Another client complained of not knowing who he was and experienced a great sense of what he called emptiness. On exploration it became clear to both of us that he was not empty of feeling (indeed he had many deep hurts and emotional wounds), but that he had so deadened himself in order not to feel his pain that he felt nothing—hence his "emptiness."

The problems of anomie (lack of identity), detachment, uninvolve-ment, and disconnection that seem so prevalent in our society come, in part, not from a philosophical crisis, but from the desensitization of our physical ground. In fearing to open our hearts and feelings to the dif-ficulties around us, we have dulled our contact with the world and our involvement with it.

Resensitizing ourselves is no simple matter; it is not merely the result of doing sensory-awareness exercises. To reawaken our senses means that we reawaken to pain and sadness as well as joy and pleasure. Not only must we come to new terms with the pain and hurt of our life his-tory, but also to a new accommodation with the joyful *and* painful realities of the present. The former requires the caring support of some-one who can help us survive our pain, and whom we trust enough to guide us through the labyrinth of confusing feelings. The latter requires that we find the courage to stand in the world and accept the fullness of life, rather than exist only half alive.

The nature of life is a continuing process of finding the courage to live in fullness. To learn to live in confrontation with the terrible realities of the world and remain unshrinking, undulled, with an open heart is the essential issue in learning to increase one's sensitivity.

The Process of Desensitization

When sensations are disturbing and it is not possible to avoid them by acting on or escaping the environmental source of the disturbance, one means of coping is to alter the perception of the sensation. Human beings are capable of dulling the impact of sensations either by reducing their quality of attention or by dulling the capacity of their organs of per-ception. This process of coping with disturbing sensations by altering the capacity for perception is called *desensitization*. Desensitization lessens the experience of discomfort, but it exacts a cost by reducing the capacity for aliveness and a full sense of self. The more blank or numbed areas you noticed during the previous experiment, the more holes there are in your experience of yourself.

Sensations can be disturbing for three basic reasons. One is that they are intrinsically uncomfortable, such as physical pain, hunger, cold. A second is that sensations signaling organismic needs become uncomfortable when they cannot be discharged or met: the need for human contact when unmet becomes painful loneliness; the need for movement unmet can become painful tension. A third reason is that sensations may conflict with strongly learned beliefs, what are called introjects in Gestalt therapy: sexual sensations and feelings are experienced as intolerable if they are believed to be "bad" or "dirty"; the natural expression of sadness at loss may be believed to be "weak" or otherwise undesirable; angry feelings are "not done in this family" and so become intolerable when experienced.

Given the difficult world in which we live, who of us has not had the need to "not feel"? People growing up in primitive or impoverished environments must cope with pain, hunger, and cold, and learn to immure themselves to this discomfort. Physical and sexual abuse foster both physical and emotional pain, which foster the need to escape one's bodily experience. Without question all of us have at least some feelings and sensations that conflict with what we have been told is "right" or "good."

Healthy grounding requires that our sensing body be lively and receptive and that we be able to focus, and sustain that focus, on the emerging sensations. Desensitization affects our ability to attend to sensation and the aliveness and vitality of our tissue. The processes involved in desensitization range from momentary avoidance to deeper and more structural processes.

Specifically we can desensitize ourselves to an experience by:

1. *Selective attention.* One avoids attending to body experience by distracting oneself, or shifts one's attention before an internal sensation becomes clear in awareness.

2. *Interference with breathing.* In order to maintain enough liveliness for adequate sensation, we must support our aliveness with our breathing. Shallow or minimal breathing effectively deadens the tissue. If you try breathing shallowly for a while, it will soon become apparent how much less lively you feel because of this restriction; even your hearing will feel less sharp. When people begin to speak of topics about which they feel conflict, the first thing I frequently notice is that they literally stop breathing for significant periods of time, exhaling or inhaling, and then pausing. This essentially freezes functioning and limits their sensation capacity, and thus controls the emerging feelings.

3. *Chronic muscular contraction.* This "squeezes off" body sensation by deadening tissue and prevents enlivening movements. You can experiment with this by lightly tensing some body part and holding that

tension. At first you may notice that area more, but eventually you will feel numbed and less lively there. If you maintain this tension long enough, you will not feel that body area at all.

Avoidance of attention and interference with breathing are active processes that can be observed in the moment-to-moment behavior in therapy. Chronic muscular tension, however, eventually becomes static and structural. It is institutionalized into the muscles and posture. Since it is, by definition, "not felt" by the person (it is a gap in awareness), it may only be noticeable by the therapist through touch. Tension desensitization results in hard, thick, and lifeless musculature, the body armor spoken of by Reich (1945/1972). In the Gestalt approach, however, we make a distinction between armoring against sensation and feeling (structural desensitization) and armoring against mobilization and action (structural retroflection), which will be discussed in later chapters.

RESENSITIZING THE SELF

Undoing desensitization involves attending to the necessary requirements for good sensation: attention, breathing, and an alive body. Techniques involve focusing and sustaining focus, work with breathing, and body-oriented work to enliven the body ground. It must be remembered, however, that technique alone does not do it. As important are the therapeutic context and relationship in which such work takes place. Without this relationship and the therapist's contact with his or her own sensation and feeling, therapeutic technique is mechanical and dull. If your application of technique is mechanical and dull, how can you convey to your client what it means to be more alive?

Focusing

Working with the attentional aspects of desensitization has long been a strength of Gestalt therapy. The essential process is one of supporting the client to focus on the body experience and to sustain that focus long enough for the sensation to become clear and differentiated, to emerge as a figure. This is done by commenting on the distractions the client creates and experimenting with the client's awareness of his or her body process. I might ask, "What is happening in your body right now?" or the ubiquitous "What are you feeling right now?" or suggest,

"Pay attention to how you are sitting"or "Stay with that some more." The aim is to shift focus from cognition to body experience and allow that experience to become important. This provides a counterbalance for the tendency of therapy to become what one client of mine has described as "talking heads."

It is important to validate that what the client reports is grounded in his or her actual, present sensation. Frequently the client answers the question, "What are you experiencing?" with preformed and convenient opinions and labels that have nothing to do with actual, present feeling. These are what clients think or *believe* they are feeling. They already know what their sensations mean before they experience them!

Equally important is the development of language to describe body experience with specificity. Since our inner experience is not public and is rarely talked about, and often inexactly felt, we frequently have not connected accurate language to our experience. Without language our sensations become even more difficult to discriminate from each other. When a client says, "I feel tired," I ask, "Where do you feel tired? How are you tired right now?" I suggest words to describe that tiredness. Is it heavy tiredness? Good tiredness? Do you feel drained or simply finished? Even if my suggested labels are inaccurate, they give clients something to reject and stimulate them to find their own description for sensations.

Breathing

Concurrent work with breathing is essential when developing sensation; in fact it is essential no matter with which part of the cycle you are working. Body work that is disconnected from breathing loses impact and control of breathing becomes a secondary defense that undermines change.

Sensation does not require particularly deep or laborious breathing for its support, or any great "charge" (unless the sensations involved are highly charged, such as fear or anger). What it does require is *continuous and regular inhalation and exhalation,* without which the body becomes frozen and awareness of bodily events is minimized. If you carefully observe a person's breathing, you will notice that when breathing stops momentarily, the whole body stiffens slightly, and the content of conversation becomes more intellectual, with little feeling background. Without the background of body sensation, the figures that form and emerge in speech are unrelated to the presently felt reality; they are abstract, cool, and partial. We keep our disowned feelings from contributing to emerging awareness by deadening our feeling body through minimal breathing.

Attention to continuous breathing is important when working with couples. I frequently find myself struggling to move a couple into their present experience of each other. It eventually becomes apparent to me that the distracted and overly rational contact in which many couples in therapy engage is due in part to one or both members losing touch with their bodily experience of looking at, touching, or talking to each other. Such disembodiment is often based on lack of breathing and functions systemically to "cool down" potential intimacy. Intimacy, because it requires softening and vulnerability, can be risky and threatening, especially when the couple's past has been full of hurt or rejection. But without it, we become starved and undernourished, and our relationships are dry and juiceless.

A couple, whom I will call Joanne and Dennis, discussed the concern that they did not know how to give each other caring. I suggested they look at each other and pay attention to what they might want from each other or want to give to the other. Like most couples who have not connected with each other for a while, they became shy and giggled like children. I laughed with them, enjoying their coltish moments of initial contact. As they settled down, it became apparent that it was difficult for them to focus on each other long enough to find out what they might want. Each would freeze his or her breathing, lose touch with the present experience, and start thinking about something. She would think about how to apply this at home and he would begin to analyze and theorize about what he was doing.

The more they allowed themselves to breathe and so be present with each other, the more they began to want to reach out to each other. The simple act of looking into each other's eyes and spontaneously touching hands moved them both, and myself, deeply. Of course, with their greater capacity for sensation in the moment came not only awareness of their love and desire for contact, but also their fears of closeness and rejection. These issues became part of the developing theme of our work and were not "cured" by a single instance of good contact. But this moment of contact and caring, supported by increased sensation through breathing, helped to provide a necessary building block for addressing such difficult issues in the future.

Enlivening

It is when desensitization has become structural, through chronic tension and deadening of tissue, that more focused work with the body is required. The issue here is how to enliven body areas that aware-ness work alone cannot enliven, because these areas are structurally limited in their sensitivity.

The most unique contribution to therapeutic work to enliven the body-self involves the use of touch. Touch, depending on its nature, can be used in a number of ways to encourage the release of desensitizing structural tension and increased awareness of one's body. Touch is es-sentially a communication that says "Notice this here" in a way that is more specific and direct in reference to the body than words alone can be. Through touch I can directly demonstrate what I want clients to notice and where I want them to focus. In this way I also communicate the quality of my presence and support more directly and specifically than with words. Combined with verbal exploration, touch is an import-ant tool for working with desensitization.

Touch can be used to directly enliven and stimulate sensation in deadened body areas, such as the use of tapping or rhythmic vibration. Light contact can give a sense of the form and surface of body areas. Touch can also be used to bring warmth and softness to braced and ar-mored areas through gentle contact and soft stroking. Where severe deadening exists, firm and deep touch may be required to directly release profound constriction and to elicit some initial body sense with which to work.

Movement also has an enlivening effect and can be used judiciously to support working with desensitization. Aerobics, bioenergetics (Lowen & Lowen, 1977), Hatha yoga, dance, and martial arts movement forms such as tai chi chuan all can be used to stimulate and open the body tissues. The important thing here is that exercise and movements not be used rigidly or mechanically. In any physical intervention, be it use of touch or movement or breathing, the interest to the Gestalt therapist is in the *experience* engendered rather than rule-book form.

It is unfortunate, and often damaging, when therapists become so at-tached to their methods and theoretical goals that they lose sight of their clients' present experience. Worse, many body-oriented methods ac-tually discount the validity of the clients' present experience of pain and discomfort or sense of readiness. They are too caught up in trying to create release or teach the client to be "correct." My interest is to pro-vide a framework for the discovery of the clients' own truth, the dis-owned parts of their experience, rather than to shape them to my own ideal. I am not always successful at remaining so true to the client's emerging self. I want my clients to feel better, and frequently believe I know what is "good for them." But when I let go of my own "shoulds," I can address their experience of their bodies in their own terms and not assault their integrity.

This is not to say that the experience of pain is always the result of method. In body areas that have been desensitized, often the first experience upon reawakening is to feel the pain of having been chronically constricted. Additionally the sensations that have been desensitized might be those of pain, suffering, and emotional hurt, and these will often be reexperienced as the person becomes more alive to his or her disowned body-self.

THE DEEPENING SELF

Judith

Judith began work with me because previous therapy had made her aware that she experienced little of her body. She felt cut off from herself and others, and frequently would feel "spaced out," meaning not fully connected to her environment, other people, or her bodily ground. She both longed and feared to be more connected to others, and would withdraw alone in her house for periods of time when relating to the world became too taxing. She was exceptionally bright and well educated, and despite periods of dissociation and constant feelings of suffering, she held a good job.

As we began to explore her sensation life, she described her sense of her body as "a head with feet." She had only vague experience of her body from her collar bone to her knees, except when she felt acute pain or illness, and described her legs as feeling like "nubs" on her body. She breathed shallowly and had strong tensions in her throat, diaphragm, and abdomen areas that restricted their expansion. Despite these restrictions she had a number of strengths that kept her growing and moving towards others. She was witty and engaging, deeply committed to social causes, and refreshing in her perspective on human events.

Although Judith was hesitant with me because of her suspicion of men, it was our initial work involving touch that cemented her trust of me. Through my touch I was able to communicate my warmth and understanding, and to provide support for her when resensitizing brought her in contact with painful feelings.

Our first work often focused on her use of her eyes. At moments of contact in our sessions, she would space out, and I would seem to recede from her as she looked at me. It became obvious to me that her eyes glazed over when this occurred: her "spacing out" was an actual distortion of her visual organs. Through physical touch to give her ownership over her facial and ocular muscles we got to the point where Judith could consciously make me "go away" and "come closer." We began to identify what made her want to distance me (I was getting closer emotionally than she wanted) so that she could act towards me directly to create distance rather than distort her own being. In this way she learned she could tell me when I was too close, and eventually this symptom diminished significantly.

The increased grounding with her environment from better visual sensation now put a premium on restoring body sensation—she was better grounded in the world, but she remained ungrounded in her inner life. Through deep touch work in her frozen musculature and constant attention to developing greater breathing capacity, Judith gradually began to sense her bodily self and the emotions she had disowned.

Like layers of sediment in a river bed, our enlivening work began to stir her solidified and desensitized body structures until they were fluid enough to move to the surface as feeling. Increasing her breathing led to tingling sensations that initially were frightening to her because being really alive was so unfamiliar. Working with her face and neck reconnected her to feelings of crying and sadness. As we moved down from the more owned territory of her head to her less owned chest, Judith began to discover feelings of deep sadness and hurt as she began to sense her heart and her longing for love. As our work approached her diaphragm, the pit of her belly, she felt for the first time truly connected to her gut—anger and rage at the mistreatment she had experienced and was experiencing. Enlivening of her belly and pelvis began to recover her sexual sensitivity and desires.

Gradually our work began to shrink the areas of desensitization and give her more room in which to exist, more ground to stand on (literally, as she also felt more of her legs). But each recovery of bodily feelings also recovered unfinished situations and old hurts that had to be worked through. Some of these restored sensations were too much to integrate at this point in her development, and Judith could not maintain her sensitivity in these areas. Nonetheless having reexperienced them gave her glimpses of what was possible for her and encouraged her to continue to work to tolerate change. Work with sensation was a predominant theme for Judith, but clearly was only the beginning of her healing rather than its end point.

Working Through

The work of resensitization obviously is not a simple technique or exercise. It is a process that involves engagement, integration, and growth. The unfinished business of one's past, as well as the feeling engendered by the present, must be brought to some new creative adjustment. The introjects and judgments about the reawakened feelings must be explored and tested against the present reality.

The phenomenon of desensitization is of great importance to any therapist who believes that body and being are inseparable. Where the body is not sensed, being is diminished.*

It therefore is relevant to work to develop lively sensitivity and body awareness with any clinical or counseling population, because to some degree we all become desensitized. But it is also true that for some clinical groups desensitization is so pervasive that it is virtually the center-point of the condition.

The disturbance known as the "borderline personality disorder" includes strong components that indicate a background of desensitization: frequent disassociative experience, identity disturbance and loss of sense of self, feelings of emptiness and hollowness, and engagement in acts that can be destructive of one's bodily life. The first phenomenon mentioned, frequent disassociative experience, should be readily understood as resulting from desensitization as described earlier in this chapter. Identity disturbance and loss of self and feelings of nothingness, sometimes called the experience of "no self," have been attributed in the analytic and psychiatric literature as resulting from a developmental gap where the person never was able to form a sense of self during a critical period of growth. Never having developed a sense of self and identity, the person thus experiences no clear well-formed "I" or sense of identity. He or she feels fragmented and diffuse.

But from my experience, particularly with somewhat higher functioning borderline clients, the experience of confusion of identity and feelings of emptiness does not arise so much from a gap in development as from the deep desensitization, and thus loss of the bodily ground for living, that they have used to cope with the abusive and difficult experience of their childhood. Without contact with one's body, one has no sense of location in the world or of one's physical presence and boundaries. Without contact with one's guts and physical responses, one's inner organismic sensations, there is only emptiness and a sense that "I am nothing." A sense of self-continuity, as opposed to fragmentation, depends upon the ability to feel one's own substance and the continuity of emotion and behavior—both bodily phenomena. It is not so much that they have no "self," as that they have come to bury their budding and fragile child self deeply in their deadened body in order to protect themselves from pain, humiliation, and abuse. When pressed or

---

*Though, under certain circumstances, it is of course adaptive to diminish one's sensitivity, such as when one is greatly distressed.

stressed, they have no bodily framework that provides continuity or sense of substance, and so they fragment and decompensate.

The tendency towards body mutilation and self-destructive behavior further supports the notion that the borderline is deeply desensitized. Borderline clients who cut themselves with razors, choke themselves, and so on, frequently report they do so "to try and feel something," or note that "it didn't hurt because I didn't feel anything." These are clear statements of a loss of bodily sensation and tell us the extent to which they have become dulled, deadened, and insensate.

Treatment of the borderline is notoriously difficult, and the above comments do not necessarily make treatment easier. Any attempt to enliven the borderline to body experience is difficult in itself because, as sensation is recovered in general, so are the specific sensations involved in pain, rage, deep hurt, fear, and grief. These emotions are difficult for such clients to assimilate unless there is enormous trust in the therapist. Enlivening work must be broken down into very small units, with as much attention paid to the client's contact with the therapist as to the client's contact with himself or herself. The therapist must be able to withstand, channel, and help the client understand the outpourings of feelings that come from developing body contact. If both client and therapist can hang in long enough and the client becomes more firmly located and grounded in bodily life, the previously unaware polarity (frequently characterized as "the hurt child") can be assimilated into adult functioning.

Chapter 8

Figure Formation and Body Process

> Our attempt ... is to recover *all* experiences con-
> comitantly—whether they be physical or mental, sen-
> sory, emotional, or verbal—for it is in the unitary
> functioning of 'body,' 'mind,' and 'environment' (these
> are all abstractions) that the lively figure/ground em-
> erges (Perls et al., 1951, p. 83).

Restoring body sensation through work on the desensitization of the
body goes a long way towards recovering one's sense of actuality, the
feeling of being in the world. In the truest sense, resensitizing ourselves
grounds us: it gives us a solid base of physical contact with our world,
and a rich background we can draw upon in our interactions.

Raw sensation alone is not, of course, sufficient to guide our
functioning, although it does form a base for functioning. It must be
organized into something meaningful in order to be important to us. In
Gestalt therapy we call this process the emergence of a *figure* against
a background.

Body sensation contributes to a figure forming in awareness. One
sensation stands out from other sensations as lively and having energy
when it has meaning to our functioning. If we can identify with that
meaning, allow it to be important to and relevant for our self, the body
figure will guide and influence our functioning.

For example, on a hot summer day, while in the garden, you eventually begin to notice sensations of dryness in your mouth and throat.
These sensations easily organize into something meaningful to you as

"thirst." At that moment whatever else you are doing—gardening, reading, sunning—the figure of "thirst" is most prominent. "Thirst"—the experience, *not* the word—is a meaningful figure that organizes a collection of sensations into a cohesive whole and, as a figure, stands out from other ongoing sensations.

Few people would divorce their sense of self from their feeling of thirst and say, "It is not me who is thirsty, it is just my body." We can easily admit that this bodily need is "I" and allow it to guide our behavior—to mobilize to get a drink. The figure of thirst can become lively and fully meaningful to our sense of self. Once satisfied through contact with water, this figure is complete and recedes into the background again.

As with the simple process of thirst, so, too, our more complex and deep emotions become figural. A feeling of sadness involves a set of body sensations that includes wateriness and tension around the eyes, and warmth and heaviness in the chest. Think of a sad occasion and you will notice the body sensations that are evoked. It is these sensations collected together that we call a feeling or emotion, that is, an emotional figure.

We must allow our sadness to have meaning to our being and so guide our functioning: to allow our tears, express our sadness, find comfort from others. To do otherwise is to leave the feeling unfinished and truncated. In Gestalt therapy these are called "unfinished figures," important experiences that have not been completed. To deny the importance of one's body experience is to deny an essential aspect of self. It draws energy from functioning. Think of what energy it would involve to keep feelings of thirst from being significant to oneself.

In the course of developing my notions of working with desensitization, I began to notice some curious problems. While people learned to recover the ability to focus on and feel their bodily life, they did not always link this sensation to who they were—their emotional and psychological functioning. Sensation did not always become part of their figure-formation process, but remained very intellectualized.

Some people who came to me highly desensitized gained more sensation yet remained separate from their sense of self. For those who initially had some contact with their body to a greater or less degree, there seemed to be a resistance to making their body experience relevant to their life functioning. They were certainly not disembodied, as was the highly desensitized person, but their body sensation seemed to have little relevance for functioning. The figures they formed were incomplete because they were separate from their bodily selves.

DISOWNERSHIP OF EXPERIENCE: PROJECTION
OF THE BODY

The common thread in these examples is that, while the body is experienced clearly, perhaps even in a minute and particularized way, there is a slippage between body experience and self. What is experienced is kept separate from the "I." The body is still considered an *object* of experience and not part of the subject. The body is thus *projected* and treated as if it is other than self.

In Gestalt therapy we define projection as an interruption of contact by treating a part of the self as if it were an object in the environment (Perls et al., 1951). In this case the experience of one's body, which in the holistic view taken here is self, is treated as if it is something that happens to or is outside the self. If the self and body experience are maintained as separate, then it is understandable that critical data for the formation of figures are missing and the impact of body feeling on a person's behavior is minimized.

One man with whom I was working seemed quite facile in his ability to describe his body experience. He could detail the resulting sensations of our sensitizing work quite minutely: "I feel warmth in my face, I just noticed tension in my throat, I can feel streaming sensations from your hands," and so on. The resulting sensations, while pleasant, did not seem to have any relevance to him.

To all appearances he seemed to be doing everything right. At that time I did not myself realize what was missing, or how to connect the sensations that he was feeling to something meaningful. The key is that, while he felt the warmth in his face, he did not feel it as *his* warmth; while he felt the tension in his throat, he did not experience it as *his* tensing; while he felt streaming sensations from my hands, he did not experience his emotional response to being touched—"I stream to meet your hands."

The projection of the body as an object rather than as self is subtler than that of desensitization. In desensitization the experience of the body is dulled and minimized; it is rendered less accessible to awareness. The sense of full actuality is lost. In its extreme form, this results in dissociation and depersonalization.

In projection, however, body sensation is experienced. There is contact with the sensory ground of experience and the body is felt as actual and real. There is clearly a higher degree of ego development and control in the body. It is a more normal process supported by our culture, religious values, and world view—the self is not corporeal but mental; thus the "I" does not refer to bodily experience. We see this highlighted in people who religiously participate in various body arts—dancers, athletes, martial artists. They often have a very finely developed kinesthetic sense of their bodies, and yet may still be cut off from themselves emotionally. They have mastered their body processes as if they were cogs and gears in a machine; their need to control their bodies indicates how out of control they feel their body-selves to be.

Projection of the body occurs because of slippage between the subject and object of experience. This disownership of the body is evident in language used to refer to body experience. For example, if asked to describe their body experience, many people respond with impersonal identifications: "The shoulder is tense," or "The neck feels compressed." The projection here is obvious in the use of "the" when referring to one's own body. This term clearly marks the body as an object distant from the sense of "I."

Some people would respond in a slightly different form: "My shoulder is tense," or "My neck feels compressed," or even "My neck is being compressed." The projection is more subtle. This way of referring to body experience is so common that it is easy to miss because most therapists do it as well! The use of the word "my" seems to imply an identity between body experience and self, but this is not necessarily the case. To say "my neck" may really be no different than saying "my car" or "my typewriter." It implies possession in the sense of *property* and the distinction between the owner and the object owned remains.

We must ask further: "Whose neck is being compressed and who is compressing it? Whose shoulder is being tensed and who is tensing it?" The tension is not caused by someone else; it is produced by oneself. A more accurate statement might be "I am tensing my shoulders" or "I am compressing my neck." In these statements the relation of self to body experience is closer and body process has become more clearly a part of the self. Therapeutic work with projection of body experience is a matter of moving:

from "It is tense" to "I am tensing"
from "It is warm" to "I am warm"
from "My leg is braced" to "I am bracing myself"
from "My back is stiffened" to "I stiffen myself"

Beyond this the full figure requires not only the connection between self and body process, but also the relation between the self and the environment:

"I am tensing . . . because I don't trust you."

"I feel warmly . . . toward you."

"I am bracing . . . against your words."

"I stiffen . . . because I'm afraid to let go and have you see me being vulnerable."

WORKING WITH PROJECTION OF BODY EXPERIENCE

The aim of therapeutic work on projection of the body is the restoration of the sense of "I" to body experience. The body must become the subject of experience so that the split between body and mind can be healed and the projected aspects of the self can be assimilated and brought into life functioning. This will allow body process to become a part of the normal figure formation, that is, the creation of unified and meaningful gestalts.

This is not a simplistic process. It demands the integration of work with sensation, careful attention to the client's language and phenomenology, and the use of linguistic "experiments." I will illustrate with an example and then discuss the principles behind the steps of the process.

Joan came to me for therapy on a number of issues that were related to her body experience. She was single and had great difficulty forming relationships. She had a history of childhood sexual abuse, about which she had few conscious memories. Joan, 25 years old at the time I saw her, came to me originally because she recently had her first conscious memory of her father forcing sex on her. This flashback had thrown her into confusion and depression, and she hoped that body-oriented therapy would allow her to recover more of her memories and feelings about these events in her past.

When she first saw me, Joan was extremely desensitized to the point of being, at times, dissociated from her body. Her musculature, particularly in her shoulders, back, and pelvis, was severely hypertonic. She found it impossible to feel many emotions, particularly sadness and anger. By the time of the session I will describe, Joan was able to feel some of her sadness, albeit from a distance, yet she was unable to cry.

In this particular session, I was working with Joan to connect her more with her breathing and the diaphragm tension that was a part of her restraint of crying movements. I was verbally instructing her to keep her breath flowing and rhythmic and, through touch, pointing out places she was tensing in her throat, face, and diaphragm. When I checked with her about her experience of this work, she noted that she felt her stomach and shoulders tensing. "I can't seem to stop them even though I know this is interfering with my breathing and stopping my sadness."

The projection of her tensing, her sense of this physical response as "other than me," is apparent here. The language she uses indicates the projective split of her experience. First Joan refers to her tensing parts as "them" rather than as "I." This signals a lack of identity between body and self. Second her report of being unable to control the tensing process, "I can't seem to stop them . . ." demonstrates the sense of there being two different selves, I and it. So the first step is to identify the projection of body experience in the lack of "I" language and the reduction of body to an object other than self.

> I asked Joan to try to exaggerate slightly the tensions she felt, and to describe the character of those tensions. I used my hands to support her exaggeration with what I could see she was doing externally. She described the tensions and resulting posture as feeling like "bracing," "stiffening," and "protecting."

The reader should find this stage of work familiar from the last chapter on sensation development. Here we are working to heighten her sensation by exaggeration and to acquire a richer and more complete verbal description of her experience. The exaggeration also begins the process of ownership because, if she can do it consciously, then she can begin to experience that it is she who is tensing.

> The heightening of her sensation and tension made it apparent to Joan that her tensing was, at least in part, a response to my touch on her abdomen and diaphragm area. She said that she felt scared of being hurt there. I asked her to try an experiment by combining her description of her tensing with her experience of fearing hurt by stating, "Jim, when you touch my stomach, I brace myself to keep you from hurting me." This felt accurate to her, and I asked her to state it to me a few more times to feel its impact on her.

This statement establishes the relationship of her body process to the environment, and the conversion from an "it," something her body does, to "I," something she does. This continues the process of ownership of the projected body experience begun in the sensitization work and blends it with linguistic and cognitive ownership. This I-statement links the body behavior, tensing, to Joan's fear of being hurt. From a mere sensation we now have a full figure. Her tension is becoming not just something that *occurs to* her, but something she *does* in response to her relationship with the environment (me).

> Joan's next comment begins to move us into the deeper work behind her projection, the work with her resistance and conflict. She commented, "It's funny, intellectually I know you won't hurt me and I trust you, but I still feel scared and needing to protect myself."

This statement still reflects some gap between her cognitive "knowledge" and the actuality of her body response.

> I next suggested that we experiment with alternating touch with no-touch so as to contrast the two. I would touch her diaphragm area lightly, then remove my hand and ask her to describe her experience. This way she could more clearly feel her physical response and what she was responding to. After a number of repetitions of this experiment, she realized what her fear was about. "When you touch me, I feel that I have to keep alert because, even 'though I trust you, I'm afraid you'll change and suddenly go farther than I can catch. So I lie here stiffly anticipating possibly being hurt."

At this point Joan is more fully owning her body response as *her* caution and anticipation. The next step was to give her a more active sense of control over our work and to link her present response to her childhood reality. Her reactions were firmly rooted in her childhood experience of sexual violation. The father she loved during the day would turn on her at night when she was helpless and least expecting it. In her terror of him, she could only lie still, stiffen herself against his violation, and submit. The only allowable expression of her self was in her stiffening, since to respond more actively risked his violence. Here, in the present, we have the opportunity of restoring her sense of control and active use of her urge to protect herself.

> I worked with her on this by having her verbally and physically (by removing my hand) say "no" when she felt the need to guard herself from my touch. This shifted her passive, structural stiffening into an active, motile process, and supported her learning to validate and respect her need to say "no." To tell her only to "let go" of her tension, or insist that she tolerate my touch and suppress her need to say "no," would have only driven her natural organismic response further underground, further alienating the projected part of her—her body response to intrusion. We continued working on full ownership of her right to protect herself and its link to her history. Later our work developed into vigorous hitting of a pad

combined with saying "no" and "get away from me" aloud. Joan began to be more connected to, and more identified with, her previously alienated response to intrusion on her body space.

Let us look at this clinical example more systematically to extract the essentials of working with body process as projection. Roughly we can delineate four steps:

1. *Identifying the projection.* Projection of body experience was first identified in Joan's use of language when describing her experience. Here I listen for the use of "it" or object language, such as "the arm," "my leg," and other indications of a felt difference between the thing being experienced and the self doing the experiencing. When body processes are experienced as if they are happening to something other than self, projection is apparent.

2. *Experiments to heighten body experience.* Having identified the projection, I next began to develop Joan's experience of her body process. This is the basic work of sensation development. Actually, step 1 emerges out of prior sensation-development work and these first two steps alternate back and forth. The experiment we used to exaggerate her tension and build descriptions of her experience both heightens her physical process and her ownership of that process, and begins to form a fuller figure by adding verbal description. The therapist's accurate support of the exaggeration process is critical here.

3. *Experimenting with I-statements.* As Joan began more clearly to experience her body response and its nature, we began to experiment with fuller identification with her body experience. It is important that the use of I-statements be framed to the client as an experiment to "try on" for accuracy. If used as a gimmick or technique, the client will merely introject the statement and superficially comply, gaining no real identification or integration of experience. The therapist must carefully construct the I-statement for experiment so that it reflects as accurately as possible the exact nature and phrasing the client has used to refer to his or her body experience. Simply making the statement is merely an exercise and not, in the Gestalt sense, a true experiment. As an experiment the statement must be experienced fully by the person, chewed and tasted thoroughly. How does it feel? What is it like to consider yourself in this way? What is your resistance to considering this a part of you? Would you try it again and look at me this time, and use your hands as emphasis?

4. *Working through resistances.* The next step was to work with Joan to more fully express her projected body impulse, in this case her anticipation of harm and the impulse to protect herself. Again the main mode of work is the experiment: expression in the here and now. Strictly

speaking we are now moving on from work with a projection per se to work with retroflection.* In this case the work centered around Joan's holding back of her impulse to express "no" (verbally and physically) so as to stop intrusion from the environment.

PROJECTION AND CONFLICT

Projection of body process functions is a way of coping with conflict over aspects of oneself that are not permitted or validated by the environment. By disidentifying with our body and rendering our physical responses other-than-self, we keep from having to acknowledge bad feelings or uncomfortable impulses: the body feels them, not me.

In Joan's case projection of her body process took place in the context of her history, when certain feelings and impulses would have been dangerous to express. As a child she was powerless in the face of her father's sexual advances. Her actual organismic expression of dislike and her want to prevent his encroachment had to be suppressed under the threat of punishment. It goes deeper than mere suppression, however. Within the family double bind her child's ego was not strong enough to maintain her own reality of her father's nighttime betrayal in the face of the implicit family rule against breaking the daytime illusion that "Daddy is good" and "Everything is fine in this family." Joan as a child, being dependent on others for survival, needed her family more than she needed her own sense of reality. Reality will frequently be sacrificed for survival. Joan could not merely suppress her truth; *she had to give up the part of her self that experienced that truth.* Her disownership was so complete that she achieved a disassociated state, projecting a large portion of her bodily life and feeling from her self, and isolating the memories of sexual violation by removing her experience of their bodily context.

Similarly aspects of our bodily nature may be in conflict (usually less severe than that above) with what we have been taught is acceptable or desirable. Many aspects of our physical nature, such as anger and sexuality, are defined as forbidden. Thus we project such elements of our self from the "I" of experience so they do not form part of the developing figures in our awareness and thus are not acted upon.

If it is important to one's parents always to be reasonable (they are frightened by strong feeling or, alternately, require a calm child to help

*Work with retroflection will be discussed more fully in following chapters.

them control their own distress), then what can a child do with feelings of anger and resentment that naturally and normally arise? They are unreasonable feelings and must be exorcised. The child disowns his or her body experience and comes to feel only the results of angry feelings, in headaches, grinding jaw, and aching back. If sexuality is seen as bad or dirty, then, the self that feels sexual, the body-self, must be disowned.

The problem comes when new situations and the natural demands of the life cycle require resources we have disowned. As long as the environment is a calm one, I can function emotionally as "always reasonable" with no need for "unreasonable" feelings. But when the inevitable change and upheaval of life require that I be in contact with my feelings in order to negotiate, to exhibit aggression so as to assert boundaries, or to release my tears to mourn fully, these are unavailable to me.

Disowned feelings, since they are experienced vaguely and apart from the self, often are expressed impulsively. When I hear reports from clients that they were "swept away" by feeling and were "not in control" of their behavior, the projection that "I am not in control of it" is obvious. The feelings or behaviors of which they have lost control are not part of the self or their need to control them would not exist.

Work with projection of the body self clearly requires more than simple reownership and experiments with I-statements. The fears and introjects that underlie the projection must be brought out and worked through. Feeling, as it is identified with, must be acted on and completed to be integrated fully into the self. Work with projection is a small part of the therapy process and must be integrated into the whole.

To finish this chapter, I would like to present another case to show a more complete unit of work emerging from projection. It will give a picture of the process of therapeutic work that is more of a piece itself. The projection is less severe and to that extent more normal.

I had been working with Steve on recovering his body sense over the course of a number of sessions. We had done work with breathing and other exercises to enliven his body and connect him to his sensation life, and he was reporting more awareness of his bodily life. On this particular occasion, he was sitting across from me when I noted a stiffness about his body position and asked him to attend to how he was sitting— with one leg crossed at the knee over the other, his torso slightly turned, the supporting foot pulled up so only the heel was resting on the floor. It was decidedly an effortful way of sitting!

I asked him to describe how that position felt. He stated, "It feels held, like I'm getting ready." Noting his use of "it" to refer to his body experience, I asked him to try the statement, "I am holding myself, I'm getting ready," and to attend to how he felt in making this statement. After trying this experiment, he commented that the statement felt accurate to him, and we spent some time developing more consciousness about his physical "readiness" through exaggeration of his posture and attention to the effect on his breathing (shallow and limited to his chest).

As he became more aware of his physical holding, I asked him to try a new statement, "I am holding myself ready in case you —," and to fill in the blank with whatever seemed appropriate. He responded, "I am holding myself ready in case you judge me or think I'm foolish. I'm holding myself ready to be hurt by you." Steve was very taken with how congruent his physical posture was with his feeling the need to guard himself.

He further noted, "I realize that I'm trying to appear relaxed to you even though my body is tense and held." I worked with him to find statements he could make to me that fit with this, such as, "I must look the way you want me to" and "I can't show you how I'm guarding myself from you." The one that grabbed him the most was, "I can't show you my true feelings." The work that ensued focused on relating this to his need to conceal his feelings from his father and his childhood feelings of being constantly on guard against his father's temper and judgmentalness.

Towards the end of this session, he was able to state to me that he was guarding his little boy inside from the chance that I might criticize him or judge his "childish" wants as foolish. I told him, "From my experience with you, it is the child parts of you I feel particularly warm towards. I want you to know that I value your little boy very much." On hearing this (and I made sure that he was in contact and listening before I spoke), Steve was able to soften his body and fear me less. He was able to hear my appreciation of his vulnerable child self, and permit himself to be less guarded and to soften physically. For the first time in our work, I saw his face lose its masklike "I'm okay" appearance. He began to recognize that he did not have to be adult and in full command to be acceptable to me. The increased contact between us which resulted allowed Steve to feel supported enough to delve further into his feelings about his father.

Chapter 9

Mobilization and Body Process

One of the most characteristic aspects of our physical presence is our sense of energy, vitality, vigor, and strength. The alacrity with which we move, the strength of our speech, the glow of our skin, our capacity to shift into action and sustain ourselves in difficulties, all tell us the degree to which we are able to mobilize for life.

From the Gestalt perspective, mobilization is not a characteristic a person has or doesn't have so much as a process in the sequence of any contact cycle. When a figure forms in awareness and orients the person towards contact with the environment, the person must mobilize for the action that will lead to that contact. The process of mobilization forms the physical base for action in the world by supplying the energy and impetus for the action that makes contact possible.

Take a basic example of action to meet a physiological need. If I am thirsty (sensation) and want water (an aware figure), I must move myself to get up from my chair and get it (action) so that I may drink it (final contact) and satisfy my thirst (post–contact). What is left out of this sequence is my preparation for action; mobilization must occur between wanting the water and getting up to obtain it. This is a subtle and easily missed aspect of the contact sequence, particularly in such simple action sequences as getting a drink of water, but it has important implications for the overall quality of my contact. If I cannot mobilize myself for action, I remain as if glued to my chair, unable to overcome the inertia of my sitting. I remain thirsty unless I am able to convince someone else to get me a drink, thus satisfying my need. Such a passive approach to my own needs has little significance in terms of a glass of water, but when spread into other aspects of life, deadens the spirit and reduces the capacity to engage with the environment.

In interpersonal contact sequences, the phase of mobilization and preparation for action is also important. Speech itself is an action in the service of contact (i.e., communication of meaning). Communication is more than just the word content of speech. Voice tone, breathing as it supports the vigor of speech, posture, gesture, and bodily stance tell us how people are mobilized behind their communication. Do they support their words appropriately with their breath? Do they literally "sit behind" what they say in terms of their posture? Do they have enough energy to carry through with their action and sustain it long enough for contact to be complete?

MOBILIZATION AND ADJUSTMENT TO THE ENVIRONMENT

A simple and commonplace example of mobilization is getting up out of a comfortable chair after a spell of sitting. If I were to ask you to begin to get up, note what you would do to prepare yourself for the execution of that action. You might take a deep inhalation, test your muscles, begin to organize your posture to get your legs and torso in the proper position. Certain muscle groups are braced and others prepare for contraction. You might notice a surge or flow of energy, or an increase in your heart rate. An observer might notice a slight flush as blood flow increases to your body periphery. Note that all of this occurs prior to, although really part of, the actual act of getting up. It is preparation and mobilization for the action itself.

The phenomena involved in mobilization are so brief for some actions that they can be easily missed by an observer. The flow of energy from its focus in figure formation to charge in mobilization and discharge in action is almost simultaneous for overlearned responses, such as turning on a light or turning the page of a book, or for reflexive actions, such as startle responses or flinching from pain. These are relatively automatic and require little buildup of energy or support from the person. The ability to quickly mobilize energy and support for action without thinking is an evolutionary gift that increases our capacity to survive crisis and emergency. Indeed, in such actions it is useless to differentiate the action from the process of mobilization. Nor do such actions require true figure formation, since the whole process is wired into our biological hardware as a reflex.

The actions described above are fairly short sequences or small preset units of action. Other actions, particularly those involving interpersonal interaction, require larger and more sustainable supplies of energy and a greater degree of self-support. It is in these sequences, because of their complexity, and frequently their association with anxiety or emotional trauma, that mobilization can be truncated or interfered with. Like all phases of the cycle of organismic self-regulation, mobilization only becomes a therapeutic concern when it is problematic.

Finding a job and completing a long-term project are examples of actions that must be sustained over long periods, as is coping with chronic illness or negotiating family crises. Such activities require sustained efforts, which, in turn, require sustained mobilization of energy and a constant, moderate level of self-support. When energy and self-support become diminished, such long action sequences appear to grind to a halt. At this point we must begin to ask what interferes with mobilization.

Another example is a large or all-out action that requires a large charge for an equivalent discharge and firm support for its intensity. In the sex act, the degree of discharge and contact in orgasm is strongly founded on the ability to mobilize and charge through full breathing and the support of full rhythmic movement. In a therapeutic situation, an example would be the expression of anger by hitting a pillow; the degree of postural support and ability to charge through breathing will affect the degree of expression and discharge in the hitting movement. Lack of power and vitality in such actions calls attention to the processes of mobilization.

In another situation, the environment may offer less support and so require greater self-support from the individual. Examples include having an argument with the boss, standing up for your viewpoint when the majority disagrees, or withstanding attempts to influence you. Having the physical capacity to support such efforts and withstand the responses from the environment is essential. Without the bodily structure and organization necessary to stand up to the crowd, one feels weak and vulnerable. Such cliches as "stand up for what's right," "stand by your man," and "to withstand pressures" speak of the unconscious but very real background that posture and body structure supply for difficult interactions.

Our fundamental capacity to mobilize through support for the emerging action and build our energy charge will have an essential effect on how we creatively adjust to variations in the organism/environment field. Without effective mobilization, life is experienced without excitement or liveliness, movement is sluggish and lackluster, and behavior is without force and pressure.

THREE REQUIREMENTS FOR MOBILIZATION

Disruption of mobilization can be observed by attending to the following questions. How does he support his action? What kind of energy does she bring into her action? How lively is his contact and so his experience of himself and the environment? How easily does she get herself moving? Can he sustain movement? These same questions can be applied to any contact situation that inevitably involves some action, and thus mobilizing for that action: reaching out for others, defending one's integrity, getting a job, negotiating with one's mate, and so on. The basic process in mobilizing for action are readiness, support, and energy charge.

Readiness

Readiness involves a sense of focus towards an action and may include cognitive and imagistic means. You may imagine the action taking place, anticipate the action with verbal descriptions, or think it through to orient yourself cognitively and perceptually. Athletes frequently take advantage of this mental "revving up" by talking to themselves before a performance or visualizing the moves they will make, as do many actors, dancers, and other performance artists. It is worth noting here that when such "rehearsal" becomes fixed and the resulting mobilization does not find fruition in action, the clinical phenomenon that results is obsessive thinking.

Readiness also involves having the required skills and capacities available (e.g., adequate muscular strength). Whereas mental rehearsal readies the neural pathways that are to be used in sequencing a complex action, sufficient muscular capacity and ability to move accurately are also essential or the action does not have sufficient power to complete itself in contact. However, it is not sufficient only to be able to imagine an action sequence and be strong enough to carry it through. One must also have the requisite skills for that particular action. We can think of training as a long phase of mobilization for the final outcome in action, say in a race or competition, where both strength and skills are developed to be discharged in the final effort.

Supports

Another element of mobilization is the readying of one's physical supports for action as reflected in posture, body alignment, and muscular tone. As one mobilizes for action, muscle tone increases, or paradoxically decreases, in the muscles that will be moved. There is a setting and bracing of posture and an enlivening of the movement systems of the body. The braced stance of the football player ready for the blow of the tackler, the beginning pose of the dancer, or the relaxed and ready stance of the martial artist are all examples of particular kinds of support for action, each according to the particular nature of the actions involved. Clearing one's throat for speech, finding a comfortable sitting position, straightening one's back, and stretching cramped muscles are all common physical preparations for action. When making an important statement at a meeting or preparing for the arrival of a loved one, we physically organize our posture to meet the required conditions of the actions, be they speaking or running to embrace. The notion of "support for action" comes from the Gestalt therapy work of Laura Perls. When we ask how a person is supported for action, we must examine how this person is physically organized so as to (1) receive the support of the environment, and (2) support himself or herself for the action to be taken.

All actions take place within the context of the environment. The most fundamental environment is that of the earth beneath us, and much of our relationship to our environmental support is reflected in whether our posture allows us to be well connected to the support of the earth. This has been called "grounding" by Lowen (1977). Some people appear solidly planted on the ground, with strong and flexible legs that allow the support of the earth to be transferred easily through the skeletal structure. The posture of others seems to displace upwards so that their upper body is top-heavy and teeters on thin and weak legs, offering them little base of support from the earth. In others the legs seem to be adequate in terms of strength, but are stiff and inflexible, as if they don't trust that the support of the earth will be there if they relax their rigid stance. People who have poor grounding through their legs have a poor base for action. They have no foundation from which to move because they have no relationship to the earth that supports their being and must spend energy posturally compensating for this gap of support.°

°This is related to the Bioenergetic concepts of grounding (Lowen, 1972). Lowen refers to grounding as one's physical and energetic connection to the fundamental support of the earth, without which we have no firm base on which to act, and without which behavior is not based on contact with reality. Lowen's notion of grounding combines the *experience* of connecting with the physical environment (considered earlier here under

In addition to this notion of the support of the environment through one's connection with the earth, there is the notion of self-support for action. Just as support of the earth anchors one's action in the environmental base, self-support anchors one's action in one's bodily capacity. Self-support refers to the posture as a whole, as it forms a base for action. To be only supported by the earth and not be self-supported would be to be lying down or sitting at rest. To be supported only by the earth (or an object such as a bed or chair) is thus to be completely passive and undifferentiated with respect to gravity. But, if in addition to being supported by the earth, we are also self-supported, then we are actively maintaining ourselves posturally in some balanced yet dynamic form—we are maintaining ourselves as upright. This requires muscular usage and body organization.

When I examine the issue of self-support, I look at whether a person can literally maintain an upright posture so as to be well organized for the action the person is to take. Does he rely totally on the environment for support, for example, by giving himself up to his chair or by leaning against a wall, or can he sit or stand using his own power and strength? Is she organized so that she is balanced within her bodily structure or must she distort her posture to counter misalignment to the pull of gravity? Is his posture such that he can easily shift into movement, or his his self-support so rigi that he must shift around before he can move from a resting position?

The practitioner is aided in perceiving problems in support for action if he or she has an understanding of the biomechanical principles of good posture. So much study has gone into this area, however, that it is impossible to do justice to its theoretical and biomechanical complexities in brief form. I refer the reader to the works of Rolf (1977), Feldenkrais (1972), Todd (1937/1959), and the essential compendium by Alexander teacher and anatomist, David Gorman (1981).

The essential effect of posture and body alignment on one's readiness for action can be made readily apparent by experimenting with various standing positions.

> First try an intentionally demobilized posture: stand without shoes, lock your knees so that there is no bend in your legs. Retract your pelvis by increasing the curvature of your lower back and pulling your buttocks back. Let your belly pouch forward and your upper

sensation) with the notion of mobilization for action through *physical supports*. In the view presented here, I find it useful to distinguish between "grounding in reality," which I see as a function of a broader sensory base than just contact with the earth, and physical supports for action, which require, among other things, a firm base on which to act, that is, the support of the earth through the legs.

body slump by collapsing your chest. Let your head hang forward. In this posture you will notice that you tend to breathe shallowly and, if you stay with it awhile, eventually you will feel tired and dull. With your legs locked into place and your balance precarious, you will also notice that it is difficult to move smoothly out of this position. Try this by assuming the posture and then shift into walking. Notice how much effort it takes to rearrange yourself for the movement.

For some people assuming this posture is very difficult because their own body organization runs in a different direction (e.g., flattened lower back, uplifted chest, and rigidly straight neck). If this is true for you, you might try emphasizing your normal posture and notice how this affects your energy, and readiness and ability to move. Others find that this experiment is no more than a slight emphasis of their normal posture, which indicates that such demobilized structure is home ground for them.

Next try a more aligned stance. This may be difficult without direct personal guidance by an outside person familiar with postural alignment, but it should at least give you some idea of what a relaxed but mobilized stance is like. Standing as before (without shoes), align your feet so they are a shoulder width apart (distance equal to the width of both your fists held together, thumb to thumb) and very slightly toed in. Let your knees bend so that they feel "soft," that is, neither locked back nor overly flexed. Imagining that your pelvis is like a bowl that sits on top of your leg bones, find a position where this bowl feels level by gently tilting your pelvis forwards and backwards until you find the midpoint. Now, keeping your body from your pelvis on down as it is, imagine that your spine is like a string of beads from your pelvis to the base of your skull. Breathing fully but softly, imagine that the crown of your skull is attached to a helium balloon that pulls your head straight up, lengthening and lifting the string of beads that is your spine.

You will notice that, as your spine lifts and elongates, the curve of your lower back straightens and relaxes spontaneously and your chest lifts slightly, allowing you a deeper inhalation. Now check your lower body to make sure your knees are still softly flexed and your pelvis is still balanced. What is this posture like? It may feel awkward if it is very different from your usual posture, and you may have muscular resistance to assuming it. How are your energy and sense of readiness different? If your typical posture is very demobilized, you will find this posture more energetic. If typically your posture is hypermobilized (very extended and "at attention"), this posture will feel more conventional to you. Experiment with shifting into walking from this posture. Most people find that their lightly flexed knees and balanced upper body allow for a more fluid shift into movement, certainly easier than the previous demobilized posture. These experiments should provide some experiential understanding of the relationship among posture, energy, and readiness for movement.

Energy Charge

A final element in mobilization for action is the building up of energy and impetus for the action. Lowen (1975) and other Reichian therapists call this building up a "charge," which can be discharged into action. This buildup of energy for action is physically evidenced by increased respiration rate, increased blood flow to peripheral organs (the skeletal muscles) and organs of action (the heart, lungs, and brain), the release of glycogen (a type of sugar for quick energy) into the bloodstream, and so on. This charge of energy is visible in the skin color and quality. Indeed we often note how one acquaintance seems so "vital and glowing" and another seems "pale and lifeless" precisely because blood flow to the body surface is linked to a person's overall charge of energy. Energy charge is experienced as liveliness, warmth, glow, and tingling, and has been described traditionally in the Gestalt literature in terms of "excitement."

The longer the action sequence or the more powerful the action behavior, the more capacity to charge oneself with energy is required to sustain it. This is true not only in the general sense of having sufficient overall charge, but also in terms of the specific muscle groups involved in behavior. For example, sexual action requires not just good energy charge for full discharge in the sex act, but specifically the capacity for charging the pelvic area of the body and allowing that charge to suffuse outwards (Reich, 1942). The act of touching requires that the surface of the hands be lively and charged for the touch itself to be vital and contactful. You can try this out for yourself.

> Try touching some object—say a smooth stone or wood carving, or better yet, a cooperative person—but before you do so, take a moment to imagine that all of the energy and blood from your touching arm are drawn away into your shoulder. Breathe shallowly and

touch, noticing the quality of the act of reaching out and contact. Try to touch again, but this time breathe slowly and deeply and imagine your breath flowing down your arm as you exhale, bringing warmth and liveliness to your fingers.

What was the quality of this reaching and touching? Most will find the second mode to be more vital, to be stronger and richer. The vitality of the action is strongly dependent on the mobilization of energy charge that goes into it.

I would digress a moment to comment on a confusion that has crept into the use of the term "energy" in Gestalt therapy. Frequently the phase I am labeling "mobilization" has been synonymously termed the phase of "energy." I believe this to be a misnomer for two reasons. One is that energy charge for action is only one of a number of the elements that go into mobilization. The second is that energy (and thus excitement, warmth, etc.) is a phenomenon that manifests in different forms and is experienced in different ways throughout the experience cycle, and is not tied exclusively to the mobilization phase. Figure 9-1 shows in schematic form how I view the phenomenon of energy throughout the whole of the cycle. It is the change in focus, intensity, and direction of energy in different phases of the cycle that gives the rhythmic pulsation spoken of by Reich (1942). Reich was concerned most with the rhythmic pulsation between mobilization (charge) and action (discharge). Gestalt therapy emphasizes the whole process, from sensation through post-contact, as the working unit in organismic self-regulation.

BODY PROCESS AND INTERFERENCE WITH MOBILIZATION

Breathing and Charge

Action requires energy for its execution. The more intense the action involved, the more energy is required for full support of the action. When action must be sustained over a long period of time, then energy also must be sustained over that period of time. If we carefully observe what body process is most directly related to the current regulation of organismic energy, breathing stands out as most relevant.

The theme of breath as related to energy and vitality has historical roots dating from the Hebrew biblical term *ruach*, which described the life that God breathed into the body which leaves at the moment of

Sensation

Figure

Mobilization

Energy diffuse;
sensations move in and
out of awareness with
little charge.

Energy becomes focused
on a figure; figure stands
out against the background
with sense of charge.

Charge increases,
building toward the
active body periphery
and musculature.

Action

Final Contact

Post-contact

Energy is discharged
into the environment
through movement
and expression.

Contact brings in
new source of energy
from the environment.

Charge settles;
energy moves back
into organismic
core for assimilation.

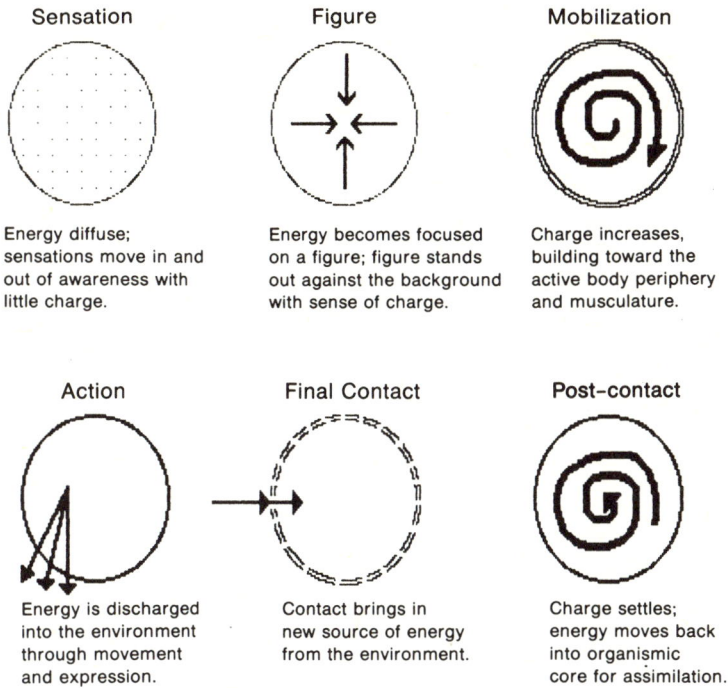

**Figure 9-1. Schematic of energy and charge as an organismic phenom-
enon throughout the cycle of experience.**

death, and also in Eastern spiritual systems and martial arts that emphasize control of consciousness and power through breath.

The modern emphasis on breathing and its psychological function
originates in Reich's work and echoes this vitalistic theme, while placing
breathing processes in the context of the post-Freudian understanding
of repression of emotion and the unconscious. Certainly while most of
the long-term supply of physical energy comes in the form of food and
drink, the moment-to-moment regulation of energy level is most apparently related to breathing. This is particularly true of one's *experienced* sense of energy and flow. This can be explored through a simple
awareness experiment.°

For a minute or two, pay careful attention to your breathing and
give a slightly greater emphasis to your inhalation than to your ex-

°Some people find the effects of increased breathing quite uncomfortable. I recom-
mend that you do not try this exercise if you are subject to anxiety attacks or have experienced previous problems with hyperventilation.

halation. In other words inhale with slightly greater vigor than you exhale. This emphasis should only be of a few degrees. After a minute or two, notice your body sensations. You may feel tingling or streaming sensations, particularly in your hands and feet, or a sense of excitement or charge. You may feel livelier, more alert, and perhaps lighter. Some people feel slightly lightheaded or anxious due to hyperventilation. If this is too uncomfortable, let your breathing return to normal and your discomfort will subside. People have very different tolerance levels for energy charge, and your discomfort from this little bit of breathing may indicate that you have some difficulty with tolerating a heightened charge.

In the Gestalt approach, given the emphasis on process and experiment, attention would be paid to the interference with mobilization through limiting breathing in the course of developing *any* therapeutic work. Breathing to charge oneself with energy might be used as an experiment to explore the experiential effects of breathing further, or to support the vigor of ongoing action and behavior. The Gestalt goal in experimenting with energy charging is not to end up "charged," which may or may not occur depending on where the particular experiment goes, but rather to attend to the *process* of charging or its interference.

When a client named Don complained to me how difficult it was for him to get anything moving in his life, I shifted my focus from his words and his heavy, plodding speech and looked at how he was supporting this particular action (talking to me) in such an immobilized way. What was apparent was how minimally he breathed, particularly during inhalation. I noted this to him and asked whether he would try giving more emphasis to his inhalation. As Don did so, he began to brighten up, color crept into his skin, and he reported feeling livelier than before. As soon as he recognized this, he suddenly stopped his breathing and sank down into his chair again. When I asked him what had happened, Don said, "I started to feel anxious and wanted to stop." To connect the process of charging to his experience of anxiety, I suggested he try saying it as, "When I begin to give myself energy I get scared and anxious." Don tried this a few times and agreed that this fit his experience.

As we experimented further, allowing him to alternate brief periods of energizing breathing with shutting down when he became too anxious, he was able to discern what it was he began to fear. For Don to become energized meant that he no longer had any excuse (his depression and immobility) not to change the things in his life about which he complained. Yet to change himself implied many risks for which he felt unready—leaving his dependent position with his parents, becoming mature and responsible, and so on. Shortly after this session, Don announced that he did not feel he could continue in therapy, and was not ready to make the changes he knew were necessary for him to move on.

I honored his decision and encouraged him to stop for the time being. Don was not yet able to move beyond this first step and to face his life more fully. Rather than my attempting to mobilize him further through extensive exercises in breathing, our exploration of his resistance to mobilizing himself allowed him to make some decisions as to what he was ready for at this time, rather than capitulating to my values or theories of what would be "good for him" or "building a charge."

Breathing to generate energy charge can also be useful to support ongoing therapeutic work, particularly work that involves physical expression. In the next example, the client was personally ready to move beyond her fear of mobilizing herself and was ready to face the actions she felt she had to take. What was not right for Don, given his life situation and capacity to support decisions, was felt to be essential for this woman, given her own stage of growth.

Throughout the long course of work with Delia, who was working to extricate herself from the deadly triangle she formed with her mother and father, we would reach a point in the work where she would be unable to summon the strength to resist the subtle entreaties to save her parents from each other. In one session this was symbolized in a dream in which she was driving across a bridge (a symbol for her of transition to a new phase) with her parents in the back seat. Suddenly the car spun off the bridge into the deep water. In the dream she was the only one who could swim and she realized that she only had the air to save one parent, or that she could save both but then must herself drown.

We acted out the dream, having Delia play its various parts. As she played her parents she would call out to be saved, but would make no attempt to help and would merely sit passively, waiting to be saved. Neither parent would make any move to swim out of the car, fully depending on Delia to rescue them.

Standing in the therapy room, Delia would look from one parent to the other, unable to make a choice, steadily becoming more and more demobilized and deflated. This was, of course, the point at which she had frequently arrived in our work with regard to her parents, and she commented that she felt ready to make a decision but did not feel strong enough to back it up. I asked her to take a softened version of the bioenergetics grounding stance (which encourages energy charge) by standing with bent knees, toe-in feet, and hands at hips, and inhaling deeply into her chest and abdomen. Through this posture and breathing, she charged with more energy and was able to begin to make statements to her parents in the dream. She was able to sustain the energy to back up her position, her voice and language becoming stronger and firmer. Eventually Delia was able to chastise her parents in the dream for their passivity, rejecting the notion that it was her job to save them, and refusing to sacrifice her life to resolve their marital difficulties.

Throughout this process I reminded her to continue her deep breathing and helped her to maintain a sense of strength in her stance as she faced the attempts of her dream parents to bend her to their will. She finished this work flushed, feeling strong and physically able to maintain her sense of strength and energy to back up her desire to step out of her parents' marital difficulties. This work became a turning point in her relationship with her parents and she was gradually able to use what she had discovered in herself to maintain her position outside their marital system and not act as a go-between. This considerably reduced her own stress and anger, and she was paradoxically more available to show her caring for her parents because she no longer felt so trapped by them.

Body Structure and Energy Charge

Sufficient energy for mobilization depends not only on the act of charging itself, but also on one's capacity to tolerate, contain, and build that charge until the organism is ready to discharge it in action. This requires, quite literally, adequate space in the body for containing the charge and the capacity of body tissues to absorb and distribute the increased charge. These are both related to body structure.

The space within the body boundaries is defined by the shape of the body structure. Where body structure is compressed, made small and narrow, there is less room to contain and store energy. Imagine a cardboard box: in its normal shape, it can hold a full complement of contents, but when crushed or flattened, its internal space is limited and little can be contained in it.

The ability of the body tissues to absorb an increased energy supply is related to their flexibility: the ability to stretch and flex allows for increased energy. A sponge is an apt metaphor. If the sponge is shrunken and dry, it is not capable of absorbing much liquid without kneading and soaking, whereas a flexible and supple sponge will quickly absorb and distribute liquid throughout. Similarly, tightly bound muscles can neither absorb nor distribute an increasing energy charge. Since body structure is maintained by muscular rigidity, this frequently limits energy capacity.

When working with persons whose body structure limits their capacity to build, store, and distribute energy, efforts to increase their breathing must be joined with body work that enables opening up of the body structure and distributing the flow of energy through the tissues. One client, a thin man with tight and stringy muscles, would come into sessions feeling tired and lackluster, unable to sustain deep therapeutic work. In addition to his thin and constrained body structure, his minimal breathing supplied him with little nourishment. When I worked with him to increase his breathing capacity, he would feel quickly flooded with uncomfortable feelings in his torso that he could not tolerate. He described it as feeling that his chest became "stuffed and tingly" and the rest of him remained deadened.

It became clear that, while breathing increased the energy in his chest, the resulting energy did not have any place to go in his narrow and constricted body space. We developed a series of stretches that, when he breathed more, he could use to open up space in his ribcage, sides, shoulders, arms, belly, and legs for the increased energy to flow into and build. With these tools he gradually came to tolerate a higher level of charge and began to sustain the energy for more difficult therapeutic work.

You can experiment with this for yourself, although the stretches I suggest won't be as carefully attuned to your own particular structural constraints as they were for my client.

> For a couple of minutes, return to the earlier exercise of giving emphasis to your inhalation. Allow your breath to gradually deepen to build more charge. Now return to normal breathing. Notice tensions or sensations of discomfort that have arisen from the deeper breathing. Do the exercise again, and this time, as you feel your energy and discomforts build, continue breathing deeply and do some gentle stretches. Raise your hands over your head and stretch upwards gently and then stretch to each side and to the rear; bend forward from your waist and gently stretch your back, extend your legs forward and stretch them gently. Now breathe normally again and notice what is different. Are you less uncomfortable? What is your sense of flow and space in your body? Your sense of liveliness? Were you able to tolerate deeper and longer breathing with less discomfort this time? If not, you may already tolerate sufficient charge,

or the stretches may not have been relevant to opening up your particular structural constraints.

In another case a periodically depressed woman who had little contact with her body would panic whenever the work we were doing to restore her body awareness would increase her normally shallow inhalations. She would have immediate symptoms of hyperventilation, such as tingling lips, cheeks, and fingers, and muscular tetany (muscle spasms) in her hands. The narrowness in her torso forced the energy she built up into her body periphery (i.e., her face and arms) because she had no space for containing such a charge in her body core. These sensations would panic her because they were both unfamiliar and uncomfortable.

Structurally her torso was constricted in her shoulders, waist, and sides. Her shoulders were narrow and pulled inwards and allowed no expansion or movement for her breathing, which she did mostly in her chest. Her waist was constricted as if she had a band around her middle drawing her in, limiting expansion of her diaphragm and abdomen in breathing. These limitations were added to by the rigidity of her ribcage, particularly along the sides of her body (lateral line), which prevented her ribs from flaring out sideways to allow more room for full breathing.

By using my hands to work with the constricting musculature and guide her to extend her breathing and awareness to her torso, we gradually increased the volume and flexibility of her shoulder girdle, diaphragm, abdomen, and sides. With each expansion she would come in touch with feelings and impulses that were frightening to her, and she now had the energy to mobilize the expression of these feelings. Initially she could only tolerate small bits of work, a little at a time, until she became more familiar with the sensations of liveliness and energy. The loosening of these body areas, combined with stronger and more mobilized sensation and feeling, also brought her into contact with long withheld emotional expression: the urge to hit as she connected her shoulders to her arms; feelings of gut anger as she connected to and opened up space in her abdomen; sobbing and sadness as her diaphragm became mobile enough to pulsate with her tears. The feelings that emerged were initially frightening to her. A gradual course of experimenting with breathing while also exploring her resistances to mobilizing her feelings was required for her to allow herself to maintain the bodily space in which to tolerate and build more energy for her functioning.

Posture and Self-Support

The issues of posture and self-support in mobilization were apparent early on in my work with Timothy. His presenting complaint was that he lacked spontaneity and felt himself to be without passion. As I got to know Timothy, I made note of his difficulty in supporting his body in an upright position. Timothy slumped in his chair and slumped when standing. His body formed an S-shape: knees hyperextended back, pelvis thrust forward curving his lower back, shoulders slumped and rounded over his collapsed chest, head and neck thrust forward.

Initially we simply explored Timothy's existing standing posture, working with him to emphasize his slump and to experiment with what it was like to look around, to walk, to present himself from this slumped and collapsed position. Timothy expressed that in this posture he felt dull, tired, uninvolved, and without energy. At the same time, this pose felt safe and familiar to him. As his awareness of his posture increased through our experiment and exaggeration, it became clearer to him just how much he had organized himself to maintain a sense of safety through demobilizing himself posturally and limiting his energy and sense of strength.

We also began to explore what a well-supported and upright posture would be like for him. I used my hands and visualization to guide Timothy in finding this posture by encouraging him to unlock his knees and let the bowl of his pelvis rock back to take the curve out of his lower back. I directed his breathing to expand his chest and shift his shoulders back, to let his spine lift and straighten, and so naturally expand his rib-cage and straighten his neck. In this posture Timothy felt strong and his voice and manner became firmer and more forceful. He reported a much greater sense of liveliness and felt tingling and energy flow streaming out to his fingertips and feet, a sign of increased charge and mobilization. In walking around the room, Timothy described himself as more "out in the world" and less withdrawn and obsessive.

One might think that simply by discovering this more mobilized posture, Timothy's difficulties might be solved. Of course, the work so far only outlined the polarities of mobilization and demobilization. He could experience how he normally stood and how he could stand with greater self-supports, but he could not maintain this new posture for long. The resistance to mobilization that made his slumped and de-mobilized posture "home ground" (i.e., the posture he always returned to) remained to be explored.

We developed this theme through a number of sessions, and what became clearer, as Timothy became more familiar with being fully upright and self-supported, was that he could maintain the posture up to a point; then he would feel weighted down and would slump under the pressure of this weight. To emphasize his experience of one side of this polarity, I acted as the weight, pressing him down with my hands until he sagged into his usual slump. Then we switched and he took the position of being the weight and pressed me down. I encouraged him to add words to the physical processes of weighting down and being weighted down.

Timothy: Now I'm upright. I feel tall and powerful. When I'm in this posture, I feel that I stand out and that I'm noticeable for a change.

Jim: I notice that even as you speak you are starting to slump in your chest and shoulders.

Timothy: Yeah, as I said, I felt that I stood out. I started to feel heavy again.

Jim: Be the weight now, and press down on me.

Timothy: (pressing down on the back of my neck and my chest with his hands): Get down you, you're standing out too much. If you do that, you'll be noticed and someone will expect something from you that you won't be able to deliver.

Jim: So you're going to protect him from the folly of being noticeable?

Timothy: That's right. If he's upright and showing his power, then he might have to show he can carry through on that promise.

Jim: The promise is that he's capable of acting on what he wants?

Timothy: Right, I don't think he's strong enough.

Jim: Switch over and let's see just how strong or weak that other part of you is.

Timothy: (now being weighted down by the pressure of my hands on his neck and chest): I hate your keeping me down. I want to stand fully in the world. [He starts to resist my weight and push back.] I'm damned tired of the safe route!

Jim: (continuing my weighting him down): But I've got to protect you from showing your strength. If you're upright, you'll be challenged and have to prove your stuff. It's too dangerous. You might fail, just like you did as a kid!

Timothy: No! I'm not the weak and gangly kid any more. [He suddenly pushes strongly against my pressure.] I'm a man now and I don't need your protection any more. [Tim grasps my hands and powerfully removes them from his chest and neck, straightens his posture into fully erect standing. He is breathing deeply in his chest and looks physically expanded.]

This vignette describes a culmination of a unit of work dealing with the mobilization of self-supports. Certainly it is not the end point of growth for Timothy, but rather the establishment of a base and resource for his continued therapy, particularly as we further developed the theme of being powerful in work and in relationships. As we explored other areas of his life, we constantly kept in mind his stance and sense of supports and the old embodied messages that he is not strong enough to deal fully with life's problems.

MOBILIZATION AND RESISTANCE

As has been illustrated in some of the case material, demobilization comes about not merely because a person does not know how to charge or support himself or herself posturally (i.e., as a behavioral deficit), but because it serves some function in maintaining his or her organismic integrity. Mobilization cannot be maintained or creates anxiety. There are implications to becoming mobilized.

Although the nature of this resistance to mobilization differs for different people, some common themes emerge. Zinker (1977) notes:

> Energy is blocked most often by fear of excitement or strong emotions ... Many individuals feel if they allow themselves to become angry, they will annihilate their environment; if they become sexual, they will be maniacal and perverse; if they express love, they will overwhelm and suffocate the other person; if they allow themselves to brag, they will be ridiculed and rejected. (p. 102)

These fears may be rooted in actual life experience, such as a history of acting out impulsively, but most often are introjects that have little or no base in any reality. Such people have been told to control themselves and not to get too excited, when there was nothing particularly wrong with their self-control or excitement. Or having lived with a parent or spouse who acted without limits, they now define even the mildest expression on their own part as "too much" and requiring control. Consequently any degree of mobilization that by implication brings them close to action, also arouses such limiting introjects. These must be explored and worked through in the course of therapy.

To allow oneself to mobilize and feel powerful, prepared, charged, and vigorous also requires that one be willing to move on from the surety of inaction into the unknown risk of action. The "safe emergency" provided in the therapeutic environment and the therapist's creativity in devising experiments with gradually increasing levels of risk afford the possibility of re-owning one's capacity for action in the world.

Chapter 10

Action and Body Process

With some degree of orientation recovered we can
then begin to regain ability to move about and manipulate ourselves and our environment constructively,
(Perls et al., 1951, p. 117).

Transformation is a process starting with simple, superficial awareness which energizes us to movement.
One way to become transformed is to act, to move one's
body, to be expressive, alive. I learned that awareness
cannot remain vital by itself inside of us, that its full
vitality is asserted in activity and, later, a sense of completion (Zinker, 1983, p. 82).

THE MOVING SELF

Almost all of our contact functions involve movement in the environment, whether it be the small subtle movements of facial expression, the
communication of gestures and body position, or larger motor actions
such as reaching out, running, and bending. From the Gestalt perspective, movement occurs not as an isolated mechanical process, but as embedded in the larger cycle of organismic self-regulation. This chapter
focuses on *movement towards final contact,* or movement as it functions
to bring the organism into contact with that aspect of the environment

that is necessary for growth, or into contact with that aspect of oneself that is disowned but seeks completion. In this way movement can be seen as a function of the self that serves to move one towards completion and wholeness. The "self" is not just a concept, idea, or psychic structure, but is a muscular self, a motile self, and an expressive self—self of bones and joints, of feet, hands, spine, and jaw.

In Chapter 2 I described the significance of emotion and self-expression and the relationship of these to movement. It is in the action phase of the cycle that the therapist becomes most concerned with the use of expressive movement and emotional release. The initiation of action signals the discharge of mobilized energy *into* the environment through the expression of feeling, movement towards the contact object, and manipulation of the environment. Body-oriented psychotherapies have been particularly noted for their use of expressive movement and the release of powerful emotions. However, frequently it is emotional expression per se that is valued so that the fullness of expression is encouraged apart from any other considerations. Expressive movement is extremely useful as a therapeutic tool, but is not an end in itself. It is a tool for discovery and for increasing the range of self-functioning and must be seen within the whole context of organismic functioning and contact with the environment to be fully assimilated as one's own. Action separated from one's functioning as a person remains split from the "I" or sense of self. Action separated from the "other" to which one is acting in relation splits the self from the environment in which needs can be completed.

The energy and support we generate in the mobilization phase find fruition when we express some kind of relevant action in our environment. Action is the discharge and utilization of mobilized energy and musculature in movement. Through action we expand ourselves into and propel ourselves through our environment, and thereby make contact within the organism/environment field.

The value that Gestalt therapists place on action and movement is one of the things that distinguishes Gestalt therapy from some other insight-oriented therapies. Awareness remains lifeless unless the blocks to the transition of that awareness into action are freed. This is what makes Gestalt therapy an *expressive* therapy as well as an insight and existential therapy. The intensive approach to the body represented in this book brings to the Gestalt approach an even greater emphasis on the use of physical expression and movement.

What distinguishes Gestalt therapy from some expressive therapies is that we look at movement within the context of the completion of organismic needs. We are not interested in movement only for its own

Table 10-1.
Some Actions as Related to the Cycle of Experience.

Sensation	Need	Action	Contact
Hunger	Food	Obtaining food	Biting, chewing, tasting, feeling satiated
Arousal	Sexual relation	Finding partner, touching copulating	Pleasure, orgasm, union
Fear	Escape from danger	Running away, pulling back	Feeling of safety
Anger	Protection from intrusion	Posturing, hardening, push-ing back, hitting	Sense of power, integrity, capacity
Yearning	Nurturance, comfort	Reaching out, asking for comfort	Softening, caring of other person, feel-ing warmed
Heart feeling	To express love	Touching, saying, gazing with soft-ness and warmth	Oneness with other, impact on self and other of your lovingness
Sadness	Mourning for losses and hurts	Crying, sobbing, voicing one's loss	Relief, comfort, healing of emo-tional wounds

sake. Movement must be grounded in sensation and feeling and bring us into appropriate contact (completion of needs) with our environment. Thus action can be defined as movement in the service of contact (completion) or *movement towards final contact.* The inability to act in a full, direct, and accurate way means that essential organismic needs will remain incomplete and unfinished. Table 10-1 gives some representative examples of possible needs, actions to serve those needs, and the resulting experience of contact.

Healthy action must be related not only to one's needs and feelings, but also to the present environment, that is, in contact with a here and now context. To reach out to others in response to one's own need for comforting will result in frustration and pain if the person you are reaching out to is unable to give to you at that moment. Similarly there is no virtue in acting on one's feelings of anger if one's actions will bring a harmful response from others, or if one's anger is based on projection rather than what is truly present.

THE ORGANISMIC IMPORTANCE OF ACTION

It is through action that we move what is inside of us—our energy, liveliness, vitality, needs, feelings—across the organism/environment boundary. It is our capacity to act fully and meaningfully in the world through which we create ourselves as powerful, able to cope, expressive of our true nature and the integrity of our boundaries. We express our commitment and courage to be fully in the world when we carry our feelings and needs into the environment: when we express our caring or sadness, protect our integrity, move with grace and exuberance, voice what is unsaid, reach out for comfort or contact. If we feel incapable of or inhibit essential actions, then we create ourselves as weak and wanting or as stuffed with needs we cannot supply and tensions we cannot discharge. An adequate capacity for acting on the environment through motoric behavior and emotional expression is essential if we are to have impact on our environment.

Motoric action is one of the pivotal points in the cycle of organismic functioning, and as such has critical importance to one's expression and experience of self. Two broad areas demonstrate the importance of motoric functioning in the healthy organism in terms of contact with the environment and sense of self. It is in these areas that psychotherapy has the most concern with movement: (1) the manipulation of the environment, and (2) the expression of self.

Manipulation of the Environment

The term "manipulation" is frequently seen, particularly in psychological circles, in light of its pejorative connotation—to control in an unfair or fraudulent way. The Latin root *manipulus* (handful) certainly implies this sense of grasping and filling one's hands. But the first dictionary definition in Webster's (1975) defines manipulation as "to work, operate or treat with or as with the hands, especially with skill" (p. 455). It is our capacity to act on our environment with skill that is so crucial to healthy functioning.

In observing young children, one is impressed (and parents exhausted) by their constant expression and activity: touching, tasting, exploring, experimenting, reacting, noise making. By acting in and on their environment, children meet many important needs: contact with novelty, which results in growth; the ability to affect and influence their environment to their own ends; the seeking of emotional contact and biological sustenance. These things cannot be obtained without movement: reaching, grasping, running, walking, vocalizing.

Although as adults our needs are more complex and we frequently use our capacity to "know" the world from our prior experience without directly acting on it, in truth our ability to manipulate our environment motorically is as essential to us as when we were children. As psychotherapists we diagnostically express our belief in its importance by examining such issues as: Does this person express a healthy curiosity in his world or is he afraid to explore? Is this person active in asking for what she wants from others or does she passively wait to be given to? Does this person move towards others actively to seek contact or away from others? In acting in the world, can this person sustain himself strongly when things are difficult or does he become exhausted and withdraw? Such questions reveal, on the one hand, the capacity to function actively and resourcefully in the world to meet one's needs, and, on the other hand, the tendency to avoid active engagement with the world, resulting in the frustration of many needs.

Usually we look no further into the manipulative capacity of the client, and in doing so ignore the bodily basis of this capacity. If a person is capable of exploration, curiosity, and manipulation, then this will be noticeable not only in verbal behavior, but also in the capacity for physical movement and the flexibility and responsivity of the musculature: arms reach out, hands grasp, legs move. Such people can shift their posture to orient to the objects of interest and contact, and they can physically support and sustain movement in, and engagement with, the environment. Where such capacity is interfered with, it is visible and palpable in the rigid muscles that restrain movement, the stillness of the body, the sunken and withdrawn (disengaged) posture and inability to sustain movement, and the lack of movement towards the surroundings and other people. Without these **physical** capacities, a person's impact on the environment is diluted or absent and he or she feels weak, ineffectual, and fearful.

The Expression of Self

I have noted earlier that the origin of the term "emotion" is from the Latin for "move outwards." The process of inner feeling translating into self-expressive movement is one of bringing a part of oneself into the environment, across the organism/environment boundary. This translation process is not something that must be consciously directed, and, if not inhibited, it occurs quite naturally. Feeling flows into expression automatically, given a reasonably receptive environment—longing becomes reaching for contact, anger becomes voicing loudly, sadness becomes crying. It might be more accurate to say that the feeling and its expression are part of the same whole. It is only our tendency to break things up into stages that fools us into seeing them as separate and distinct "things" as opposed to a continuous process that appears different in different parts of a time sequence. Feeling becomes expression in the environment and the whole is emotion.

In expressing our inner life, we accomplish a number of things. First, we discharge energy and tension built up from mobilization; we discharge our "readiness to act" through action. Second, we communicate to our environment our inner state so that we can elicit a response. Third, by our awareness of our action, we shape and support our sense of self.

Mobilized feeling by its very nature moves toward discharge. It has a "pressure" that must be willfully (although not necessarily consciously) controlled. If I become sad, my feeling will naturally seek outlet or discharge in the form of crying or sobbing, which involves some push and release outward through movement—forceful exhalation, sounds, tears. If I perceive the environment as dangerous or unsupportive of my expression of sadness, I must muscularly bind up this flow and will have to tense. Chronic binding of expression is easily seen in tense, frozen musculature and overbound body structure whose tension *restricts movement*.

Expression of feeling not only discharges tension, but is a contact function. It communicates and connects us to others and to our environment at large. It is only by expressing what I need clearly that others can respond to me. And unless the quality of my expression is congruent with the quality of my inner feeling, I am not likely to get an appropriate response from others. I was presented with this dilemma recently when I attempted tell a close friend about some emotionally significant events in my life. His response was low-key and I felt hurt and unheard, emotionally unsupported by him. When we discussed this, it became apparent that I had presented myself to my friend in such an unemotional way that he had no idea just how important the events were to me. I had so limited the emotion in my facial expression and tone of voice that all he could hear was a brief and unemotional sentence that had little impact on him. Accurate communication of feeling requires not only words, but also facial expression, vocal volume, and gestural and postural emphasis. The limitation or inhibition of self-expression and communication requires that bodily movement be restricted and inhibited.

For example, a woman was unable to convey a consistent message to others when she became angry. She smiled and softened her voice while saying, "I'm angry at what you did," and assumed a pliant and submissive body posture. The nonverbal portion of her message tended to negate the verbal statement. As we experimented with what it was like to support her verbal message with a serious facial expression and stronger stance and voice by pushing against me as she emphasized each word, *"I'm angry at what you did,"* she experienced herself as having more impact and effect in conveying her feelings.

Finally, through expressive movement we not only make contact in the "external" environment, but with aspects of our own self. Most psychological theories tend towards a structural view of the self: the self consists of "things" such as self-image, self-concept, positive and negative representations. These are seen as defined structures that we have acquired through experience and, once acquired, we need do nothing to maintain them. They have object-like status.

The founders of Gestalt therapy (Perls et al., 1951) have emphasized that the self is not a fixed given so much as it is created through contacting. That is, I do not *have* a negative self-image; rather, I *experience* myself negatively through something I *do*—e.g., by critizing myself or behaving in ways inconsistent with my values, or by creating visual images of myself that are unpleasant. Similarly I do not "have" a self-image as powerful so much as I experience my power through my behavior and action, that is, by experiencing the power of my feelings and my impact on the world.

It is only in contact (by experiencing) that we are aware of "self." Action in the world serves as a major source of experience whereby we are given a sense of self-reflection. If your movement is weak and ineffectual, you will feel yourself to be weak and ineffectual and cannot experience a sense of power and strength. If you cannot cry from your diaphragm and belly, your "depths," then you cannot experience the deep core of your "sad self." If you are muscularly constricted and constrained, then you cannot experience your expansiveness and openness. One's self is found and made through experience (contact), of which motor behavior (action) is an essential part.

Requirements of Healthy Action

Healthy action requires a number of conditions for the organism.° The musculature must be capable of flexible movement and have ade-

---

°It is essential that the reader understand that by highlighting what we are capable of in terms of movement and action we are not setting standards to which either therapists or clients should conform. By knowing what is required for full action, we are in a better position to perceive the nature of blocks to full action, and to bring these into the realm of awareness and experiment. This allows us to appreciate the resistance to full action (how inhibition of full action is a part of organismic self-regulation) and choose to try fuller action, or legitimately remain as one is.

quate strength. Whether in the form of gross movement such as running or hitting, or the fine muscular patterns of facial expression, gesture, or manipulation, all actions involve movement and muscular activity. If movement is restrained, structurally limited in range, or painful, or one's muscular strength and capacity are not adequate to the task, then the actions taken will be limited or inadequate. For example, if you want to reach out to others but restrain your arms at your side, you will have difficulty completing your need. If you wish to express your joy in movement but are structurally bound up and muscularly inflexible in your movements, you cannot fully express your internal feeling. Similarly, to communicate your love, anger, or other feelings is difficult if your facial musculature is immobile or if you inhibit your words by choking off your voice.

A second organismic requirement is the exhalation phase of breathing, particularly in more vigorous movements, and the release of energy and tension. Whereas full and complete inhalation seems to mobilize and energize the organism, full and complete exhalation allows for the discharge of energy and gives focus and strength to one's movement. You can explore this yourself through a simple experiment.

> Exhale and hold your breath, then try punching the air with your fist a couple of times. Then try the same punching motion inhaling with each punch. What does this feel like? How powerful or strong were these punches? Now try vigorously exhaling on the outward thrust of each punch. Do you feel any difference in your focus or sense of strength of your punch?

Most people find that punching with the exhalation gives them a greater sense of power and focus, and results in a greater degree of discharge of mobilized energy. Inhibition of your exhalation, particularly when you are charged and mobilized for action, not only weakens the action, but also leaves you pent up with energy, which must be muscularly bound through chronic tension.

RETROFLECTION: ACTING ON THE SELF RATHER THAN IN THE ENVIRONMENT

When action can find completion in the environment, there is little inhibition of movement. A need emerges, action is engaged in to bring the need to fruition, and contact is made in the environment to achieve satisfaction. I require comfort. I seek out those who care about me and ask to be comforted, and we sit together or talk or hold each other. Or I feel intruded on, and speak up, telling the other to back off; I obtain some space and therefore some relief. Of course, not all transactions go so smoothly. Those from whom I seek comfort may not be able to give me that comfort at the time I feel I need it or in quite the way I desire. Those intruding on my territory may feel they have as much right to the space as I. More extended negotiation of needs is required in the real world, and this requires that we have some way of modulating and containing impulses and the movements that express them until the balance of the organism/environment field can be achieved. The need must be contained and the actions restrained to varying degrees. This is an aspect of maturity and a hallmark of civilization—the modulating of raw needs and self-centered behavior through inhibition of movement, impulse, and action.

The world in which we live has stumbling blocks to easy action on the basis of our needs. But often the environment, particularly the human environment, goes beyond this and acts with destructiveness toward the expression of self in the environment. Action, rather than merely being problematic, is negated by others, and even the desire for action becomes punished. If, when I reach out for comfort, I am criticized for being needy or called a leech or always refused, then I learn not just to modulate my action, but to stop the act of reaching out. I may even come to identify with the implication that I am not worthy of receiving comfort from anyone. If, when I try to act out of my want for independence, standing on my own two feet and exploring the world on my own, I am rejected because "Don't you like Mummy any more?" or "How can you do this to me?" then I come to inhibit my movements of exploration and restrain the support of my legs.

The authors of *Gestalt Therapy* note, "It is, rather, in the big, overt movements which we make in our environment that we run our greatest risks of incurring humiliation, suffering embarrassment, or in various ways bringing down punishment on ourselves" (Perls et al., 1951, p. 117). If expressions of anger, sadness, disgust, love, desire, or fear are regularly met with punishment, criticism, or rejection, one learns to stop the bodily expressions of these feelings by inhibiting the movements that form them—the vocalizations in the throat, the expelling of breath in sobbing, the angry flash of the eyes or the sad face, the movements of pushing away, grasping, or striking out, of reaching out or escaping.

Forms of Retroflection

The process by which movement is inhibited or distorted is called *retroflection* in Gestalt therapy. Retroflection means to turn back onto oneself, and is thought of as doing to oneself what was originally directed toward the environment. Many retroflections are the literal reversal onto oneself of the action one wants to do to the environment. Many psychosomatic symptoms fall within this category of literal reversals of movement. When I asked a woman with globulus hystericus (sensations of choking and strangling in her throat) to show me with her hands what her throat felt like, she became suddenly aware of her fury at her mother whose throat she wanted to have in her hands to strangle. This woman quite literally choked herself rather than allowing herself to feel her desire to choke her mother. Lost to her awareness, the act of choking remained in operation as a seemingly isolated physical symptom.

Another form of retroflective behavior occurs when movement towards the environment is physically inhibited, usually just as it begins. Rather than having been actually reversed and performed on oneself, movement is countered by equal muscular force in the opposing muscle groups. An example is the inhibition of hitting. In a reversal the hitting would be directed toward oneself (suicide, self-mutilation, smacking one's knee, pinching oneself). If the movement is stopped in its early phases, it is much less obvious and may appear only as a tension (force and counterforce) of the shoulders and biceps or a clenched but immobile fist. Muscles are mobilized but withheld from movement; there is a balance of tension between the muscles involved in the desired action and muscles antagonistic to the action. Where this kind of retroflection is persistent, there is a characteristic bunching and overdevelopment of muscle groups from the resulting isometric forces, as well as the pain of constantly compressed joints, such as disc problems, bursitis, or soreness of muscles and joints.

Retroflection is also seen in doing to oneself what one wants from the environment, such as holding oneself instead of asking to be held by others or complimenting oneself when what is sought is approval from others. Again the self is substituted for the environment. In this form of retroflection, what is inhibited is the actions involved in reaching out, in asking for help and comfort, in showing the feeling that wants communication and contact. People who cannot move themselves physically into contact with others or reach out with their arms and facial expression or use their voice to ask for support become insular and isolated. They complain of loneliness and frequently project the blame for this on others. Fear of rejection and criticism seems to form the basis for such retroflection. The body structure may be folded in on itself: rounding one's shoulders over the chest, curling the neck forward, crossing the arms and legs as if to hug oneself, or stroking and patting oneself for comfort.

Retroflection and Polarities

Implicit in any retroflection is a split of the person's functioning into opposing forces, in Gestalt terms, a polarity. For example, when a movement or self-expression is stopped, the polarity includes one part that is acting/expressing and another part that is stopping the action/expression—a part that, kinesthetically, says "move" and a part that says "stop." In the reversal of action, the person takes on the roles of both the actor and the environment. An internal polarity is created in which the person is both the subject and object of the action. With the impulse to act comes a fear of the reaction from the environment so that the expression is redirected back onto oneself. As in the stopping of movement, there is also a "yes" and a "no" to the movement or self-expression, and the bind between these opposing forces (the need to act and the fear of the consequences) results in muscular tension and immobility.

Simple relaxation or manual release of tension, say, through exercises or deep massage, is not sufficient to undo retroflective tension. If the conflict between the parts of the self or of the expressive act and the negating environment (now internalized) is not resolved, the tension will recreate itself. We can neither eliminate the impulse to act nor eliminate the need to stop or deflect that impulse simply by releasing the tension or urging the person to let go. This only pushes one or the other further out of awareness, where it continues to function nonetheless.

For example, the musculature of the chest and diaphragm are the foundation of the expression of sadness in the act of crying or sobbing. Tensions in these areas are frequently the retroflection of crying and sadness. To teach a person to relax these muscles by an act of will may certainly release the holding tension, but it renders the muscles flaccid and demobilized so that the crying remains unexpressed. Both the stopping and the expression are controlled. To "break down the armor" of the holding tensions may release crying, often because of the pain involved in such breaking through of tension, but negates whatever is valid and real about the person's need not to cry. What is required is that both parts be made aware and expressed so that the conflict can be worked through, so that what belongs to the environment can be sorted out from what belongs to oneself, and both the "cry" and the "don't cry" become assimilated.

One client blocked her crying in this way, and in the course of our work she recalled how she had to stifle her sobs as a little girl escaping with her parents from the Nazis in Europe. The part of her that said, "No, I must not cry," was an essential part of her ability to survive danger, and it required some devoted work on her part to acquire ownership over both her tears and her need to stop them. It was only by honoring the lifegiving nature of stopping her crying that she could test the safety of the present environment for herself so as to experience in all of her being that she could now afford to let down her guard.

For another client, this same process of stopping his crying was rooted in his constant self-criticism for being unmanly. When he felt sad, he would brace and toughen himself, and, since one must soften the body to allow for the pulsation of crying to occur, he could no longer cry. His self-criticism was clearly connected to his father's disapproval and criticism. Simply to break down his holding against crying might allow him to experience his tears, but would do little to return his self-criticism to the environment. He would be able to cry, but also would be more vulnerable to his harsh internalized father. Additionally we do not want him to get rid of his bodily capacity for toughness, but rather to apply it against his father's criticisms and not against himself. True assimilation requires that the polarities that belong to the environment be returned to the environment. In this case it was necessary to externalize the harsh self-judgment as introjected from his father without losing his capacity for criticalness and discernment or the toughness to defend himself from the criticism. The latter are essential contact functions and belong to him and not the environment.

Clients rarely directly express these polarities— "One part of me wants to cry (or yell/reach out/strike back) but another part won't allow it." The typical complaint is, "I want to (express or act in some way) and can't," with no ownership or awareness of the "can't" part of the process. There is often even less differentiation— "I feel stuck," or "My wife just left me and I can't understand why I feel so tense"—or there are isolated somatic symptoms, such as, "I feel so tense in my stomach (shoulders/ neck/etc.)."

Therapeutic practice requires that we be able to locate the retroflec-tions as they exist, bring them into awareness, develop ownership over the polarities and expressive movements intrinsic to them, and find a new creative adjustment between self and environment and with one's own organismic functioning.

Body Structure as Retroflection

In our normal functioning in the world, all of us utilize retroflection, more or less by choice, to manage and modulate our contact with others. I may decide not to say everything on my mind, and this will be present in that moment as a tightening of my lips and throat. I may want to reach out and touch a friend to reassure him, but hold back my arm because the setting may not seem appropriate or he may not be receptive to such support in this particular moment. In the moment-to-moment regulation of action and contact, Gestalt therapy sees retroflection as functional and necessary for self-regulation.

It is when we retroflect our actions chronically, pervasively, and without awareness that we distort our functioning and misshape our bodily life. If I characteristically do not say what is "on my mind," or more accurately, what comes to my lips (since "mind" is not understood as separate from the body process in Gestalt therapy), then the counter tensions with which I prevent my mouth and throat from uttering the words as they arise become structured into my body. I become literally tight-lipped and constricted in my throat. If I constantly inhibit my urges to reach out, then I become structurally bound up in my shoulders in order to counter any impulse I have to reach out to others.

The force/counterforce of retroflection becomes static and structural if the retroflection is habitual because the conflict between acting and not acting remains chronically unresolved and unaware. A pattern of retroflected tensions develops and is visible in: muscular development, because the chronic isometric tension of agonist and antagonist (opposing muscle groups) builds up the muscles; in postural distribution, as the countering tensions pull body parts out of alignment or movement is only partially expressed; and even in the distribution of body fat, as poor circulation and energy flow through chronically bound-up areas become layered with fat, just as a slow section of a river collects sediment.

In retroflection each postural disturbance, nexus of muscular tension, or immobilized body area is frozen movement. It is (it does not merely represent) a movement towards contact and the countering of that movement. In this way the polarities of act/stop, of yes/no, of move/stay are always present in the ongoing body process and the unfinished situation is always alive. By paying attention to such body structures, we can bring the polarities into present awareness and discover, rather than interpret, the movements that are being countered; we can then work through the conflicts between parts of the self (or self and environment) that maintain the organism in partial and incomplete expression.

EXPLORING RETROFLECTION IN BODY PROCESS

There are a number of ways to explore and elucidate retroflections and to gain entry into a unit of work in the domain of action. First and foremost, is the ability of the practitioner to see and locate variations in body structure and the underlying muscular tensions and postural displacements. This is the basis on which work with body process rests. What you can't "see," (do not have a framework and set of standards for registering perceptually), you cannot work with. Chapter 4 on body structure introduces this notion, but the reader should understand that work in this area requires more extensive training and an understanding of biomechanical functioning than can be obtained through this text.

When such variations in structure are identified, the next step is to develop awareness of their presence and ownership of their nature. If I notice that my client sits with her chest collapsed and her shoulders curled forward, my identification of this does not necessarily mean that she is aware of her posture or that she experiences it as something she does. In addition, she might have no sense of how this posturing has significance for her life and way of being or for her symptoms. The first step is to develop her sensory grounding in how she sits, to locate what is experienced as "I" and what as "it," and to connect what she is doing physically to her experience of herself and the environment.

This work has already been detailed in Chapters 7 and 8, on sensation and figure formation, and I mention it here to highlight the importance of the cycle as a whole for therapeutic work in any of the specific phases. Too many body-oriented therapists move too quickly to act on and change what they see. The result is that they work assiduously on what they, as therapists, see in a client's body process but which the client does not own or with which the client has no direct experience. Such work can rarely be assimilated by the client because the awareness is *not owned*. Work with sensation and figure formation forms the basis for experiment with movement and structure, and will be constantly returned to throughout any unit of work.

Let me continue with the above example. The client has now become conscious of how she is sitting, and how this affects her breathing and sense of space inside; she has located some of the tensions by which she holds herself curled forward and collapsed, and has some sense of how she experiences me as she sits with me in this way. We have experimented with attention, breathing, and touch to enliven her sensation—perhaps I have used my hands to gently exaggerate and emphasize the posture so she can feel herself more clearly. I have suggested some "I" statements to explore the aspects of her structure she identifies as her own and those she experiences as alienated. She has stated, "I am pressing in on myself . . . I am squeezed in my chest . . . I am curled forward."

Understanding that retroflection and the resulting body structure are a process of polarities, I become interested in differentiating the parts: Who is pressing in and who is being pressed on? Who is squeezing and who is being squeezed? Who is curling forward and in relation to what? I ask these questions not to determine the answers for the client, but to frame for myself the direction of our experimenting together. How can we emphasize and differentiate each part of the polarity in her behavior and awareness?

One experiment is for the therapist to act as the holding tension so that the client can clearly experience the other side. I might use my hands to press, gently but firmly, on her chest or to curl her shoulders forward and work with her on what it is like to be the pressed-on polarity. Or I might have her do this to me, playing out the side that presses down and making this polarity clearer. Another possibility would be to have her resist my curling her forward so that we can find the movement or expression that is being stopped by the holding-back tensions. As each polarity becomes physically expressed, we also begin to give them voice and so initiate a dialogue between the split-off parts.

An example of the use of such experiments took place during a meeting with a colleague with whom I work. I was complaining of lower back pain and he offered to work with me on identifying it more clearly. He asked me to describe the tension as I experienced it. I said, "It feels like a pinching tension, pinching my bones together." We spent some time locating exactly where I experienced the pinching and what was being pinched muscularly. My colleague then suggested that he act as the pinching, and with my assent, he firmly grasped my back in this area. I immediately wanted to lean forward against his "holding me back," and I expressed this physically by struggling against his pinching me. My statements went something like, "I'm tired of you holding me back. Let me go. I've got to move forward and you won't let me." The more firmly I tried to move forward, the more he pinched me, and the angrier I became at being held back.

At this point he suggested I switch and act as the pincher. Grasping him, I began to identify with what it is like to hold him back, to prevent him from moving forward. Putting this into words as well as actions, I said, "I won't let you go forward, I'm going to stop you," which gradually became, "I can't let you go forward, it's too risky. You'll get into trouble if I don't stop you." As we continued to play out these polarities and discuss them, the issue became clearer to me. I was at that time struggling with writing the earlier chapters on the use of touch in therapy. I felt stuck and unable to move forward with this chapter, and the parallel of the writing process with this emerging polarity became obvious to me. I felt it was essential to the integrity of my work to write frankly about all aspects of working with body process, yet I work in a professionally conservative town and was concerned that I would be seen as an oddball and a "fringe type."

In the course of the dialogue, he worked with me to sort out what was realistic concern from what was self-criticism and self-doubt. I recognized that, while it is true that the professional community was conservative, most of my perception of this was in the limits I place on myself and tactics with which I scare myself (i.e., projections), rather than an accurate description of what would happen if I were "too different." He then asked me, "How is it that you'd pinch those critical professionals if you could?" Laughing, I declared, shaking my fists, "I'm not going to restrict myself to meet your damned narrow definitions of what is legitimate. I know my truth and I won't be pressed into a box trying to act as I don't believe." My colleague and I knew that I was speaking both to my imagined professional critics and to my own self-critic, finally pinching back instead of pinching myself.

I said to my colleague, "I don't believe I need to scare myself any longer. I can cope with being seen as different and unusual and with seeing myself this way as well." My back tension eased considerably from this work, although I would discover myself tensing again whenever I faced a point in my writing that aroused my old fears of being different. These occasions required me to stop and attend to how I was becoming self-critical and scared of being honest about my work, to examine what was realistic about that fear, and to mobilize some of the aggression directed towards myself back to the environment.

This work illustrates some of the possible components in developing work with retroflection. We started with a current awareness (back pain) and developed a more differentiated sensation (pinching). Ownership for each side came through taking on different parts of the resistance, with the therapist acting as if he were the other side. The polarity became apparent and the work began to sort out my introjected and projected criticalness from my caution and self-integrity. Finally, the aggression that had been turned on myself could be redirected towards the environment.

The easy description of this work, as in any condensed case description, conceals the amount of background and preparation that went into it. I have had much experience in attending to my body process and verbalizing my polarities. I am also very familiar with my self-criticalness and had already worked through much about this life theme in prior therapy. With many clients, working simply to experience each side physically and verbally may be sufficient. Expression cannot outpace differentiation, and until each part is clear, as well as what separates them into parts, they cannot be integrated through contact into the resolved whole.

This is illustrated by a client who experienced tension in his chest muscles. We had been exploring this tension as "armoring and protecting." I asked him if he would allow me to use my hand to act as protection for him so that he could experience what it was like not to have to work so hard to protect himself. Sitting at his side, I placed my hand on his chest at the nexus of the tension, and as he felt the protection of my hand, he began to soften and release some of this tension. Eventually his softening brought on deep sobs, and he grasped my hand to his body to make sure I would not leave him unprotected. It was more than enough for him to assimilate the experience of allowing himself to be protected by another person, and to experience the deep sadness in him that moved to be released. This was a sufficient unit of work; additional development of polarities would occur in future therapy as he came to experience more clearly the parts involved and his relationship to others.

WORKING WITH EXPRESSIVE MOVEMENT

The use of movements that are emotionally expressive has been frequently associated with body-oriented therapies. Hitting a cushion and other forms of physical acting out have even become stereotypes of Gestalt therapy and, indeed, unsophisticated and poorly trained therapists frequently take the use of therapeutic expression of emotion out of context and claim they are practicing "Gestalt." Yet expressive movement and vocalization can be extraordinarily useful in therapy: they have the ability to expand and recover the full range of organismic functioning and to reverse the direction of retroflective muscular effort from the self back onto the environment. To use expressive movement accurately, the therapist must have an idea of the therapeutic context within which such movement is used and the aims toward which it is directed.

Lowen and Lowen (1977) give an excellent compendium of expressive physical exercises and movements in their manual of bioenergetic exercises. These include hitting or kicking a pad, vocalizing emotionally laden phrases or sounds, imitating movements involved in a temper tantrum, hitting a pad with an object such as a tennis racket, twisting and "strangling" a towel, rhythmically and sexually or aggressively moving the pelvis, reaching out with the lips and arms, and utilizing various stretches and positions to induce muscular vibration. In accordance with the aims of a Reichian approach, these movements are to break down the constricting body armor that prevents full expression; developmental conflicts can then be worked through and the spontaneous and vibrant natural character [called the "genital character" by Reich (1945/1972),] can be restored. In the bioenergetics approach, these movements are practiced as deliberate exercises at first, with the idea that as one lets go with the movement, one will spontaneously evoke or stimulate the release of repressed (that is, blocked by muscular tension) feelings.

Although Gestalt body-oriented therapists may use similar expressive movements in the course of therapy, they are seen in a slightly different context and philosophy, which, in turn, modify how they are applied. One difference has already been described as that of the understanding of resistance—in this case the resistance to expression through retroflection. Because of our view of resistance, we prefer not to use movements to break down tension so much as to explore both sides of the polarity, so that energy directed towards the self can eventually be redirected towards the environment.

In the Gestalt approach, movement is seen as part of a whole cycle of organismic functioning and does not occur separate from sensation, awareness, and contact. That is, expression occurs from organismic need and is directed towards contact with the environment or one's self. Our concern is not with the movement *per se*, but with its relation to overall organismic functioning: Where does it come from in one's awareness and experience? What is the nature of the movement itself and how is it prevented? What object is it directed towards?

Because of our emphasis on experience in the present, we tend to develop expressive movement out of what occurs in the here and now— for example, from an apparent theme of work or from the present experience of body process or body structure. There is much less emphasis on doing an expressive movement to evoke or stimulate a theme for work because this is usually more rooted in the therapist's awareness of the client than in the client's experience of himself or herself. This brings us to the concern in Gestalt therapy with ownership and assimilation. Movement that is "given" by the therapist, or where the emphasis is on doing it fully or correctly, frequently results in imitation, and often in little ownership of the expression. The client does not experience the feeling as originating from the self and the movement remains an imitative exercise.

Because of these concerns, the use of expressive movement in a Gestalt approach to body process uses the form of *experiment* rather than exercise. Movements evolve out of what is occurring in the here and now and so may vary in form depending on the experience from which they evolve. The emphasis is not on doing the movement as fully as possible, but rather on doing it fully enough for the movement to be experienced clearly and ownership to be acquired. The emphasis is not on making something happen, but on discovering what *does* happen, and so takes into account the critical phenomenon of ownership, or its absence, and resistance.

Expressive movement in therapy can be developed from a number of starting points and along many different avenues. That the starting point can be either body-oriented or purely verbal well illustrates the continuity possible in therapeutic work and the holistic view of human functioning.

Movement and Expression from Theme

One starting point for developing expressive movement is the theme of a therapy session as it is verbalized by the client or therapist. For example, a client may be discussing how he can't seem to speak up with his wife and tell her what he feels. As a Gestalt therapist, I am most interested in how (as opposed to why) his speaking up is interfered with, and as a body-oriented therapist, I am particularly interested in the physical process of his literally voicing what he feels. So I might ask him if he would pick two or three of the important feelings he wishes to convey to his wife and voice these to me in a series of statements while I pay attention to the quality of his expression.

As he experiments with statements such as, "I feel very hurt when you snap at me," and "I love you very much and I don't know how to tell you that sometimes," I notice how he constricts his throat and tightens his diaphragm as he speaks, diminishing his voice. I point this out to him and demonstrate, through touch, the areas he constricts. I then ask him to try the experiment again, paying attention to what these tensions feel like. He comments, "It seems that I'm trying to cut down the volume of my voice by tightening these muscles." I ask him to emphasize that process more by following each statement of feeling with "but I must keep quiet" while he tightens further in his throat and diaphragm.

He smiles at this notion, and then repeats the statements over and over with my encouragement. Eventually he virtually shouts his feeling statement, while following it with a hushed and constricted "but I must keep quiet." I support both the naturally evolving release of his voice and the alternating constriction of his voice by using my hands as emphasis and encouraging appropriate breathing with each mode. As the experiment winds down, we discuss and sort through the old beliefs (introjects) he has acquired that mandate his silence about his feelings: One must keep one's feelings to oneself because no one wants to hear them. There is no justification for "burdening" another with your own concerns. You'll just be rejected if you reveal what you feel.

The physical underpinnings for a theme that was arrived at through verbal description were explored and extended in the form of an experiment. We elucidated the resistance to voicing physically and, in this particular piece of work, even arrived at some spontaneous release of constriction by giving room to both the resistance and the expression. Other verbalized themes could be treated the same way.

For example, a client complains of having difficulty withstanding the barrage of questions and criticisms tossed at her by her family whenever she visits home. Interested again in how she physically organizes herself to cope with such a barrage, we experiment with my tossing pillows at her "as if they are comments from your family," and we explore various approaches to coping with such a barrage. Does she feel better when she bats them back at me? Would she rather dodge them, step on them, or kick them? Which responses work for her and which do not? By grounding the possible choices in her physical process, she now has an immediately apprehendable physical "sense" of what works and what does not in this situation. It is a simple matter to translate her physical responses to the tossed pillows into more specific verbal or nonverbal responses to her family's pressures, although perhaps not so simple for her to use them with her family.

Expression and Movement from Metaphor

Similar to developing movement from theme, such work can also be developed from a metaphor or figure of speech. Many figures of speech have an explicit body orientation—"to stand on one's own two feet" or "to have backbone"—and these can be readily expanded into physical expressions. We can explore the physical dimensions of standing on one's own two feet: how you feel strong and how you feel weak when standing, how your self-support is undermined (the resistance), what you have to do to mobilize to withstand outside pressures or burdens (by my acting as the outside force through pushing or loading you down).

The same is true for metaphors that arise during therapy. One woman complained of her promiscuity, describing herself as "a mattress." I wanted to enliven her deadpan expression of this very important issue in her life and so suggested that she lie on the floor "like a mattress" while I placed pillows symbolizing men on top of her one by one. As the experiment progressed, her passivity and helplessness changed to resentment, and then fury, as each pillow was added to the pile. By acting out the metaphor in physical (and exaggerated) terms, she came to feel her passive and disowned resentment to being a mattress for men. She began by bragging about her exploits while complaining about her unhappiness; now she had a definite physical experience of the part of her that abhorred being in such a position.

Expression and Movement from Micro-Actions

One of the classic Gestalt means of attending to retroflection and developing movement work to explore and undo the retroflection has been through attention to what I will call *micro-actions,* that is, small, self-directed movements that occur in the course of normal conversation and verbal therapeutic work. These micro-actions include tapping or swinging the foot, touching, stroking or holding into body areas, and small shifts in posture and sitting position.

Such experiments exaggerate these movements so as to make their intent more apparent, and then to find some way to express this towards the environment so as to reverse the course of the retroflection. For example, a client begins to move his foot as we discuss a problem at home. Bringing this to his attention, I ask him to exaggerate the movement. He does this until his foot movement becomes a kicking motion. We explore what it is like to kick a bolster while he verbalizes about his dilemma at home. As he does so, the contrast becomes apparent to him between the flatness of his voice and upper body energy as he speaks and the vigorous and aggressive action of his lower body in kicking. I ask him to express his concern about home to me from each of these parts of himself alternately (instead of both at once), first from the flat and energyless style, and then the same statements while he vigorously kicks the bolster. After trying out a number of statements in this way, the contrast between his flat and unemotional complaining and his firm and aggressive demands as he kicks is quite marked. He notes that his flat style is how he usually complains to his wife, despite the fact that he feels tense and angry with her, as with the feeling evoked when he kicks the bolster. We continue the work, examining his fears of, and beliefs about, bringing his concerns to his wife in a more active and impactful way.

Development of Expressive Work from Body Structure

The previous three avenues along which to develop expressive or movement-oriented work involved some emphasis on verbalization. Formulating ways of representing a theme or metaphor in physical terms are two of the most obvious departure points for most therapists. The third departure point, that of attending to the ongoing micro-actions, is the first departure point that blends what the person is *doing* with what the person is *saying,* and is common to the traditional practice of Gestalt therapy. The expressive movement evolves directly out of present body process and is exaggerated as opposed to prescribed (as with rote exercises).

The fourth starting point for developing expressive movement is from the existing body structure as opposed to an ongoing movement, i.e., from the particular way in which the person has shaped his or her posture, breathing, muscular development, body armor (braced or rigid areas), and so on. Much about the body which seems static and structural is, when converted into process, really inhibited movement. By attending to the pattern of body structure, this movement can be discovered and then recovered for expressive functioning.

For example, I had been working with a man on developing his awareness of the way he was structured to habitually "narrow" himself. Working from a standing position, we noted how he held his arms close to his sides, stiffening the sides of his rib cage so that his breathing did not expand sideways, raising his shoulders up, and otherwise drawing himself into a narrow space. He posturally appeared as if he were squeezing himself between confines on either side which provided him no room to expand himself. Through our work he had come to experience how little room he allowed himself to take up.

We first developed his awareness of his body structure as it existed, through exaggeration, I-statements, and through my acting as the resistance for him by using my hands to narrow and restrict him further. We then began to explore how he could widen himself—the opposite polarity. I worked with him to discover how to breathe into the sides of his rib cage and find out what expanding himself in this direction could be like. I used deep tissue work to give more range to the constricted musculature by which he pinned his arms to his sides and raised his shoulders towards his ears.

On one occasion I asked him to go back to exaggerating his narrow structure, to hold it for a moment, and then to gradually move into a more expansive stance. Starting in his constricted posture, with his arms pinned to his sides, he began to inhale, allowing his torso and rib cage to expand. As he exhaled, his arms gradually rose in front of him and then opened and moved out to each side. I asked him to repeat this sequence—drawing himself up into a narrow stance while inhaling, and then pushing outwards while exhaling—and to add more of his body to each movement.

When I asked him to tell me his experience of this movement sequence he described it as "recoiling and then pushing away." I then asked him to think about what he had had to recoil from as a little boy. In repeating the movement he recalled how he had witnessed his father's drunken rages against his mother. Caught between his desire to protect her and his fear of being himself beaten by his crazed father, he had often drawn himself into a corner of the room behind some furniture. There he would remain, trying to hide while witnessing the ensuing violence.

While his recoiling and fear had become part of his narrow body structure and habitual fearful approach to life, what had never been expressed was his physical impulse to protect his mother and push his father away from her. I worked with him to bring this into full expression, having him push me away and make the statements "as if to your father" that he had wanted to say as a child but could not because of the danger of acting. This movement work initiated a process of re-owning his capacity to act strongly in the world, being able to risk expanding himself and "standing out," and putting him in a position where he could truly mourn his helplessness as a child.

This work, starting from his existing stance in the world, moved from finding the polarity or "counter stance" to his confining body structure to evolving the movement between the positions. This movement could then be readily identified as two kinds of active expressions—one of recoiling and the other of pushing back—and the previously unexpressed impulse could finally be expressed in the environment and worked through.

Development of Expressive Work from Spontaneous Body Process

The fifth point of departure for developing expressive movement is entirely nonverbal in origin, and usually only occurs within the context of ongoing physical intervention, such as work with touch, breathing, muscular release, and certain exercises. During the course of such body work, spontaneous changes often take place in body structure or muscular organization, which, with proper support and encouragement through the therapist's verbal and nonverbal communications, can be developed into expressive movements or emotional release.

Such work is illustrated by a session during which I was using touch to encourage a client to find how to release his hyperinflated chest. We had been working with his breathing using guided awareness and touch, then began to focus on his difficulty with dropping his chest as he exhaled. Instead of exploring the process of resistance to letting down his chest, which we had done at other times in our work, we simply continued to attend to his breathing. As he exhaled I gently pushed on his chest so that he could experience how much more drop was possible in his chest. Eventually I noticed a spontaneous spasmodic movement taking place as he exhaled, which I simply emphasized by imitating it with my hands as I pressed with his exhalation. As we continued, tensions began to appear in his throat and face, which I addressed with soft, feather-like touches to encourage him to let go. As tension appeared in his belly muscles, I placed my other hand on his belly to make supportive contact and he began spontaneously to cry. By my rocking his body along with his crying, the cries enlarged and his previously rigid chest began to join with the natural expulsive movements of crying on his exhalation.

Gradually his crying subsided, and it was only then that we spoke of what had occurred. By finding ways to encourage the emerging body process during the course of body-focused work, this man was able to allow his body structure to "give," and the complementary action the structure was protecting emerged. This was possible in part because of the extensive support he received through my touch, as well as from the groundwork supplied by our earlier therapeutic explorations. His awareness was of needing no longer to keep his tears hidden from view, and of discovering he could follow the direction encouraged by my touch and let his chest drop into his emerging feeling of sadness.

An example on the other end of the emotional continuum took place while I was working with a client to release tense back muscles. As we worked, with her lying on her stomach on a pad, I noticed her legs were beginning to tense with each movement of her back muscles. I encouraged her to attend to this and allow the movement to expand. Eventually this subtle tension developed into kicking motion and I encouraged her to kick into the pad and vocalize while I continued to work with the tension of her back muscles. As she mobilized her pelvis and back to participate in this action of kicking, her back muscles began to release and a fluid and powerful expression of aggression emerged. After the movement reached a peak, I asked her to wind down, and we began to explore what it was like for her to do this movement. She reported that as she expanded the movement, she began to experience that she was tired of holding back (note the play on words—holding back and holding her back tightly), and her kicking became getting free of her restrictions—"kicking loose." We continued this work, looking at the things in her life she wanted to "kick loose from" and what required her to hold herself back.

Body techniques of deep breathing and hyperventilation or stress on muscle groups will often cause similar spontaneous muscular vibrations and spasmodic movements (Reich, 1942), which can be similarly encouraged into emotional expression. But my experience with such techniques, both as a practitioner and a participant, is that the release often takes the client by surprise and is experienced as something that "happened to me," and not as *something of one's own* that is allowed to emerge. Such experiences may remain as interesting and even frightening carthartic events, but they stand apart from oneself and produce little change in perception or behavior. While the neurotic client will simply isolate such an event or become anxious, those clients who are more seriously disturbed or have more tenuous ego strength may become flooded by such interventions, and even decompensate if too much emotion emerges at once.

GENERAL COMMENTS

It should be apparent from the work described in this chapter that work with expressive movement and undoing retroflected action can result in the release and expression of powerful emotions and vigorous and often aggressive behaviors. This requires that the therapist be competent in managing and guiding such work, and not be anxious about the presence of strong feeling. This is not work for therapeutic novices, despite the fact that novice therapists frequently are attracted to such expressive work because they see it as more significant and "real" than the basic work of awareness. Expert training and supervision are essential for proper use of such therapeutic technique, and one's own therapy is mandatory to develop the capacity to tolerate strong feelings.

Catharsis is not significant in and of itself, even though it is often dramatic. Work with developing expressive movement requires a base of awareness, relationship to the therapist, and a well-managed therapeutic context to be useful. The emotional expression or expressive actions that occur in the therapy room need to be linked to their *appro-*

priate counterparts in the client's current situation to be applied in the less dramatic form healthy daily living requires. The fact that kicking is used to develop contact with one's physical capacity for assertion does not imply, of course, that such action is used when standing up to one's boss! It is the contact with one's feeling of power that results from such physical expression and the effect of this on one's self-perception that are important. This contact must find a relevant and appropriate form in situations outside the therapy room.

Chapter 11

Contact, Final Contact and Body Process

> ... the organism persists by assimilating the novel, by change and growth ... Primarily, contact is the awareness of, and behavior toward, the assimilable novelty; and the rejection of the unassimilable novelty (Perls et al., 1951, p. 230).

The word "contact" is frequently spoken in almost mystical terms. When we "make contact" with one another, we often refer to an intangible sense of connection, presence, or awareness of the other person in a way that is close and personal. A situation of "high contact" has a sense of immediacy and presence and charge, whether it is warm and positive in nature, such as having a heart-to-heart talk, or unsettling and difficult, such as participating in an argument.

In Gestalt therapy we refer to contact as that which occurs "at the boundary between organism and environment," at the meeting of self and other. The opening quotation refers to contact as the assimilation of novelty by which growth and change take place. When we are "in contact," we are experiencing that meeting at the boundary that separates and defines our self and that of the other (or the object) we are contacting.

If action is the extension of our organismic self into the environment, then the stage of contact is the meeting of one's self with the other: "The point at which one experiences the 'me' in relation to that which is not 'me' and through this contact, both are more clearly experienced

... not only a sense of one's self, but also the sense of whatever impinges at this boundary, whatever looms at the contact boundary and even merges into it" (Polster & Polster, 1973, pp. 102–103).

This definition of boundary implies that to have contact is not merely to meet at the boundary, to brush up against it, but that it involves some kind of exchange. In contact we take something across our self boundary and render it into some form that is usable for our growth. We not only bring the environment up close, but into our self, where we can use it for our growth. Without taking anything in, we meet but are not nourished. To open our individual boundary to the other and come more in touch with the environment, the field in which we are embedded, requires that we meet the environment, the object we are contacting, in an active and selective way.

Perls' seminal work on Gestalt therapy (1947/1969) took his prototype for the contact process from the infant's intake of food. He noted that it was an infant's development of teeth that altered the process of growth from that of a passive being who must introject (swallow whole) what is given to it, to that of an active being who can determine what is taken in. Initially the infant is confined to the automatic intake of what is presented and involuntary regurgitation of what is organismically unsatisfying. With teeth the infant can chew, spit, and be selective about what is taken in.°

These descriptions, as abstractions and generalities about contact, give us the notion that contact is per se an obscure and intangible process. Contact indeed has its intangible aspect, that is, the experience itself is in many ways beyond verbal description. But there is another aspect to the process of contact that is grounded in very tangible and physical functioning: the bodily basis of contact. For example, the boundary between myself and others consists not only of the characteristics and beliefs about myself that define me as distinct and different from others [an "I boundary" as Polster and Polster (1973) refer to it], but also has bodily form—my skin, the space I maintain around me, the way I define my presence through posture and gesture. Similarly the basis of discrimination between "assimilable" or "unassimilable" novelty (how we select or reject what we are to take in across our boundary) is not merely a process of mental review, but is also rooted in bodily *feel* of the contact as it occurs. In addition, much of our contact with the environ-

---

°However, even Perls greatly underestimated the age at which some form of selectivity at the boundary occurs. Even before the development of teeth, infants demonstrate such boundary processes as turning their heads away and the selective use of attention such as visual scanning. Later the development of the child's motor capacity in walking adds increased autonomy and aggressiveness to the developing child's management of contact.

ment is in and of itself physical in nature. For example, touch contact involves the boundary surface of our skin and muscles, eye contact involves the use of our visual apparatus, and much of our interpersonal contact involves the negotiation of physical space through gesture and movement. In this chapter I will focus on the bodily nature of our self boundary in contact and on the physical basis of exchange at the boundary.

BODY AS BOUNDARY

Before continuing I would like to call your attention to your own boundary process.

> Spend a minute or two shuttling your attention between being aware of yourself and being aware of your environment. Do this slowly, first attending to yourself for a bit, then shifting to attend to that which is "outside" your self.

What defines the difference between your self and your environment? Where is the line, the separation point, where you meet other? You might experience this separation point as where your skin and the air meet. Or you might experience "your" space as extending beyond your tangible boundary into some space surrounding you. Is this defined by how you are sitting or "containing" that space posturally? For example, I am sitting cross-legged and I experience the space enclosed by my pelvis and crossed legs as "within" my boundary. Or you might not experience any clear differentiation between inside and outside, your self and your environment. (This is also, of course, a statement about your present bounding—that you don't experience a defined boundary.)

> Now, to experiment a bit further, try two different bodily attitudes so that you can examine how changes in your physical bounding of yourself affect your contact with your environment. First try relaxing and softening your body as much as you can—soften your gaze and facial muscles, allow your shoulders and breathing to relax, soften the whole "surface" of your body as much as possible, and then attend to your environment again. What is your contact like? Now intentionally firm up your muscles and the surface of your body. What is different about this contact?

Whatever specific thing you noticed, it is likely that there was some important difference in the quality of your experience of contact from one bodily attitude to the other. Your sense of relationship and receptivity was probably quite different in quality from one mode to the other.

These experiments are intended to heighten your awareness of the relationship of your bodily being to your self boundary and how this affects the quality and nature of your contact with your environment. Changes in your bodily "stance" alter how you relate to others, what you take in and how you take it in. Similarly how you organize yourself physically both affects and reflects how you are related to your environment. Let us examine more specifically the components and nature of body boundaries.

The authors of *Gestalt Therapy* describe four critical boundary functions (Perls et al., 1951):

> . . . an organism lives in its environment by maintaining its difference and, more importantly, by assimilating the environment to its difference; and it is at the boundary, that dangers are rejected, obstacles are overcome, and the assimilable is selected and appropriated (p. 230)

These functions—(1) the maintenance of difference, (2) the rejection of danger, (3) coping with obstacles, and (4) the selection and appropriation of assimilable novelty—are rooted in our body process. How we maintain, modulate, select, and prevent contact at the boundary are evident in the way we create and express our body-self.

The Body as a Boundary Layer

In a purely objective sense, we would have to define the skin surface as the most obvious material body boundary. Our skin literally contains the "me" as separate and distinct from "other." But our notion of boundaries is not based on a concern with material structures per se so much as with boundaries as an ongoing process of relationship—as modulated and changed over time—and as the place where contact is experienced. You will recall that the opening quotation described contact as "the awareness of, and behavior toward" the novel. In this sense to define the body boundary as equivalent to the skin is overly simplistic. We cannot really use our skin in an aware way to modulate contact (i.e., it cannot "behave"), and we experience contact at other-than-skin places. (See Figure 11-1.)

Proximal boundary space: Space around body within range of touch, intimate distance.

Boundary layer: Superficial musculature, skin, body openings.

Organism

Distal boundary space: Space around body outside range of touch, social distance.

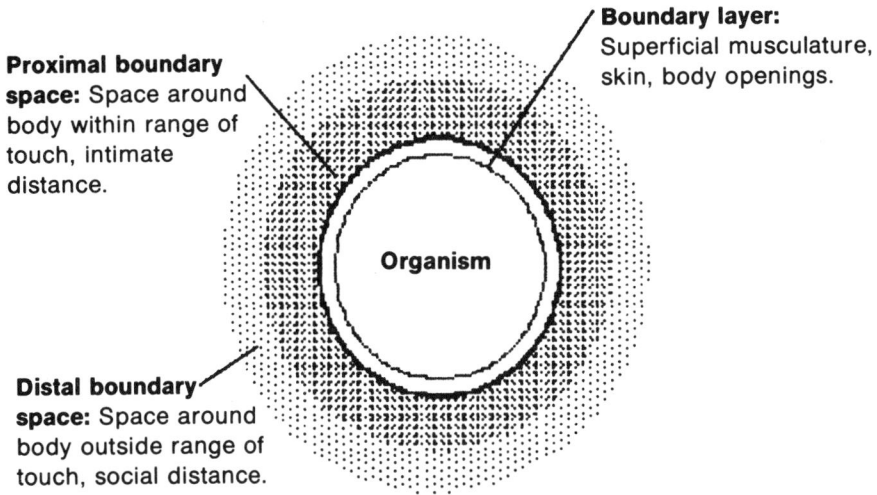

Figure 11-1. Schematic of boundary layer and space. The density and thickness of the boundary layer and space vary according to the needs of the given contact.

Vis-à-vis contact with the surrounding environment field, it is our underlying superficial musculature in conjunction with the skin surface that forms our essential body boundary layer.[°] It is our capacity to harden and soften this muscular/skin layer—in a real sense, to open and close ourselves to contact—that provides the physical process by which we can moderate what we take in from the environment and alter our experience of differentiation from the environment. The previous experiment illustrates the relevance of one's muscular state to the quality and nature of contact.

Contraction of superficial muscles serves to give greater definition to one's sense of boundary by bringing the body surface layer into high relief, thus making one's sense of self firmer and more definite. This is illustrated in the extreme by the "macho" body stance, which typically involves a hypererect posture and a rigid and unyielding body surface, both due to a high degree of muscular tension. Superficial muscular contraction also serves to reduce the permeability of oneself to the environ-

---

[°]I will speak here mostly of contact with the environment as distinct from the process of contact with alienated parts of oneself which I have discussed in previous chapters, particularly in the chapters on sensation and figure formation.

ment so that less comes in, and acts as a kind of filter or modulator for contact. This can be easily illustrated by having someone touch you—say, on your shoulder—while you tense and brace your muscles, then while you let those muscles soften and relax. In the former you will probably experience the touch as shallow, as if on top of your skin, and in the latter you will probably feel the touch to be entering more deeply. By regulating your body boundary layer, you change the permeability of yourself to contact, and thus the assimilation of the novel experience. In the first case, you maintain the difference between self and other and only minimally assimilate it to your self; in the second you reduce your sense of differentiation and allow the other to enter into your boundary, where it can be assimilated for growth and nourishment.

The relaxation and softening of the superficial muscular layer render one's boundary more permeable to contact and intake, and allow a momentary blending of self and other. It is an alteration in the figure of experience: instead of the figure of self against the background of the other, the other is experienced as figural and one's self as background. A softer body boundary is more vulnerable and receptive to the environment because of this permeability, while also less able to select and reject the environment.

This notion of muscular contraction/relaxation as modulating contact is true not only for the body surface in general, but also for two of the major contact apertures—the mouth and the eyes. If you make a suspicious face, you will notice a narrowing and hardening of the muscles around your eyes and mouth, as if to restrict the possibility of anything coming in which is not carefully considered. All of the common facial expressions that imply the restriction or rejection of others involve some hardening of the body boundary and closing off of the contact apertures: the tight and downturned mouth of a sour or bitter expression, the narrowed eyes and hardened face of a guarded expression, the tightly clamped jaw and tensed brow of an angry expression. On the opposite side, we have the gullible slack jaw, the wide-eyed innocent, the relaxed lips and jaws of an open expression, all of which imply that whatever is presented by the environment is received and taken in.

Even the hearing apertures can be indirectly restricted by boundary layer modulation. Although we cannot literally "close" our ears, little children know well that in order not to hear the teacher who is berating the, they can harden their body boundary and avoid eye contact, frequently enabling them to not listen to a word that is said. Adults acknowledge this auditory boundary when they demand, "You look at me when I talk to you," knowing that they do not feel heard when the child is looking away.

The Body and Boundary Space

It would be a vast oversimplification of the contact experience to suggest that the self boundary begins and ends at the skin/muscle surface. This would ignore the large body of knowledge from ethologists and social psychologists on the importance of personal space, interpersonal distance, and territory. Our management and maintenance of the personal space that extends beyond and surrounds our body imply that our self boundaries may often include a part of the environmental field. For example, a stranger may sit down next to you and, without actually touching you, nonetheless feel too close for comfort. Despite the fact that the stranger was not intruding on your body boundary in any tangible way, his or her presence within a certain definite distance seemed to intrude on your person.

This *boundary space,* our sensitivity to interpersonal distance, is highly related to a fundamental need to protect and maintain the integrity of our self boundaries. It is the capacity to create and adjust this boundary space that (1) allows us to regulate the pace and intensity of novel contact by regulating our actual distance from others, and (2) helps us to reduce the actual impingement of contact on our body boundary layer to assimilable proportions. You will recall the earlier quotation that outlined the essential functions of the contact boundary: (1) the maintenance of difference, (2) rejection of danger, (3) coping with obstacles, and (4) the selection and appropriation of assimilable novelty. The boundary space is the first stage where these functions are exercised, and without which we feel pressed in and intruded upon by the environment. Our boundary space is, in a sense, a buffer area for our self, the place where "me" and "environment" diffuse into one another, and which by its existence allows the more differentiated boundary layer to function well.

The term "space" in no way implies that this is preset or static. Like the permeability of the boundary layer itself, the actual amount of surrounding space we experience as "mine" varies according to our particular organismic needs and perceptions, as well as the conditions of the environment. For example, if you compare the personal space you require with a stranger with that you require with your parents, you will probably find them to be quite different. Similarly you can probably recall times when you have been either more "touchy" or more "open" because of shifts in your own sense of self, which had a profound effect on the space you needed to feel comfortable. Our boundary space, like our boundary layer, is in the process of constantly being formed and

reformed, drawn closer or pushed out further, defined and rede-
fined.

The ways in which we regulate, modify, and communicate our boundary space are mostly nonverbal, that is, through body process. We can
roughly divide this into two domains (the exact physical distance
of which will vary with the particular organism/environment conditions):

1. *Distal boundary space.* This is the regulation of the outer range of
one's boundary space: that space we cannot directly act on to regulate
(e.g., by touch) but experience as important enough to regulate in
some form.

2. *Proximal boundary space.* This involves the regulation of the boundary space that is relatively close to the body boundary layer: that space
within the range where we can touch or be touched and thus can act and
be acted on directly.

In the regulation of the distal boundary space, we can either modulate our distance from objects (including people) by moving ourselves
through space, or by communicating our distance requirements to the
other. Body processes relevant here are (1) the capacity to find a "comfortable" distance (which implies being able to sense our body signals of
comfort/discomfort), (2) gross motor activity by which we move through
space, and (3) the use of both verbal and body language (such as posture, gesture, voice tone, and facial expression) to signal to others the
distance we require. If you ignore the verbalized content of a conversation and simply observe the physical responses, you will notice that
much of the body process is geared toward the negotiation and regulation of this boundary space.

In the proximal boundary space, we can regulate distance directly by
gross motor action, such as pushing someone away or using our hands to
prevent the other from moving closer, or more indirectly, through adjusting our body position, such as leaning back with the upper body to
"set back" from the other or turning aside to present less of the contact-
able body front to the other.

ISSUES AT THE BOUNDARY

In the therapeutic process, our concerns with contact extend to three
critical issues relating to body process at the boundary:

1. *The ability to modulate the form and pace of contact.* Unless one can influence the form of contact and the pace at which it occurs, the contact easily becomes overwhelming and results in a loss of self as the "other" crowds the self into the background. The ability to modulate the form and pace of contact rests largely on the capacity to fluidly adjust the boundary space through movement, posture, and communication (verbal or nonverbal) that are congruent with one's current needs for self–regulation.

2. *The permeability of the boundary layer.* The second issue is the capacity to moderate the permeability of one's body boundary layer as is appropriate for the contact and the context. Good contact requires enough differentiation of self such that the other is clearly perceived, yet there is enough openness to let the energy of contact into the self. It also requires the appropriate ability to close one's boundary to protect against unwanted (unassimilable) intrusion or danger. As I have described earlier, the body process of the boundary layer is an intrinsic part of managing this aspect of contact.

3. *Discrimination of the experience of contact.* This is analogous to the process of tasting in Perls' oral metaphor for contact. Schaler (1980) calls this the "taste factor," which he sees as essential for fully autonomous functioning. In relation to body process, I see it as crucial that, in the course of any contact episode, one is able to perceive the impact of the contact on one's organism and sense of self. This requires the ability to attend to one's bodily sensations, feelings, and responses—the holistic bodily form of "tasting" to discover: "Is this contact palatable?" "Do I feel safe or in danger?" "Am I maintaining my sense of self?" This is the discrimination between that which is assimilable and can be taken in, and that which is unassimilable and must be rejected.

It should be clear by now that the adjustment of contact at the boundary functions best as a fluid and context-related process. There is no fixed form of boundary that is better than any other in an absolute sense. Rather it is the capacity to adjust one's boundary and boundary space that is essential to healthy functioning. Problems in fluidly adjusting oneself to contact and the contact process itself are the relevant focus of therapeutic attention, and it is these boundary functions that are the relevant focus of body-oriented therapeutic work.

INTROJECTION AND REACTION FORMATION
TO INTROJECTION

Problems during contact generally occur when there is some difficulty with the modulation of the form and pace of contact through the negotiation of boundary space, with the permeability of the boundary layer, or with discrimination of the experience of contact. Without these capacities one is at the mercy of external forces. One's boundary tends to be overwhelmed, and one's self is crowded out by the environment. You can imagine a house in the middle of a field with no trees to act as wind breaks and all of its windows wide open. With each gust of wind, everything in the house is blown about. Everything must be weighted down and constant attention given to when the next gust will come. The occupant's energy is constantly reacting to the environment (the force of the wind) and little is left over to pursue his or her own interests.

This boundary situation is called *introjection* in Gestalt therapy and is described as "to swallow down whole what does not belong in your organism" (Perls et al., 1951, p. 199).* Its Latin root defines it as *to throw (jacere) within (in)* and connotes the taking in across one's boundary in an unselective, uncontrolled, or unregulated fashion. That which has been thrown in and not rendered in assimilable form sits around in undigestable lumps, eventually crowding out the organismic space available for new experience.

The tendency to meet the environment as an open house seems related to growing up with adults who regularly intrude themselves on one's boundaries through: expectations for performance; constant rules and regulations for conduct; demands that one adapt oneself to their narcissistic requirements.** With such intrusion the growing child's own perceptions and needs are constantly displaced by those of others, and regulation of contact at the child's boundary is disturbed.

Against such boundary pressures, the child has two basic options: (1) to give up the self in the service of the other, burying his or her own

---

*Readers familiar with psychoanalysis will recognize an important difference between the use of this term in Gestalt therapy and its use in psychoanalytic theory. In psychoanalytic theory introjection is referred to as a requirement of healthy adjustment because of the value placed on identification, whereas in Gestalt therapy it is considered an important initial but incomplete stage of development because it is by nature not assimilated to the self.

**These narcissistic requirements include their need for self-esteem and appreciation; pressure to adopt their particular world view as "truth" regardless of one's own perceptions; demands that one meet their needs for sexual contact, either through emotional liaison or actual sexual behavior.

needs deeply out of reach where they do not clash with the introjected needs of the other; or (2) to compensate by closing his or her boundaries to any contact that might be foreign and unassimilable and/or attacking any approach to his or her boundary as a preventive measure. The first option is analogous to the house buffeted by the wind, with the occupant barricaded deep in an inner room—while he or she is safe from the intruding wind, the rest of the house cannot be lived in with any comfort. The second option is analogous to the occupant shutting all the windows, rendering the house impermeable to any movement of air, and setting out large fans to counterblast any breeze that might blow on the outer walls.

The essential dilemma is the same even though the contact style is apparently opposite—the dilemma being the selection of the assimilable novelty and the rejection of the unassimilable novelty. In the first option, no nourishment results from contact because there is no self available to do the work of assimilating that which is taken in across the boundary. In the second option, little of anything is taken in so that there is little to assimilate. The dilemma is that of introjection or reaction formation to introjection. In reference to the bodily nature of each of these basic options, the first can be described as resulting from *underbounding* and the second from *overbounding.* Therapeutic work with either consists of developing awareness of the ways in which one gets stuck in managing one's boundary process, and recovering the capacity to bound oneself flexibly and responsively. To return to the house analogy one more time, this means learning that one can regulate the openness of the windows to allow fresh air and sunlight in and to plant wind breaks as needed to provide some buffer without building walls to contact.

Underbounding

Carla came to see me because, in working with her prior therapist, she recognized that she was very out of touch with her body. It became readily apparent in our work that her lack of contact with herself was much more general and pervasive than this. She was exceptionally bright and capable in her work but was easily overwhelmed by interpersonal difficulties, particularly the aggression and anger of others. She would virtually collapse at the end of each work week, and spend much of the weekend in bed, trying to marshal her resources. As I got to know her, I began to recognize a pattern in her difficulty in coping with interpersonal contact in her life. In her love life, her school experiences, and her work life, Carla described linking up with men in the roles of lovers, teachers, and bosses who abused and manipulated her. She had begun to recognize that this did not just happen, but that there must be some way in which she participated in setting up such repeated occurrences in her life.

As I worked with her to develop awareness of her physical process, her way of managing her bodily boundary and space with me became similar to her description of what happened elsewhere in her life. For example, once I reached over to touch her to show her something about her posture that I noticed, and she literally collapsed inwards on herself. She was unable to tell me what happened; all she was aware of was suddenly "spacing out" and feeling disassociated. Another time I was having difficulty with my contact lenses and rather abruptly moved my chair closer so that I could see her better, and Carla again seemed to collapse inwards. This time she was able to report that it was my closeness that "caused" her to collapse, and that the only reason she had not felt completely overwhelmed (and so had to "space out") was that since I was not touching her, she did not have to completely withdraw from me.

From this we began to attend carefully to her experience of her boundaries with me, experimenting with different distances and how she responded to each with her posture and feelings. It became apparent to both of us that Carla had little experience of her physical space and boundaries until they were violated. She typically sat either in a childlike and unguarded pose or completely collapsed inwards and out of contact. Carla would become acutely aware of others after they had come too close to her physically or emotionally. However, she had little awareness of her own social space with others and tended to lean and position herself closely to others whether she felt particularly intimate with them or not, and whether the situation was an intimate one or not. There was no seductiveness about this that I could see; it was merely that she had no consciousness of her boundaries and so could do little to adjust her distance with others. It was no wonder she felt overwhelmed and violated by the unexpected, although frequently understandable, overly personal response to her. By the time she recognized that she was overwhelmed by the contact, the other person was already "inside" her boundary, and she could only react by retreat and withdrawal or by explosive bursts of rage that would succeed in driving the other away. All of this was, of course, after the fact of her losing her sense of boundary so that she was constantly engaged in recovering what she had lost, as opposed to operating in the world from a place of integrity.

Our work on this theme developed through small experiments with distance and closeness until Carla was comfortable enough to experiment more directly with how she bounded herself, or in this case did not bound herself, in a physical way. Carla had been talking about an upcoming meeting where she was afraid she would not be able to withstand the pushiness of her colleagues. I became interested in linking our physical work with her boundary space to her concerns about the upcoming meeting. For this I borrowed an exercise from tai chi chuan, a Chinese martial art, used to practice receiving and working with another person's movement and energy. I asked her to stand across from me so that we were close enough to be able to touch each other's shoulder with our arms outstretched. With her arm raised in front of her, I carefully made contact with her wrist with my palm so that I could gently push against her arm. In this way Carla had a way of creating space for herself as she needed to (by pushing my hand away with her arm) while we could look at how she received and coped with the pressure at her boundary when I pushed her arm towards her body.

When I first slowly pushed against her arm, there was no significant resistance to my pressure until I had her arm pinned against her chest so that she had no option for movement. Carla noted that it was as if she had let me "into her skin" and she could only collapse into herself (her body) and retreat from my pressure. I could feel her give up her body surface as her superficial muscular layer became limp and toneless and her posture folded inward, collapsing around my pressure. She yielded her boundary to my pressure, and this inevitably resulted in her sense of herself being displaced out of her awareness. When I asked her to imagine that I was one of the colleagues with whom she had difficulty, she similarly allowed me in until her arm was pinned to her chest, but at this point she suddenly tensed and angrily pushed me away. Again this was identical to how she reacted to this person at work: she would yield to his pressure until eventually she could not tolerate it any longer, and then would lash out in anger to get him "out of her space," as she put it.

We continued this experiment, except I asked her to attend more carefully to her sense of space right from the start and to see if she could locate when I felt "too close" and how she knew it. As I pushed slowly towards her, Carla commented, "Now I see, it's when I begin to collapse that I've *already* let you in too far. I don't pay any attention to my body saying 'that's enough.' It doesn't even occur to me that I can stop you, that I have the right to any more space." We began to experiment with having her stop my hand or guide it away from her with her arm at various distances from her body. Each time she paid careful attention to her bodily reaction to that particular distance—whether she experienced it as "inside" or "outside" her boundary, whether she felt she had room for her "self" (did not need to withdraw), and so on. After finding her comfortable boundary with me I asked her to imagine that I was various other people in her life, and had her find her comfortable boundary distance. With some people she felt in danger even before we were within touching distance, and others she could allow much closer before she felt she was giving up her boundary.

This experiment certainly did not cure Carla's problems with underbounding. What it did do was to ground the nature of her interpersonal difficulties in her bodily use and give her a clear enough experience of what it physically felt like to neglect or honor her need to maintain the integrity of her personal space. This provided a framework that was widely applicable to her life, whether she was coping with physical contact, verbal contact, or contact with others' ideas.

By underbounding Carla was overly permeable to contact with others. She would let the other into her so far that her sense of "I" would be displaced. Carla would retreat into her body core, with a soft and yielding surface musculature over palpable but much deeper muscular tensions. It was the explosive pressure of this core self that would frequently emerge as rageful reactions. This is like a defensive line in a battle: the retreating troops fall back to one position after another in the face of enemy attack, eventually retreating into less and less space within their own borders. Just as a country cannot maintain its identity as a nation without intact borders, a person cannot maintain identity without intact personal boundaries. Each becomes occupied by foreign troops, unassimilable introjects that displace the native needs, functions, and identity.

By reestablishing her bodily sense of boundary, Carla could more competently modulate the form and pace of contact so as to select or reject what was assimilable to herself rather than whatever was pressed on her. In turn she gave less unaware invitations for the kind of contact she did not really want or could not tolerate. Because her boundary was clear to her, and thus was communicated to others through her body language and posture, Carla had fewer surprises of suddenly discovering that someone had moved in on her space.

Overbounding

Resistance to introjection at the stage of contact is frequently seen in a more active form than the passive collapse of boundary integrity described with Carla. Instead of giving up one's "self" to the intrusion of the other, the body boundary is hardened and made impervious and a high degree of boundary space distance is maintained so that the self is certain to be maintained at all costs. [This has some similarities to the re-sistance called "egotism" by Perls et al., (1951); however, my use of the term "overbounding" is more descriptive of the bodily processes I am trying to emphasize.] The overbound person creates a shell whenever contact with his or her boundary is threatened. Experience has led the person to distrust the demands of others on personal integrity. If this becomes stylistic (i.e., chronic), then overbounding can be seen struc-turally in the hard and unyielding quality of the superficial body tissue. Ida Rolf has likened such hardening to a case of mistaken identity (Feitis, 1978), where muscles, whose function is movement, are made to act like bones, whose function is support and protection.

This mode of coping with potentially intrusive contact probably evolves later in the child's development than underbounding. Under-bounding and subsequent introjection of the other seems to result because there is no sense of a differentiated "I" from which to respond. However, overbounding, since it requires more motor development to harden one's body boundary and active work to maintain boundary dis-tance, implies a greater degree of differentiation of self and ego strength, and hence a more developed organism. But the price for the ability to maintain one's organismic integrity through overbounding is that, while harmful contact is less likely to get in, so is nourishing con-tact. The overbound person reports feeling insulated and untouched by others, lonely and isolated. Life seems empty because there is little that is novel or fresh or nourishing. The overbound person fears opening up to others because this results in a loss of control and the potential danger of introjection and loss of self. The necessary ability to physically soften, to be accessible to others, and to take in the other and feel "filled" by contact is missing. Unaware of how confrontive and abrasive he or she is when approached by others (so as to keep ample boundary space), the overbound person may feel chronically rejected by others, misunderstood, and treated in an uncaring manner, particularly when others understandably react with anger.

Paul was born in war-torn central Europe during World War II. From the outset of our work together, which took place off and on over a num-ber of years, his guardedness and structurally hardened body boundary were significant themes. Paul was referred to me by his therapist, who, sensitive to the importance of body process in the therapeutic issues they were addressing, wanted to support Paul to develop greater body awareness. Paul was raised mostly by his mother as his father was a soldier who only infrequently was home. His mother, clearly over-whelmed by the deprivations and trials of the war and single parent-hood, demanded strict compliance from Paul, blaming him for her suffering and loneliness. His sense of his childhood was of a harsh and cold world where he tried hard to please his parents but seldom seemed rewarded by love or gentleness.

In our initial work, it became apparent that, despite his sophisticated knowledge of therapy and his understanding that body work would be "good for him" (note the introjection implicit here), he experienced any physical work as threatening and painful, and was very guarded against physical contact. Paul's muscles were hard and unyielding, particularly in his shoulders and neck, chest, diaphragm, and abdomen. He was not muscularly overdeveloped, as is frequently true of the overbound person, but was nonetheless physically taut and well-shielded—something like skin stretched over a frame. His face was also taut and muscled, with a tense jaw and a narrowed and heavy-browed expression around his eyes.

In the first periods of our work together, I focused on deep work on the tense musculature to encourage Paul to release some of his tension and postural holding, particularly as this affected his breathing. At that time I had not conceptualized Paul's body process as relating to boundary issues and worked within a more traditional model of looking at all tension in terms of emotional inhibition. This accorded with Paul's own eagerness "finally to let go" of his chronic and painful muscle tension. His response to this deep touch work was predictable retrospectively, in that he found any deep-tissue work excruciating, carrying emotional overtones of being hurt and beaten (a common occurrence for him in his childhood). When he was able to release some tension, Paul would experience feelings of anger and disgust, or alternately sadness and tears. These he would allow partially to emerge and then, feeling scared and vulnerable, he would quickly suppress them.

I finally began to recognize that in our mutual eagerness to "get rid" of his tension, we were ignoring the obvious fact of his guardedness and fear—and the intrinsic importance of his mode of self-protection: his sensitivity to contact at his body boundary and fear of boundary loss. Shifting the focus of attention to his body boundary, I worked with him to clearly experience his guarded bodily stance and boundary tension through exaggeration of his posture and attention to his facial expression. I also used experiments such as those with Carla, which heightened his sense of his bodily reactions to closeness with me. Eventually Paul was able to express his suspiciousness of me—how he experienced me as "not safe," as "cold, distant, uncaring," and how he was afraid I would shame and embarrass him if he let down his guard.

As we sorted out what he was reacting to that was actually relevant to his experience of *me* (since I am indeed distant and cool sometimes), and what was not relevant to what he knew about me (he knew I was safe and would not intentionally hurt him), Paul recognized these feelings as descriptive of his relationship with his mother. Each time he reached out to her, she would criticize and shame him. To be open to her or to want something from her was to risk humiliation and ridicule. To maintain any sense of integrity around her, he had hardened himself and resigned himself to asking for little. Paradoxically, as Paul owned more of the necessity for his boundedness, he was more able to allow me to work with touch, now in a gentle fashion, to release some of his tension. With each new physical release, particularly in the areas of his diaphragm and throat, he would first feel his deep disgust and anger at what he had been subjected to, and then could allow himself to feel his loneliness and isolation.

Paul returned to therapy after one of his long breaks, reporting that he had been able to allow his wife and friends to be closer and to trust them more. He was having dreams of falling and melting, which frightened him, but he felt more able to tolerate this. With me he was much more trusting and open, less automatically guarded towards my touch and able to tell me what I was doing that he didn't like without lashing out.

Finally in one session Paul was lying on the work table while I was using soft touch to encourage him to release tension in his chest and eyes. He told me that he was feeling an emerging sadness but was struggling with whether it was safe to let go. I asked him, "What do you need from me to feel safe?" He paused, then looked up at me and replied shyly, "I need to know that my sadness is not disgusting for you," and burst into deep sobs. Since I was already sitting next to him, I placed my hands on his shoulders and he hesitantly moved to be held by me. As he yielded to being held, his sobs deepened more and more. I could feel his body boundary soften and warm under my hands. His tears finally subsided and Paul looked at me, for the first time without his characteristic suspicious expression. He was surprised and relieved, and somewhat hesitant about being out in the world so openly. He asked me a few more times to reassure him that I did not think ill of his feelings. I received a note from him later describing the tremendous impact of this culminating session and acknowledging that such openness was very hard for him to maintain. Of course, all such peak experiences are impossible to sustain for any length of time. Its relevance is not in whether the actual peak can be maintained so much as in the degree to which Paul can now respond to contact from his experience of the actual present—its actual safety or danger. As he completes his unfinished business with his past, he can exercise a different way of being at his boundary that is valid for him in the present.

WORKING THROUGH INTROJECTION— DEPTH BODY-ORIENTED WORK

When some restoration of awareness and flexible functioning of the body boundary layer and boundary space has occurred, the link between the intake of contact in general with the intake of food may become apparent. Many persons who have had difficulty with managing their boundaries at contact, either by overbounding or underbounding, also have deep tensions in the areas of the mouth and jaw, the throat and base of the skull, the chest and upper back, and the diaphragm. Treated separately or as "segments" (as in Reichian therapy), these tensions are extremely difficult to release. It is only when they are seen and worked with as a *unit*, based on the processes of intake across the boundary and assimilation, that these tensions acquire meaning for therapeutic work.

It was mentioned earlier that Perls based his original model of contact on the oral intake of food and the subsequent development of teeth that allowed for selective assimilation rather than mere introjection (swallowing whole). I believe that this model has been a misleading one for understanding many kinds of engagement "at the boundary." Most contact process is more like tactile engagement than like the taking in of food. Much of our boundary negotiation is experienced "as if" we must cope with the impact of the environment with our total body surface. Thus I can speak of introjection of, or reaction formation towards, contact with one's heart, sexuality, or space because all of these relate to our bodily nature and can be "touched on" by others.

But the oral model is still quite relevant to many other forms of introjection at the boundary and oral phenomena appear when working with the body *intake pathway*, which is centered around the intake of food. This is, of course, the pathway that includes the lips and mouth, jaw, throat, channel through the chest and upper back, diaphragm, and belly. This is the pathway through which food is taken in, chewed, swallowed, and digested, as well as the pathway through which undigestable "stuff" (no longer food since it is unassimilable) is spit out, vomited up, disgorged, and cast out of the body. Much of what needs to be worked through in terms of introjection is experienced physically as resistance along this intake pathway, that is, as if resisting the intake of food.

One client who came to me initially for help with chronic muscular spasms in his upper back would cough vigorously every time we did any deep muscular release work in his upper back or chest. Eventually he would spit up large quantities of phlegm and saliva. He was a highly cultured man whose soft-spoken manner contrasted sharply with his highly muscled, rigid, and overbounded body structure. As we began to link his previously unaware "killer" stance (from standing work) with the outpouring of mucus each time he released in his chest and back through hands-on work, he became aware of how much "crap I had to swallow from other kids" growing up in the rough city streets of his childhood. In order not to have to "swallow" any more humiliation, he, as a sensitive young boy, learned how to tightly bound himself and posture in a way that communicated, "If you come any closer, I'll kill you!" As an adult, his getting rid of the accumulated foreign material (undigested introject) in the form of mucus and verbalization, allowed him to "clear himself out," as he put it, and redefine his relationship to the world.

Another client demonstrated a similar phenomenon related to different issues. Kate's body structure was light and fragile and she easily collapsed into depression and tears. She had extremely tense muscles in her jaw and throat and diaphragm and it was these areas on which we focused first. After having acquired some ability to release a portion of these tensions, we were exploring her unyielding rigidity in her jaw. To emphasize this I asked Kate to bite down on a rolled piece of towel. She grasped the towel firmly in her teeth and an aggressive look came into her eyes. When I asked Kate to emphasize this by making a noise, she growled like a dog with a stick, thus mobilizing her tight throat and diaphragm, and then began to gag and cough. Each time she bit down and started to make a sound, she would feel her gorge rise as if to vomit.

For a long time, this phenomenon remained an isolated body response without any connection to its larger meaning. But it was clear that we could not foster any more release of these tensions without somehow discovering what it was Kate had to disgorge but resisted. Concurrently, in working with other aspects of her underbounding and loss of self, Kate was now discovering her own needs and beginning to insist that others respect her boundaries rather than merely succumbing to their pressures. She would frequently find herself at some choice point where, if she were to respect her own boundary, she would feel "that I'll make myself less of a woman." I eventually recognized this resistance point as being the kernel of an old introject—unintegrated (because it was in conflict with her emerging sense of self) and so clearly unassimilated material.

I pushed Kate to specify exactly how she would be less of a woman if she did what she wanted and maintained her boundary with others. She made statements such as, "If I put myself before others even once, I'll be less of a woman." "If I disagree with my mother's criticism of the way I dress, I'll be saying to her that I'm not feminine enough." And, "If I act tough and firm on issues I believe in, I'll be less of a woman." As she did so, she could feel that characteristic rising of her gorge and nausea. After each statement of how she would be "less of a woman," I suggested that she acknowledge the validity of her body response by answering, "That makes me sick!" I simultaneously supported her awareness of her jaw, throat, and diaphragm through my touch. As this dialogue took shape, Kate noted that the statements she was making encompassed all of her mother's strictures and disapproval of her for being a tomboy as a child. Kate eventually gave in to her mother's chastising so as to become a "proper woman."

We restructured the experiment having Kate first play out her mother's image of proper womanhood and then, paying attention to her bodily reaction to this view, expressing her disgust with and protest to what she had passively swallowed. With each "ejection" of her mother's standards for womanly conduct, she experienced less nausea and tension and I could see her stand more firmly and clearly in her body boundary. Kate's jaw/throat tension and the nauseous tension in her belly became important signals of when she was trespassing her intrinsic needs by virtue of some unassimilated standards from the past. Each ejection of unassimilated material allowed Kate to further re-own her body boundary and she required less body resistance against her own intrinsic disgust.

In working with underbounding at contact, the overriding theme for therapy is making the boundary, and thus the self, more substantial and firm, and connecting the core, where the self has retreated, to the surface. In terms of body process this means:

1. *Postural collapse and loss of energy at the body surface.* This constitutes the yielding of self to the contact object and the inevitable introjection of the other.

2. *Loss or lack of superficial muscular tone and capacity.* This functions as the loss of the boundary layer such that the differentiation between self and other is minimized.

3. *Poor or inappropriate maintenance of physical space and distance.* This results in feeling crowded and intruded on by others, or difficulty in keeping others from inappropriately touching.

4. *Reference to external rules and standards* to determine one's response to contact rather than the actual bodily response to what is taken in. This results in a lack of discrimination.

The therapist cannot simply take for granted that when the client says "That's okay" or "That's not okay" or "I agree" in response to some contact episode, the client is responding out of his or her *self,* rather than out of introjected beliefs and standards. If such responses are congruent with one's organism as a whole, then there will be a clear bodily component, a "gut feel" to the response. The therapist must ask such questions as: "How do you know that you agree?" "Where do you feel your agreement?" "Does any part of you *not* like what just happened?" With each clarification of the client's intrinsic response (in contrast to how he or she has been taught he or she "should" respond), the self-boundary becomes firmer and clearer.

One client who was in turmoil over an important life decision could not distinguish the "right" choice. On investigating her confusion, it was apparent that all the options from which she was trying to choose were what others wanted her to do: her parents, her husband, her children. She completely lost her sense of self in this storm of other voices. It was not until we placed these people "outside" of her by giving them locations in the therapy room that she could begin to distinguish any internal sensations of her own wants in the matter.

Therapeutic work with overbounding takes an opposite direction as its major theme, that of making the self-boundary more flexible and permeable to contact. In this work we pay careful attention to:

1. *Postural rigidity and lack of "give" of the body boundary layer.* This must be brought to awareness through use of physical touch and experiments with body structure so that the stiff maintenance of one's boundary is experienced as something one *does* rather than something that "just happens" or as something done to oneself. The unaware bodily statement of "No, don't come in, don't come close," which is made via body boundary rigidity and tension, must become an aware and verbal "No, I won't *let* you in," before any choice or discrimination is possible.

2. *Hypersensitivity to boundary space.* Overbound persons must become aware of their needs for space and the ways in which they habitually make space for themselves, and the resulting interpersonal effects. Experiments with touch and placement about the room can

begin to build a clearer sense of the importance of this sensitivity. Work with projection clarifies how they read "threat" into situations where there is none.

3. *Therapist's contact style.* Although in overbounding the boundary space is managed in a way that is behaviorally opposite to that in underbounding (by responding vigorously to even small encroachments and maintaining a lot of distance from others), the underlying fear is similar—that if I let anything in, I will lose myself. It is only the conclusion that is different—I will give up myself (in underbounding) or I will maintain myself at all costs (in overbounding). But this does imply that therapeutic technique must be different until the common fear is reached. It is essential that the therapist maintain a gentle and respectful presence, particularly during the delicate phase of exploring the reality at the boundary.

Under these conditions rather remarkable work can be done, even for individuals who otherwise find interpersonal contact very problematic. If we value the necessity of organismic body boundaries, and the important ways in which people have shaped the process of their self-regulation to manage environments where maintaining boundaries has been difficult, we create options for a new creative adjustment that can free energy for nourishing relationships.

FINAL CONTACT

Contact culminates in the experience of *final contact,* the moment of meeting when the boundary between self and other disappears. This is the moment of orgasm; the completion of a project; the point at which one looks into the eyes of the beloved, who becomes "all"; when one's thirst is slaked and the cool and soothing water is for that moment all that exists; the point in conversation where a sense of connection is achieved. These examples are peak experiences, but the momentary letting go of self in final contact occurs, albeit less dramatically, even in less urgent contacts. Since "boundary" is a perceptual term, one no longer perceives a separation between self and other. Without this dissolving of boundary for this moment of final contact, the organism would absorb nothing new into itself and no nourishment and growth could occur. With the boundary temporarily dissolved, the "I" is less prominent and the other (or object of contact) is fully realized: "The feeling of absorption is 'self–forgetful'; it attends completely to its object; and since this object fills the entire field . . . the object becomes a 'Thou,' it is what is addressed. The 'I' lapses altogether into attentive feeling . . . " (Perls et al., 1951, p. 418)

This is really just a small part of the whole cycle, yet experientially has much impact. The same things that make contact problematic, over- and underbounding, result in diminishment of final contact. They are really just phases of the same part of the cycle after all. The underbound person experiences little to let go of, so that little final peak or culmination can be experienced. The "other" is already so prominent that it constantly displaces the "I," but in a way that has been intrusive. The experiencing self has been lost and there is no blending of self and other.

The overbound person has so well organized his or her functioning to prevent loss of self that he or she cannot afford to "let go" into the final contact where true exchange and intake of energy and new experience can occur. His or her self-containment cannot allow for the confluence of final contact where self and other become one.

Of course, other resistances can also intefere with final contact. At this moment one can project, so that instead of the *actuality* of the other, one "experiences" only one's images or guesses about them. Or one can desensitize and dull the moment of final contact so that the experience of the other is less prominent in that moment, and less potentially overwhelming. The therapeutic principles already discussed can be applied here as well: attention to breathing and energy; elucidation of perception and sensation; and increasing fluidity of boundaries during the cycle.

Chapter 12

Withdrawal, Assimilation, and Body Process

> Psychologically, the passage from aware contact to un-
> aware assimilation has a deep pathos. For the figure of
> contact filled the world, was excitement, all the excite-
> ment there was; but in the aftermath it is seen to be a
> small change in the field. This is the Faustian pathos,
> when one says, "Stay! thou art so fair!" but to effectuate
> this saying would be just to inhibit the orgasm, the
> swallowing, or the learning (Perls, et al., 1951, p.
> 422)

Final contact is often misconceived as the culminating point of the experience cycle. While the need that has been organizing behavior has found completion through contact (or, more accurately, through the contact*ing*), the organism is not in a position to make energy available to the next emerging figure until certain tasks have been achieved to "make room" for what is to emerge. Final contact, as thrilling and "high" as it may be, must find an end, so that what has been gleaned from the contact can be assimilated, and so that something new and fresh can emerge in its own right without contamination from the previous event. In order for this "finishing" to occur, we speak of the phase of *withdrawal from contact.*

The importance of the withdrawal phase of the cycle is barely apparent in many contacts. In completing the contact of reading a book, for example, we often require little more to finish than closing the cover, orienting ourselves for a moment and getting up from our chair. In completing a light social conversation, we ritualize our finishing process down to a simple "Good to talk to you, bye now."

Our passage through withdrawal is equivalent to the intensity and nature of the contact in which we have been engaged. Where the contact has been light, brief, and with little intensity and exchange of material, the associated withdrawal phase is brief, stands out very little, and requires little digestion and assimilation of the experience. Where little of one's self has been dissolved in meeting the other, then little energy is required to re-form one's self and shift the focus back toward one's organism.

It is with more intense and demanding contacts that the need for withdrawal, and the impact of letting go of the contact, is felt more keenly. An intense conversation, for example, where much is discussed, exchanged, and learned from the other is rarely "finished" when the conversation is ended. We may spend additional time thinking about, imagining, and rehashing the conversation as we digest its impact on us and fit what we have learned into our preexisting way of understanding. Until this takes place, we are still "in the conversation," despite the fact that the actual talk has ceased, and it remains prominent in our attention.

Similarly, contacts that have developed or taken place over long periods of time, like shorter but intense contacts, may require equivalent attention to finishing and withdrawal. A major project that has culminated in its goal, such as writing a book, making a sale, or courting a lover, frequently results in a withdrawal and assimilation period, which many people interpret as depression. This is the well-known "postpartum blues" and often signals a reassessment and reorganization of one's self after being organized intensely around a major goal or figure. Even within the course of such major projects or events, the intensity of contact requires mini-withdrawal periods, natural breaks, and pauses that allow us to return to the contact refreshed.

Gestalt therapy views human process as cyclical, and as a Gestalt therapist I place value on the rhythmic punctuation that the withdrawal phase provides. This bias, however, runs somewhat counter to that common to Western culture, particularly in the United States. Zinker (1977) observes:

> There is a rhythm between contact and withdrawal. One learns how to pay attention to one's needs, how to go about satisfying them, then to withdraw and rest. Being constantly mobilized is also a kind of sickness, a sickness of not having peace . . . Our culture reflects a prejudice against experiencing this natural rhythm. (pp. 109–110)

With our intense emphasis on the work ethic, and on perfection and performance, the natural phase of withdrawal is often labeled as laziness, because to outward appearances we may seem unproductive. We have, as a culture, little appreciation for the work of digesting, the work of finishing, the work of reconnecting with ourselves and clearing our internal space so that new and fresh experience can emerge. A television commercial for beer pushes this view by proclaiming, "Who says you can't have it all?"—taking advantage of our national madness in pursuit of the perfect "don't lose out on anything" life-style. This difficulty in coming to grips with one's limits in life seems to be often confused, in our culture, with the pursuit of happiness.

Contrast this attitude with that expressed by the ancient Chinese philosopher Lao-Tzu (1955):

> To take all you want
> Is never as good
> As to stop when you should.
> Scheme and be sharp
> And you'll not keep it long.
> One never can guard
> His home when it's full
> Of jade and fine gold:
> Wealth, power and pride
> Bequeath their own doom.
> When fame and success
> Come to you, then retire.
> This is the ordained Way.
>   (p. 61)

It is perhaps because of our western bias for action and contacts that little has actually been written about the withdrawal phase of the cycle in Gestalt therapy literature, and certainly even less in the standard literature of psychotherapy. Like the culture out of which our methods of psychotherapy have evolved, we seem to have been more preoccupied with the action and contact aspects of the cycle than with the natural polarity of withdrawal. Much of the literature that does focus on withdrawal from contact tends to emphasize its negative or pathological side, such as the literature on attachment separation anxiety (Bowlby, 1960) or loss (Searles, 1981, 1985), or see it only in developmental terms (Mahler, 1972; Winnicott, 1960).

It is perhaps the particular work I do and the particular issues of many clients who are attracted to body-oriented therapy that have demanded I understand better the fundamental organismic need for withdrawal. Attending to one's body process requires slowing down and moving inwards, two tasks typical of the withdrawal phase. I have often found these tasks to be difficult for people to accomplish.

Additionally, many of my clients are hardworking, high achievers who seek body-oriented therapy because their high-pressure lives keep them tense and anxious, unable to let down and relax. I quickly discovered that relaxation or tension release alone (e.g., through physical manipulation) was not sufficient to accomplish change. Such techniques did not address clients' *resistance* to slowing down and their *resistance* to giving themselves breaks in the cycle of their lives. These clients approached relaxation or body-awareness work in the same way they approached other life tasks: as another skill to be perfected and goal to be achieved. Doing relaxation or muscular release work often became simply another demand on themselves—like climbing the career ladder, jogging, doing quality time, or doing relationships.

Most of the observations here are derived from my clinical experience and thus will need to be examined in practice by others for clinical usefulness and validity. Nevertheless, it seems important to me that we begin to explore this area in more depth, and I offer the material in this chapter to stimulate discussion about this often neglected aspect of human functioning, withdrawal from contact.

ELEMENTS OF THE WITHDRAWAL PHASE

At some point final contact ends, either by choice through satiation (we have had enough), or through extrinsic factors that cause us to move on (time is up, the other withdraws). Contact may end gradually or abruptly, and the ending may be wanted or unwanted by one or both of the parties involved. Regardless of the way in which final contact ends or the specific reasons contact becomes a bounded event, one is faced with some necessary tasks in order to complete the present cycle and allow for the next cycle to occur.

In the previous chapter, I described how, at final contact, the boundary between self and environment has been "dissolved" or rendered permeable. By this I mean that the "I" is less clearly delineated in awareness since, in final contact, the object of contact is most figural. If the "other" is a person, then at final contact you feel yourself to be connected to, or perhaps even merged with, him or her. If your contact is with an activity, such as work, then in final contact you are completely absorbed in that work, the work "fills the world," as the opening quotation of this chapter describes it. That there is also frequently a fluidity of the body boundary in these moments, as discussed in the previous chapter, illustrates the dissolving of boundary as well.

Completion of the cycle involves a reversal of the previous direction of the organism's energy and awareness toward the environment. Just as in earlier phases of the cycle, I see body process as a intrinsic part of the phenomena of the withdrawal phase. The phenomena outlined below might be thought of as a set of tasks to be accomplished rather than as a strict sequence of activities, and are derived from phenomenological observation of the contact process. Depending on the nature of the particular contact involved, certain elements will stand out as more relevant than others.

Disengagement

The ending of final contact in its broadest sense involves a shift in focus from "that which is contacted" to the "self that has been in contact." This shift in attention accomplishes the first major task of completing a given experience, that of *disengaging from contact*. In order to disengage one must let go of the intensity of contact and relinquish the peak experience. Usually this shift of focus is signaled by some inner signs of satiation—the contact has been enough, at least for the moment. "Inner signs" refers to bodily sensations, such as fatigue, dulling of one's perceptual intensity, a sense of fullness or sufficiency in one's belly, an overall bodily sense of pleasure we call satisfaction.

In addition to the bodily signals of satiation that herald the first shift of focus from the environment back to self, there may also be body movements to separate oneself physically from the other. For example, as an involving conversation ends, I find myself shifting from having been leaning forward into the conversation to settling back into my chair. This both separates me physically from the person with whom I have been conversing, and supports me experientially in settling back into myself and disengaging from the other person. Even in the course of our conversation there may be momentary points of disengagement where I break eye contact, turn my body somewhat askance, or lean back and momentarily separate myself from the other person. Similarly, in the midst of an intense writing session, I may lean back, take a breath, step away from the desk, or otherwise disengage or find temporary distance from my task.

Relinquishing contact and making some movement to separate the self from the environment/other puts one in a position to give more equal attention to the self. In contact, awareness is mostly taken up by the thing with which one is in contact; the other crowds out, for that time, one's awareness of self. To disengage and physically separate is to return to a more balanced attention to oneself. Difficulty in disengaging results in the self being chronically crowded out by the other—a state of *confluence* or blending of self with other.

Another necessary process of disengagement is that of slowing down and quieting oneself. This is particularly noticeable when the contact has been intense, involving, or pressured. The following experiment will give you an opportunity to explore your own current responses to this aspect of disengagement.

> Close your eyes and over the course of three or four minutes allow your breathing to slow down. Gradually lengthen your inhalations and exhalations, and allow a slight pause to occur after each exhalation. As you attend to your inner experience, notice the ease or difficulty with which you slow down, the amount of inner "noise" you experience, and any distractions from this quieting process.

This might be a simple process for you. Or you may find yourself raising objections to slowing down, or feeling pressured to "get going" or "stop wasting time." If this occurs, try to note these pressures or objections to withdrawing, then continue to attend to your inner process for as long as you feel comfortable.

For some people, disengaging from contact with the environment is natural and spontaneous. They can detach their attention from externals and locate it within; they can allow themselves to settle and slow down; they can allow for not always being active and doing something. For others the process of withdrawal generates anxiety and discomfort. They may feel constantly distracted by thoughts or images, and feel pressured to be active and working on something continuously. Some people report that when they detach their attention from objects or other people, they feel a void or emptiness, and have little sense of their own self. They seem to experience little sense of self outside of their relation to others or their activities. Still others find that, despite perhaps an initial difficulty in shifting their focus, the process of withdrawal forms a welcome respite in their normally hurried pace.

Re-forming the Self Boundary

Having disengaged from the other, there is a natural movement toward *re-forming* of one's boundary, or to put it another way, of rebounding the self. Having separated oneself from the contact, one can more fully differentiate one's sense of self from the contact. This is supported by the heightening of the bodily sense of self. Body space locates and defines what "I" is as distinct from what "not I" is. In withdrawing from contact, it becomes important to reaffirm one's bodily sense of self and, as it were, relocate oneself.

> Take a minute after reading this sentence to disengage yourself from the contact of reading this chapter, shift your attention to the space inside your body, and notice where you locate your sense of "I." Where do you "sit" inside after disengaging from reading? Take your time discovering this.
>
> Where were you located? In your eyes? In the space of your head? In your body as a whole or someplace within your torso? Did you feel located by your thinking or by pictures in your head? In the surface musculature of your face? Or perhaps you found yourself outside your body space?
>
> Is this location a comfortable one for you or uncomfortable? Do you feel "at home" there or that you just ended up there? Is this familiar to you or unfamiliar? Do you feel that you have adequate space or do you feel crowded?
>
> Try stating the results of this experiment: "When I am not out in the world I return to my _____ (name your location) and I am _____ (comfortable/uncomfortable, familiar/unfamiliar, cramped/have space).

This sense of location is a subtle thing. Each of us has a home ground we tend to return to when not engaged in the world. For some, visual imagery or thinking is the most roomy, or at least easily accessible, place to which to return. Others find specific body spaces or areas where they reside. For some, thoughts and images might be too crowded, or their bodily space is too dense, painful, or desensitized to offer comfortable "lounging." Without clear space within which to locate oneself, withdrawal from contact can be very difficult. The only comfortable or easy place to be is outside oneself, constantly engaged, or in one's thinking, constantly cogitating and obsessed.

If you will, try another brief experiment in changing your location of awareness.

> First pick out some interesting object nearby and look at it very carefully. Don't just gaze at it; examine all of the contours and shadings and textures of what you are seeing. Take a stance of interest and absorption in what you are seeing. Try this now.

Where was your "I" located in this way of seeing? To what degree did you feel your body and how you were sitting while you did this? You might have experienced yourself as being, as it were, "in" the object, or as if out in the space between your body and the thing you were seeing. If you were very absorbed in what you were seeing, it is likely that you recall little of what was happening to your bodily sense of yourself for that moment.

> Now try this from a different stance. Looking at the same or a different object, keep your location of your awareness behind your eyes, looking out at what you are seeing. Look as carefully as you can while still maintaining a sense of being located inside yourself. Try this for a while.

Where did you locate yourself—in your eyes, your head, anyplace else? Were you able to summon as much visual richness of detail compared with the previous experiment? Were you more or less in touch with your bodily experience while you looked? Did you feel more involved or cooler and more distant?

Experiencing oneself as bounded within one's skin assists in detaching from the contact object and so reaffirming one's sense of self. This is the concrete physical manifestation of what has been called, in other contexts, individuation. Readers familiar with child development literature will recognize that the importance of experiencing oneself as being "inside one's own skin" has also been noted by child development theorists as an essential aspect of infant development. Winnicott (1960) and Mahler (1972, 1974), extending Freud's notion of the "body ego," describe the importance of this body sense of self for the infant's ability to break the symbiotic bond with the primary caretaker and embark on the road to a more separate and differentiated existence. Winnicott (1960) comments, "As a further development, there comes into existence what might be called a limiting membrane, which to some extent (in health) is equated with the surface of the skin and has a position between the infant's 'me' and his 'not-me'" (p. 589).

From the viewpoint of Gestalt therapy, the process of separation and individuation outlined in child development literature is not one that is accomplished (or not) only at a given point in one's childhood. Rather it is characteristic of the *ongoing* contact and withdrawal process. Reforming the "me within the body" is accomplished over and over again as we contact the environment, dissolving to some extent our sense of boundedness, and then return to a more bounded sense of self.

Most of us have had times in our lives (for some it is characteristic) when we have been extremely busy for an extended period (that is, a period of constant action and contact). If you would, recall a recent time when this was true for you. Did you ever feel during this that you were so busy that you had "lost touch" with yourself? Did you ever find that you had skipped a meal or ignored your fatigue, then suddenly "woke up" and realized you had been out of touch with your needs? What was it that allowed you to come back into yourself?

Assimilation and Closure

If we simply discharged a need and returned to homeostasis, little would be accomplished other than mechanistic stimulus and response. The aim of contact, as described in Gestalt therapy, is that the self-boundary is now redrawn to *include* the new experience or material engendered by contact. It is the *assimilation* of this new material or experience that results in growth. Every interaction with the environment has some impact, its degree varying with the intensity and meaning of the interaction. This impact engenders in us emotional and other body responses, and it is necessary to sort through and fit this impact into our previous experience. A new gestalt (whole) emerges from this assimilation process. The effect of contact is thus to engender something new, not merely a return to a preexisting homeostasis.

Clearly assimilation often merely begins at this point in the cycle and may continue even as we enter into new experience cycles. The authors of *Gestalt Therapy* (Perls et al., 1951) felt that most of assimilation occurred outside of awareness, just as the digestion of food requires no conscious attention. I believe, however, that assimilation is a much more active process and involves much conscious sorting, and thus our awareness. As we sort through and assimilate the results of a contact episode, we work to fit the new experience into our old framework—we cogitate, compare, look at what fits and what doesn't, and so on.

Assimilation also involves an awareness of the impact of contact on oneself in terms of its completeness. We sense what is finished and what is unfinished for us in terms of the need that originally organized our behavior. With this may come an acknowledgment of what cannot be finished.

Closure marks the full turn of the organismic circle. Ideally one might hope that the need that initiated the cycle has either found completion through its satisfaction or, if unsatisfied, there is an adjustment to the lack of closure. Closure may be experienced as a sense of calm and settling. What was embarked upon has found fruition; the natural urge toward closure has been satisfied. But closure may also bring with it a sense of loss and mourning. If the event has been an unpleasant struggle, what is it like to be without the struggle? What parts of the struggle did you relish even if other parts of it cost you dearly? Almost all endings, even endings of unpleasant situations, involve aspects of both relief and loss. Even the culmination of happy events can be paradoxically coupled with a sense of loss.

Long-hoped-for achievements bring the thrill of victory and the loss of the excitement and charge experienced in working for it. Leaving a job you hate brings relief, but you may also miss the comraderie, the special friends, or even the heat of the battle. If the event has been a positive one, stimulating or exciting, then you may experience the ending of that stimulation as a loss. I recall how surprised I was to be feeling a deep sadness as my wife and I drove to our honeymoon. Eventually I realized that, although I felt great joy in our marriage, the event of marrying also marked the end of a life stage for me. I felt keenly that I was suddenly leaving my childhood behind. This entailed both relief and sadness for me — relief that I was finally leaving behind many of my insecurities of childhood, and sadness for those pleasures and hopes I could no longer have in the same way. As I stopped insisting to myself that I shouldn't feel sad on my honeymoon, I could allow for that curious bittersweet feeling that comes from appreciating the paradox of polarities in life. To recognize the loss of my childhood gave me more room, eventually, to fully appreciate my joy in marriage as well. Finishing inevitably contains ambivalent elements, although we frequently deny our mixed feelings or are talked out of them by friends and family: "It's over now, why aren't you happy?" or "You're finally rid of that jerk, so stop crying."

RESISTANCES TO THE PROCESS OF WITHDRAWAL

When I work with clients who live past-paced, highly charged lives, who constantly work and produce without pause, or those whose lives center continuously around others, I pay careful attention to the possibility of a lack of withdrawal in their lives. As I familiarize myself with their history and life situation, I note their complaints of being overburdened and overwhelmed, constantly pressured, fatigued but unable to rest, feeling that they have never done enough and that they are never quite adequate to their task. I also note the lack of flow and rhythm in their lives as they report virtually unbroken activity followed by collapse and exhaustion, rather than rhythmic and periodic pauses and breaks.

In the here and now of the therapy hour I see in action the same processes that generate these symptomatic complaints. Some people have difficulty knowing when they have explored a topic to their satisfaction, that is, when a contact has been "enough." They have no sense of their own satiation. Some people are unable to find a focus in sessions; everything demands their attention at once and they have no quiet background from which figures can emerge with clarity. Others may experience pauses or silences as anxious moments and will talk merely to fill the space and ease the discomfort created by such pauses. They fear that if they slow down, they will lose their momentum and become passive and lazy, or that if they stop even for a moment, a tidal wave of demands will drown them. Some people comment, when asked to slow or pause, "But if I am not *doing* something (proving myself/attached to others/working hard) what good am I?"

In the previous chapter, we saw the dilemma of moving into contact and final contact: the fear that if one allows contact to *occur,* one's self will be lost or endangered. The dilemma in withdrawal phase centers around expectations of what would happen if contact with the environment were to cease. The issues involved have to do with losses of various kinds: loss of self, loss of or abandonment by the other, and experiences engendered by loss such as mourning, grief, and anger. The particular nature of the loss experienced is related to the point in the withdrawal phase in question. I will try to describe how these issues form the "unfinished business" that can interfere with the course of normal withdrawal: disengaging from contact, re–forming of the self-boundary, and assimilation and closure.

Interruptions to Disengaging

This resistance frequently occurs as anxiety and fear that if one lets go of the contact, the self will not exist—the self only exists when engaged in activity, or when engaged with others. Most commonly these fears seem to be related to familial introjects that equate self-worth with performance of activities. The family value is on doing and producing, and the devaluation of being (unconditional worth). This becomes institutionalized as fear of inactivity, and a lack of self-worth without an activity to prove one's value. The manifest resistance will be in the form of difficulty in letting go of the active mode, slowing of one's pace, and shifting one's attention from the environment to the self.

As the experiential work earlier demonstrated, one aspect of disengaging from contact is that of slowing down. If slowing down was relatively easy during that exercise, then it may be difficult to conceive of the monumental difficulty this engenders for some people. One of my clients described himself as an "action junkie." He was very involved in athletic purusits, lived a busy professional and social life, and came to me because he wanted to learn more about how to release some of the tension he accumulated in the course of his busy life. Any work we did of an active nature, such as work with his posture or generating movement experiments, he took to easily and naturally. When I began to work with him on the body work table where he had to slow down and pay attention to his "insides," work that required him to disengage and withdraw from activity in the environment, a different picture emerged.

At first he found it difficult even to close his eyes and turn his attention inwards. He would become restless and talkative, distracting his attention to himself by barraging me with questions and comments. I would answer his questions enough to help him bind his anxiety, then gently and consistently use verbal instruction and touch to remind him to pay attention to his body experience. As he became more able to slow down a bit and finally shift his attention inwards, he started to shake and tremor, his muscles jumping spasmodically. At first this remained an isolated body experience, without any clear feeling. Over time, as we developed verbal experiments to owning this as "I am shaking" and "I am jumpy," he recognized that it was not just "My body is shaking," but, "I feel frightened."

On my urging him to be more specific, he was eventually able to state that he was afraid that if he slowed down and was not constantly doing something, then he would be worthless. As our work continued, we began to expose and work through his family's introjects (rules), which held that a person was valued only for producing—thus his belief that if he was not "doing," he would become "nothing," without value.

Difficulties in Re-forming the Self-Boundary

As one shifts to the task of re-forming the self-boundary, difficulties will often be seen in the form of disorientation, feelings of emptiness, and fear of being abandoned to this inner emptiness. One of the essential problems here is that such people, due to a great degree of desensitization, have little sense of their physical substance and location as they disengage and withdraw. Having no embodied place to locate themselves outside of contact with others, they maintain a state of confluence with others and are dependent on others for their sense of self.

One client, a vivacious and very socially active woman, constantly centered her life around other people. Most of her concerns in therapy were with others' responses and actions toward her, and her responses and actions toward them. Once, as she spoke of her interactions with others, she complained of having no clear sense of herself except as others defined her. I asked her whether she had any clear sense of herself as she was speaking to me. She noted that, in fact, she was so focused on how I was responding to her story that she had no idea of herself. We spent some time experientially investigating where she experienced her "self" as she talked to me, and eventually she was able to describe that she felt herself to be existing on her body surface, particularly her eyes and face, and that she had little sense of her insides. At one point I suggested that she experiment with locating herself inside her body by closing her eyes, using the sensations of her breathing to help ground herself kinesthetically in her torso, and, staying in touch with these sensations, to look at me "from sitting inside yourself."

With what I only later realized was an act of great courage and trust on her part, she tried this out. As she tried to move into her body-self, she lost any sense of my presence with her and became overwhelmed with feelings of being abandoned and lost. She became frightened and burst into tears. To re-form her self was for her to be completely disconnected from the other. We worked gradually—shuttling back and forth between her visual contact with me and her kinesthetic contact with her body experience—to form a middle ground where she could experience herself, while also perceiving my presence as background. As this became possible, we were able to shift attention to transforming her retroflected loneliness into anger at being emotionally abandoned by her parents, and mourning the loss of a consistent parental presence in her childhood.

Interference with Assimilation and Closure

As described in this chapter, the process of assimilation and finishing involves coming to terms with the impact that interaction in the environment has on us. Some interactions do not come to fruition, others have significant elements of frustration, and still others end with a sense of loss. If we have not been able to express and come to terms with our resulting feelings of disappointment, anger, grief, and mourning, then we are left with unfinished situations that interfere with the resolution of similar instances of withdrawal and closure. We become unable to assimilate current contacts because our energy is still taken up in trying to finish previous contacts.

One of the most common difficulties in resolving such feelings is that others around us are unable to support or acknowledge the expression of these feelings: "No use crying over spilled milk," "Big boys don't cry," "What have you got to feel upset about?" and other denials of the validity of our organismic reactions to difficult endings. When our feelings are pronounced invalid, are denied, or go unrecognized by significant others around us, we resort to various ways to manage the double bind of "feeling what I should not feel." Retroflection, turning against the self, is one way in which such situations are frequently coped with: frustration with others becomes one's own failure, anger over the quality of contact becomes self-criticism, grief for the loss of others becomes depression without apparent source, lack of fulfillment by others becomes one's own inner emptiness.

It is in the here and now experience of the processes of withdrawal and closure in the therapy hour where unfinished business with previous endings can come into focus, and the retroflected feelings can be identified and expressed toward the environment. The therapist can encourage resolution by generating experiments that heighten the client's experience of the withdrawal process, and by validating the reality of feelings of sadness, anger, or disappointment.* This allows for assimilation and closure, and frees the organismic energy that has been stuck with the unfinished situation so one can move on to new experiences.

The case that follows describes a person whose major therapeutic work centered around problems in the withdrawal phase of experience. Through it I will illustrate the use of body process in identifying difficulties, generating experiments, and working through these issues. The work with Kevin draws from the spectrum of body process intervention that has been discussed during the course of this book—sensitization, ownership of the projected body, mobilization, and emotional expression—and shows the integration of this technique into a therapeutic whole.

KEVIN'S SEARCH

Kevin came to therapy in an acute version of the depression and anxiety to which he had been subject for most of his youth and adult life. Increased responsibility at his job had been more than he could handle and he had become unable to cope. In his late 30s, he was an executive who had worked hard and achieved a good position in his company, yet felt that whatever he had achieved was not enough. He chastised himself constantly for not taking on more projects, yet felt overwhelmed and exhausted by the tasks in which he was already engaged.

Initially our work focused on helping him manage and put into

---

*This view is directly counter to the traditional psychoanalytic drive theory that views such feelings arise as a result of conflicts within the individual.

perspective the demands with which he had to contend, both those of his job responsibilities and those of his own perfectionism. Little of this initial work involved body-oriented work. Although this early phase of our work provided Kevin with some relief, as some of his acute distress and initial complaints dissipated, a new theme emerged. Embedded in his constant sense of misery and failure was his inability to pause, even for a moment, other than by collapsing into exhaustion and sleep. It was as if Kevin had only an "on" or "off" switch, with no modulation in between. It became quickly apparent in our work that this was not merely a simple matter of not pausing, but that he *could not* stop, this is, he experienced an active resistance to ceasing his constant work.

The Process of Disengagement

Kevin's constant engagement was represented in its most basic form when, after complaining to me that he was tremendously overworked and needed a break, he laid out a list of tasks he must accomplish in the therapy hour. I pointed out how speedy and rushed he was, and that it was my impression he needed to use therapy to experiment with doing *less*, rather than therapy becoming an extension of his list of tasks and demands on himself. He considered this and agreed.

Accordingly we began to experiment more directly with the process of pausing and slowing down. I did this initially by encouraging Kevin to pause at times during his opening story and asking if his telling of the story was rooted in his bodily needs. Eventually Kevin was able to discern that his physical sense was one of pressure and exhaustion and that, if he were to follow his bodily need rather than his "head" pressure to talk continuously, he would "allow my body to rest" (note the disownership implied by his language). With my support we experimented with ways he could find some comfort, rest, and pause in sessions, even if only for brief moments.

Over time Kevin's awareness of his bodily need for stopping and withdrawal from activity and contact made the therapy hour one of the few moments in his life when he could give himself pause. He began coming into sessions and requesting that he take the time to rest. During this period I would have him lie down to give his whole body support for withdrawal, and would use gentle touch to teach him how to slow down further. I thought of this phase as one of learning how to *disengage from contact.* Initially Kevin required much external support from me to allow himself to disengage from his busy-ness and activity. Eventually he acquired enough experience to know when he needed to disengage, even if he could not yet initiate it for himself.

Recontacting the Self

At this point a new issue evolved for Kevin: when he wasn't "in his head," thinking, talking to himself or others, imagining or working on something—he had no place else to be. He experienced his body space as either full of discomfort and so to be avoided, or as a blank void. Without discomfort he hardly felt his body-self at all, and so had no place in which to locate himself other than in his head, where the activity of thinking and verbalization gave him some sense of his being.

Accordingly our work focused on developing his bodily sense (work with desensitization) so that Kevin had *someplace to be when not engaged in activity*. I used touch to enliven his taut and sensation-deadened tissue, and worked to expand the space in his narrow torso through breathing. As Kevin came to feel his body more, he began to discover an alternative place in which he could locate himself. This place was his belly, where he now had sensory access and some degree of ownership.

As Kevin became better able to enter his bodily space, he was less inclined to complain and tell stories in therapy. Instead he became motivated to "find himself" in each session, to find his sense of inner substance and being that he would lose touch with in his externally oriented and high-pressure life. Body-focused work became the essential entry point to help Kevin slow down, breathe, disengage himself from his life activities, and give him a sense of location by shifting his awareness into his belly and torso. I marked this second stage as the process of *recontacting the self*.

Our work on the process of disengagement from contact and recontacting his sense of self formed the first essential steps in grappling with the process of withdrawal for Kevin. This initial work was certainly therapeutic in and of itself, and yet did not in any way cure the distress Kevin felt; rather it set the stage for deeper work. The therapeutic issues that eventually emerged were part of a developmental process involving the acquisition of certain organismic capabilities. Having the capacity to slow down, disengage from unceasing activity, and recontact his body-self allowed Kevin to begin to make contact with feelings often intrinsic to the process of withdrawal: feelings of emptiness, loneliness, and abandonment.

Confronting the Emptiness

A paradox appeared as Kevin gained more sensory contact with his body, particularly his torso. The more he experienced this area of himself, the more he began to perceive an inner sense of emptiness and nothingness. When I asked him what he felt as he shifted his awareness into his belly, he would describe himself as feeling "empty" and "hollow" inside. At first I assumed that this phenomenon was due to a lack of sensation (as I have described in my earlier discussion of desensitization and numbness in one's body). It soon became apparent that Kevin's sense of emptiness and hollowness, rather than being the *result* of a lack of feeling, was simply his report of *what he felt* when he came into contact with this area. At my suggestion he experimented with I-statements to further his identification with this feeling: "I am empty inside. I am hollow and unfilled." To experience these feelings of emptiness was initially quite frightening to Kevin. For most of his life, Kevin had pushed aside any awareness of this inner void through activity and work and such distractions as sex and drugs. It was only the groundwork of our relationship and the above mentioned skills that allowed him to face and tolerate these feelings.

I explored with Kevin what specifically frightened him about feeling his emptiness. He replied, "It just confirms to me that I am really just nothing, that I'm worthless." He continued to speak of his sense of emptiness in his life, how his feelings made no sense, there was no reason for it, he had everything he needed and yet felt empty, he had no right to complain. At this point he concluded that he was basically flawed as a person, that there was something missing in him for which he had only himself to blame.

I recall that, at the time, I felt puzzled and struggled with trying to understand what to do with all of this, particularly with the bleak conclusions he had come to as a result of my encouraging him to stay with and confront his feelings of emptiness. All I had done was succeed in making Kevin more depressed and hopeless.

When he first started in therapy, Kevin had little clear memory of his childhood. He described his parents as good, kind, but unremarkable people, and his growing up as ordinary until his adolescence, when he became rebellious and troubled. He dated his troubles and dissatisfaction in life to that time. What impressed me was the lack of context for the distress and bitterness he felt so keenly as an adult. In describing his history, it was as if there were two different lives: an ordinary and normal childhood, somewhat rose-colored, then a sudden anger and rebellion in adolescence that had settled into a bitter and distressed adulthood. It was as if a tree growing in good soil had suddenly, and without apparent reason, became stunted and twisted in its growth. Consequently, having no way to attribute his anger and depression to external events in his life, Kevin naturally concluded that he was basically flawed. This, of course, added to his sense of failure and inadequacy with which he evaluated his work and his relationships.

The first shift in the pattern came when I was able to recognize that both Kevin's feeling of emptiness and his rejection of his right to feel that emptiness could be seen as forms of retroflection, that is, *as things that at one time were done to him but which he now does to himself.* I asked Kevin to test this experientially by suggesting he say, as if to his parents, "You give me so little that you make me feel empty inside." At first Kevin refused to try this out, insisting that this couldn't be true of his parents. I countered that if it wasn't true, then there would be no harm in saying it, and he could only know by trying it out. Kevin eventually summoned the courage to try the statement aloud. With each statement "as if" to his parents, Kevin's eyes began to tear. He reported feeling very sad, as if mourning. He did not understand why he felt such grief, but what he said felt accurate to him.

This initiated a new stage in our work. Each time Kevin was able to withdraw from his frenetic activity and contact in the world, he was able to get in touch with certain fundamental body experiences. We can think of this as a shift of figures: by maintaining the current environment as a powerful and engaging figure of awareness, his bodily feeling of inner emptiness would remain in the background and unaware. He worked to keep them out of awareness because, when he experienced his emptiness, he had no context for his feeling, and so to get in touch with this feeling only made him feel badly about himself.

Our work began to fill in the context in which his bodily feeling took place. As these feelings emerged into awareness, we experimented with stating them "as if" they were legitimate responses to growing up in his family (and thus had a context), instead of as symptoms that occurred to him in isolation. When Kevin withdrew and the feeling of emptiness emerged, I asked him to "try on" such statements as, "It is so empty here in this family" or "There is not enough here for me." When he withdrew and experienced internal pressure and demands on himself to do more, I asked him to try, "I can never do enough for you. I can never rest in try-ing to win your attention." When Kevin felt unjustified for feeling miser-able, I had him try, "You always made me feel I had no right to ask any-thing of you." When he moved inwards and described a deep sense of loneliness, I asked him to experiment with such statements as, "You leave me alone and unsupported."

Gradually Kevin began to recollect his growing up differently than

---

*In addition to the understanding of retroflection derived from Gestalt therapy, this in-sight was stimulated for me at the time by Alice Miller's (1984) conception of symptoms as enactments of what, as children, people have been subjected to. This is similar to the Ges-talt notion of retroflection, but Miller emphasizes behavior as a communication of uncons-cious historical situations rather than, as has been typical of the traditional Gestalt notion of retroflection, the restraint of an organismic action.

he had originally described it to me. He began to see that his household was not the mildly rosy place he had imagined it to be. Although not entirely without some expressions of warmth, there was also much coolness, distance, and difficulty in giving love. In particular he began to see that his parents had very little warmth or love for each other, that he was emotionally at odds and distant from his siblings, that his father, who portrayed an image of extrovertedness outside the family, had been expressionless and withdrawn at home. Kevin began to distinguish between the appearances of warmth and the genuine article, which, it became clearer, was often lacking. Seeing this, Kevin began to mourn for his empty, lonely, and unwarmed childhood.

What, in isolation, seemed like depression, in context became more clearly a true sadness. What without context he had experienced as "his" emptiness—a personal characteristic that had no relationship to a real event—he could now acknowledge as the emptiness to which he was *subject* as a child but had no support for acknowledging. Now that it could be experienced, Kevin could begin to fully mourn what he had lost and what could never be.

Return and Renewal

With Kevin's recognition of his great sadness and sense of loss as a chronically unfinished piece of business came, eventually, our recognition of his unacknowledged and contained anger at his family. Therapeutic attention then shifted to working with his demobilized body structure and gradual physical expression and ownership of his denied power and anger. Issues relating to these forms of therapy have already been discussed in earlier chapters and I will not detail them here. I only wish to point out that the process engendered by our work on the withdrawal phase was not an end point in itself, but rather brought Kevin to the point where other figures of interest could now emerge against a new background and themselves be brought to closure.

So, too, does the finishing of any essential organismic cycle free energy and attention for some new cycle: attention to some other unfinished business, the emergence of some new figure, continued growth and development. Accomplished withdrawal and closure are the ending of one cycle, only to make room for the emergence and energizing of some other cycle. This is the rhythm of forming and completing "gestalts" (wholes), the interruption of which forms the attention point for our work as therapists, and the success of which results in growth.

Appendix

A Comparison of Reichian
and Gestalt Therapies

Of the major approaches to psychotherapy, there are only two that I believe can be considered truly integrated therapies, as defined in this book. These are therapies based on the work of Wilhelm Reich, and Gestalt therapy. Although these two approaches have many similarities and have in common a holistic viewpoint, and certain elements of the Gestalt approach have been derived or influenced by Reich's work (Smith, 1975), they have many important differences. These differences are frequently glossed over by those who attempt to combine their methods and philosophies. Because of this confusion I have provided this appendix to elucidate what seem to me to be critical differences between these approaches.

By exploring the uniqueness of each, I also hope to make clearer that so-called "combination" therapies (e.g., Gestalt and Reichian therapy, Gestalt and Alexander method, Reichian and Rolfing) are really misnomers. One may use a technique or principle in Reichian therapy derived from Gestalt therapy, or a technique or principle derived from Alexander method in Gestalt therapy, but one cannot "synthesize" the two unless their philosophies and world views are compatible. To truly integrate different approaches requires either that one approach borrow techniques or principles from another and alter them to fit its philosophy, or that both are altered to create a new whole. In either case the use of "and" (as in Gestalt "and" Alexander method) is a misnomer, since the resulting work is really either the assimilation of technique from one method into another, or something entirely different from its origins.

WILHELM REICH: FATHER OF UNIFIED APPROACHES TO THERAPY

In early days of psychoanalysis, a student of Freud named Wilhelm Reich began to grapple with some of the critical problems in the development of psychoanalytic technique (Reich, 1945/1972). He was very concerned with two major issues. One was to understand the nature of libido (sexual energy): "I was looking for the *energy source of the neurosis,* its somatic core" (Reich, 1973, p. 98). The second issue was to evolve ways to understand and deal with patients' resistance to the therapeutic process.

With reference to the second question, Reich began to notice that his patients each had a characteristic style, a way of acting. Linking his observations to the emerging notions of character formation, he noted that this style seemed to serve as a defense in therapy, as a way of screening out the analyst's interpretations and thus preventing change. He called this style the "character" or "character resistance." His crucial observation was that character resistance was not simply a matter of cognitive organization, that is, purely mental in nature. Reich did an unusual thing for an analyst of his day in that he sat across from his clients, and actually looked at them, instead of only listening to their verbalizations. He observed that this stylistic way of being was part of the way in which clients moved, held their posture, modulated their voice, and tensed their muscles.

An example would be the client whose aloofness and haughtiness serve to keep the analyst at a distance and "beneath" the patient, thus rendering the interpretations of the analyst ineffective. Another would be the subservient patient whose body is cowed and diminished, and so prevents by his superficial compliance the uncovering of aggressive impulses. Reich felt that unless the character resistance was dealt with, the interpretation of the underlying conflicts would be defended against; the character *is* the defense or "armor" against interpretation. Interpretation was not sufficient, the armor itself must first be removed.

Reich connected his first question, that of the nature of libido in its physical form, with his growing understanding of character resistance,

Comparison of Reichian and Gestalt Therapy Approaches to Body Process and Intervention

	Reichian	Gestalt
Sensation	The result of energy flow and motility.	The material out of which figures are formed that organize contact with the environment.
Tension	Serves to block the flow of energy and thus limits expressive movement. Related to the degree of inner conflict.	Retroflection of movement or desensitization of sensation. Interrupts contact with the environment.
Resistance	Physically manifest as tension. A defense to be broken down so that the "true" impulse can be expressed	An expression of the self (i.e., an ego-function) to be made aware and active rather than static and passive; then expressed so that full choice can be made.
Intervention	Breathing, exercises, and direct pressure on tense areas to break down resistance and bring out underlying impulse. Analysis of psychic conflicts.	Development of sensation, restoration of felt sense of self, experiments with awareness and expression. Assimilation of unassimilated material.
Goal	Full expression and flow of impulse and ability to armor when appropriate. The genital character.	Organismic self-regulation and good contact with environment.

and so achieved the first integrated somatic psychotherapy. His initial technique for breaking down character resistance (later called character armor) was to focus intensely on and verbally describe the clients' manner, body language, and posture. As clients became more conscious of their ways of defending themselves physically through mental and bodily attitudes, Reich began to observe tremendous generalized reactions.

Reich (1973/1942) describes one of the first such occurrences:

> In Copenhagen, in 1933, I treated a man who offered considerable resistance to the uncovering of his passive homosexual fantasies. This resistance was overtly expressed in the extremely stiff attitude of his throat and neck ("stiff-necked"). A concentrated attack on his defense finally caused him to

yield. though in an alarming way. For three days he was taken by acute manifestations of vegetative shock. The pallor of his face changed rapidly from white to yellow to blue. His skin was spotted and motley. He experienced violent pains in the neck and back of the head. His heartbeat was rapid and pounding. He had diarrhea, felt tired and seemed to have lost control... *Affects had broken through somatically after the patient had relinquished his attitude of psychic defense.* Apparently, the stiff neck, which emphasized austere masculinity, had bound vegetative energies which now broke loose in an uncontrolled and chaotic manner. (p. 269) [Italics from original]

From this and other clinical observation, Reich formulated the principle that "sexual energy can be bound by chronic muscular tensions" (Reich, 1972, p. 270). Since muscular armoring and character armor were considered by Reich to be functionally identical, it followed that the muscular tension and character armoring served to bind libido energy and affect (as a function of libido). In diagramatic form:

Muscular tension = Character defense = Binding of sexual energy

Reich's concretization of Freud's abstract notion of libido and his notion of the functional identity between a body phenomenon (muscular holding and tension) and an emotional, and thus psychological, phenomenon (the defense) were the key to the development of somatic approaches to therapy. They implied that mental and physical phenomena were a unity and could be available to *both* psychological and somatic intervention.

Reich went on to develop somatic techniques using breathing and expressive movement to liberate emotion, and direct contact work to loosen tight muscles. All of this was to supplement the analytic work of interpretation and resolution of archaic conflicts. His aim was to break down the defense through its physical manifestation and resolve the underlying conflicts of the instincts. His goal was the ideal of the "genital character"—a person with flexible and unfixed body (and thus character) armor who could fully surrender to the pulsation and spread of feeling of the sexual orgasm. Reich later attempted to extend his concept of libido energy as a physical energy to social and geophysical realms. We will not be concerned with these later views here, as they are only peripherally related to the process of psychotherapy.

Reich, then, was the first person to clearly link body functioning and psychological functioning as an intrinsic whole. He also formulated the first somatic methodology or "body work" with psychotherapeutic aims: the freeing of blocked affect and psychic energy as a function of developmental conflicts and fixations. Modern extensions of his work are seen in medical orgonomy (Baker, 1967) and in neo-Reichian approaches best represented by Alexander Lowen's bioenergetics (1975). Lowen extended Reich's formulations of character types (Lowen, 1958) and developed many new techniques of somatic intervention (Lowen & Lowen, 1977). His prolific writings form a background for much of this present volume (Lowen, 1965, 1967, 1972, 1980, 1983).

The Second Approach: Somatic Emphasis in Gestalt Therapy

As we look at the later development of interest in body processes in the therapeutic context, we come first to the developing work of Frederick Perls, the founder of Gestalt therapy. Perls was at one time an analysand of Reich while both were still in Germany. Perls was clearly influenced by Reich's writings on character and somatic process. After Freud, Reich was the most frequently referenced author in Perls' seminal work *Ego, Hunger and Aggression* (Perls, 1947/1969), followed by F. M. Alexander, another writer on posture and muscular organization and founder of the Alexander technique (Alexander, 1971; Barlow, 1973). Perls' background and that of his collaborators—Laura Perls, who, in addition to being a psychologist had a strong interest in modern dance and eurythmics, and Paul Goodman, who had been an early patient of Lowen (Goodman, 1977)—gave Gestalt therapy a strong emphasis on body phenomena from its inception.

Perls, after Reich, saw muscular tension as functioning to repress impulses and emotionally meaningful movement. He captured this view in his conception of retroflection—muscular holding as the turning back onto the self of actions one wanted to perform on the environment: "The motoric system has to a great extent lost its function as a working, active, world-bound system and, by retroflection, has become the jailer rather than the assistant of important biological needs" (Perls, 1947/ 1969, p. 229).

Perls differed most from Reich in his interpretation of body processes in two major ways. First, Perls saw physical expression and withholding of expression in the context of contact with the environment in order to meet organismic needs. Thus he saw the organism/person always in relation to its environment, and not only organized around internal conflicts and events. In this way bodily expression and being were viewed in light of their function in contact with the environment. The withholding of expression (retroflection) emerged from the need to withhold contact in a dangerous situation.

Second, Perls was interested in the body not just for its potential of movement and expression, but also in terms of the phenomenology or experience of the body by the client. His concern was with the client's sense of self, the "I" of experience, as an embodied self. To be in touch with one's "self" is, then, to be in touch with the actual felt-sense of one's embodiment, as well as one's motoric expression of self in contact with the environment. For Perls the first step was concentration on body sensation to restore the body sense of the client, and *then* to undo the muscular repressions: "Our aim is—through concentration—to re-establish the Ego-functions, to dissolve the rigidity of the "body" and the pertrified Ego, the "character"... Through full contact with the neurotic symptom you will be in a position to dissolve it" (Perls, 1947/1969, p. 229).

The emphasis on body awareness and concentration on sensation and somatic experience in order to restore the sense of "I," of ego-function, was the first step in working through neurosis. This is a crucial difference from Reich's approach, not merely because of the emphasis on sensation and awareness instead of expression, but in what it implied about the nature of resistance. To Reich the muscular resistance was a defense that impeded the course of therapy and proper functioning, and therefore must be broken down and eliminated. To Perls and the Gestalt therapist, the muscular tension is an ego-function, part of the self, albeit disowned and unaware. To break it down or eliminate it per se would be to eliminate part of the self and "the patient will be left less than he is" (Perls, et al., 1951, p. 286). The authors go on to comment:

> What must be the result of hammering at the resistances? Anxious and guilty, assailed by a frontal attack, the patient represses the entire whole. Supposing that in sum there has been a gain, bound energy is released. Yet the patient has importantly lost his own weapons and his orientation in the world; the new available energy cannot work and prove itself in experience. (p. 285)

Perls (1947/1969) was equally critical of methods that attempted to train the body mechanically to relax or change posture. These approaches ignore the emotional meanings of tension and posture and encourage the sense of split between self and body by teaching control of the body by the ego, rather than integrating ego and body.

> Unfortunately deliberate relaxation—even if carried out as thoroughly as Jacobson prescribes it in *You Must Relax*—is insufficient. It has the same disadvantage as have superficial resolutions; though you might be able to relax if you concentrate on relaxation, in any state of excitement the "mus-

cular armour" is bound to return. Moreover, Jacobson, like F. M. Alexander, neglects the meaning of contractions as repressors ... We must also not overlook the fact that the tonus of a healthy, motoric system is neither hyper- nor hypo-tonic; it is elastic, alert. Relaxation, if carried out according to Jacobson's instructions, might lead to a state of flaccid paralysis—to a hypo-tonus. (pp. 229–230)

In addition to working with the experience of the body as self through body awareness and concentration, the original Gestalt methodology placed much emphasis on breathing and nonverbal communication. Perls et al., (1951) commented that anxiety was excitement in the absence of breathing. Other somatic aspects of Gestalt technique included physical expression of the retroflected impulses, that is, acting on what has been withheld through emotionally expressive movement, and work with posture, stance, and physical supports.[*]

THE LIMITATIONS OF BODY WORK IN TRADITIONAL GESTALT THERAPY

Although the emphasis on body process and phenomena is essential to Gestalt philosophy and methodology, traditional practice has some important limitations in the breadth of body-oriented technique. It is these limitations that have prompted therapists to attempt to combine the rich, holistic framework of Gestalt therapy with other methods that have a greater depth of somatically based intervention: the "Gestalt and" approaches mentioned earlier.

For example, Gestalt therapy has not itself developed as full a range of somatically focused techniques as have the Reichian and many purely somatic approaches such as the Feldenkrais method and Rolfing. Gestalt therapy has also lacked an explicit base and rationale for hands-on work, that is, therapeutic work through touch. The understanding of the relation of breathing .to emotional work in Gestalt therapy has been rudimentary compared with the Reichian approach, and in my opinion even erroneous (as in the Perls et al. (1951) comment that anxiety is excitement without breathing).

Yet the basis clearly exists in Gestalt therapy for a more complete understanding of body processes in therapy. A more differentiated understanding of the process and use of breathing, a methodology and

---

[*]Laura Perls is the originator of much of our present attention to posture as a support for organismic process.

rationale for the therapeutic use of touch, and a more complete understanding of the use of physical expression of emotion in therapy are completely compatible with existing Gestalt therapy. In the present volume, I hope, at least in part, to remedy this situation, and to outline an integrated approach to depth work with the body in therapy from a Gestalt perspective.

References

Alexander, F. M. (1971). *The resurrection of the body.* New York: Dover.

Baker, E. F. (1967). *Man in the trap.* New York: Collier.

Barlow, W. (1973). *The Alexander Technique.* New York: Knopf.

Berne, E. (1964). *Games people play.* New York: Ballantine Books.

Boethius, A. M. S. (1963). *The Consolation of philosophy.* Carbondale, Illinois: Southern Illinois University Press.

Bohm, D. (1980). *Wholeness and the implicate order.* Boston: Ark.

Bowlby, J. (1960). Separation anxiety. *The International Journal of Psycho-Analysis, 41,* 89–113.

Burton, A., & Heller, L. G. (1964). The touching of the body. *The Psychoanalytic Review,* 1(1), 122–134.

Colby, K. M. (1951). *A primer for psychotherapists.* New York: Ronald Press.

Darbonne, A. (1976). Creative balance: An integration of Gestalt, bioenergetics and Rolfing. In C. Hatcher & P. Himelstein (Eds.), *The handbook of gestalt therapy* (pp. 602–614). New York: Jason Aronson.

Don, N. S. (1980). The story of Wendy: A case study in multi-modality therapy. In S. Boorstein (Ed.), *Transpersonal psychotherapy* (pp. 267–296). Palo Alto, Calif.: Science and Behavior Books.

Dychtwald, K. (1977). *Body-mind.* New York: Jove.

Ellis, A. (1962). *Reason and emotion in psychotherapy.* New York: Lyle Stuart.

Ellis, A., & Harper, R. A. (1968). *A guide to rational living.* New York: Lyle Stuart.

Feitis, R. (Ed.) (1978). *Ida Rolf talks about Rolfing and physical reality.* New York: HarperCollins.

Feldenkrais, M. (1972). *Awareness through movement.* New York: HarperCollins.

Freud, S. (1938/1966). *The basic writings of Sigmund Freud* (A. Brill, Ed.). New York: Modern Library.

Goodman, P. (1977). *Nature heals: the psychological essays of Paul Goodman* (T. Stoehr, Ed.). New York: Dutton.

Gorman, D. (1981). *The body moveable* (Vol. I, II & III). Vancouver: Ampersand Press.

Herman, J. (1992). *Trauma and recovery.* New York: Basic Books.

Karon, B. (1976). The psychoanalytic treatment of schizophrenia. In P. Magaro (Ed.), *The construction of madness* (pp. 181–212). New York: Pergamon.

Keleman, S. (1979). *Somatic reality.* Berkeley, Calif.: Center Press.

Keleman, S. (1985). *Emotional anatomy.* Berkeley, Calif.: Center Press.

Kelly, C. (1976). New techniques in vision improvement. In D. Boadella (Ed.), *In the wake of Reich* (pp. 351–381). London: Coventure.

Kernberg, O. F. (1975). *Borderline conditions and pathological narcissism.* New York: Jason Aronson.

Kogan, G. (Ed.) (1980). *Your body works: A guide to health, energy and balance.* Berkeley, Calif.: Transformations Press.

Kurtz, R., & Prestera, H. (1976). *The body reveals.* New York: HarperCollins.

Lao-Tzu (1955). *The way of life.* (R. B. Blakney, Trans.). New York: New American Library.

Lowen, A. (1958). *The language of the body.* New York: Collier.

Lowen, A. (1965). *Love and orgasm.* New York: New American Library.

Lowen, A. (1967). *The betrayal of the body.* New York: Collier.

Lowen, A. (1972). *Depression and the body.* New York: Viking Penguin.

Lowen, A. (1975). *Bioenergetics.* New York: Viking Penguin.

Lowen, A. (1980). *Fear of life.* New York: Collier.

Lowen, A. (1983). *Narcissism.* New York: Macmillan.

Lowen, A., & Lowen, L. (1977). *The way to vibrant health.* New York: HarperCollins.

McDougall, J. (1989). *Theatres of the body: A psychoanalytic view of psychosomatic illness.* New York: Norton.

Mahler, M. S. (1972). On the first three subphases of the separation-individuation process. *International Journal of Psycho-Analysis, 53* 333–338.

Mahler, M. S. (1974). Symbiosis and individuation: The psychological birth of the human infant. *Psychoanalytic Study of the Child, 29,* 89–106.

Mehl, L. E. (1981). *Mind and matter: Foundations for holistic health.* Berkeley, Calif.: Mindbody Press.

Miller, A. (1983). *For your own good.* New York: Farrar, Straus & Giroux.

Miller, A. (1984). *Thou shalt not be aware.* New York: Farrar, Straus & Giroux.

Mindell, A. (1982). *Dreambody.* Santa Monica: Sigo Press.

Perls, F. S. (1947/1969). *Ego, hunger and aggression.* New York: Vintage.

Perls, F. S. (1969). *Gestalt therapy verbatim.* Moab, Utah: Real People Press.

Perls, F. S., Hefferline, R. F., & Goodman, P. (1951). *Gestalt therapy.* New York: Julian.

Polster, E., & Polster, M. (1973). *Gestalt therapy integrated.* New York: Vintage.

Reich, W. (1942). *The function of the orgasm.* New York: Orgone Institute.

Reich, W. (1945/1962). *The sexual revolution.* New York: Farrar, Straus and Cudahy.

Reich, W. (1945/1972). *Character analysis.* New York: Simon & Schuster.

Reich, W. (1942/1973). *The function of the orgasm.* New York: Simon & Schuster.

Rogers, C. R. (1951). *Client-centered therapy: Its current practice, implications and theory.* Boston: Houghton, 1951.

Rolf, I. P. (1977). *Rolfing: The integration of human structures.* New York: Harper-Collins.

Rubenfeld, I. (1984). An interview with Ilana Rubenfeld. *Therapy Now, 1*(1), 8–9.

Rywerant, J. (1983). *The Feldenkrais method: Teaching by handling.* San Francisco: HarperCollins.

Schaler, J. (1980). Taste factor in autonomous function. *Gestalt Journal, 3*(2), 21–23.

Schutz, W., & Turner, E. (1977). *Body fantasy.* San Francisco: HarperCollins.

Searles, H. F. (1982). Some aspects of separation and loss in psychoanalytic therapy with borderline patients (1981). In P. L. Giovacchini & L. B. Boyer (Eds.), *Technical factors in the treatment of the severely disturbed patient* (pp. 136-160). New York: Jason Aronson.

Searles, H. F. (1985). Separation and loss in psychoanalytic therapy with borderline patients: Further remarks. *The American Journal of Psychoanalysis, 45*(1), 9-27.

Sheldon, W. H., Stevens, S. S., & Turner, W. B. (1940). *The varieties of human physique.* New York: HarperCollins.

Smith, E. W. (1975). The role of early Reichian theory in the development of Gestalt therapy. *Psychotherapy: Theory, Research and Practice, 12*(33), 268-272.

Todd, M. E. (1937/1959). *The thinking body.* New York: Dance Horizons.

Webster's New World Dictionary (1975). New York: Avenal Books.

Winnicott, D. W. (1960). The theory of the parent-infant relationship. *International Journal of Psycho-Analysis, 41,* 585-595.

Wolpe, J. (1961). The systematic desensitization treatment of neuroses. *Journal of Nervous and Mental Disease, 132,* 189-203.

Zinker, J. (1977). *Creative process in Gestalt therapy.* New York: Brunner/Mazel.

Zinker, J. (1983). Searching for clarity. *Pilgrimage, 11*(2), 79-85.

Index